Meeting the Needs of Ethnic Minority Children

A Handbook for Professionals

D0183630

of related interest

Group Work with Children and Adolescents
A Handbook
Edited by Kedar Nath Dwivedi
ISBN 1 85302 157 1

How and Why Children Hate
A Study of Conscious and Unconscious Sources
Edited by Ved Varma
ISBN 1 85302 116 4 hb
ISBN 1 85302 185 7 pb

How and Why Children Fail
Edited by Ved Varma
ISBN 1 85302 108 3 hb
ISBN 1 85302 186 5 pb

Project-Based Group Work Facilitator's Manual
Young People, Youth Workers and Projects
Andy Gibson and Gaynor Clarke
ISBN 1 85302 169 5

Parenting Teenagers
Bob Myers
ISBN 1 85302 366 3

Meeting the Needs
of Ethnic Minority Children

A Handbook for Professionals

Edited by
Kedar Nath Dwivedi and Ved Prakash Varma

Jessica Kingsley Publishers
London and Bristol, Pennsylvania

'The Immigrant (West Indian) Child in School' was originally published as 'Stresses in Immigrant Children' in Varma, V. (ed) *Stresses in Handicapped Children*. London: University of London Press.

First published in the United Kingdom in 1996 by
Jessica Kingsley Publishers Ltd
116 Pentonville Road
London N1 9JB, England
and
1900 Frost Road, Suite 101
Bristol, PA 19007, U S A

Copyright © 1996 Jessica Kingsley Publishers

Library of Congress Cataloging in Publication Data
A CIP catalogue record for this book is available from the Library of Congress

British Library Cataloguing in Publication Data
Meeting the Needs of Ethnic Minority
Children
I. Dwivedi, Kedar Nath II. Varma, Ved P.
362.797

ISBN 1 85302 294 2

Printed and Bound in Great Britain by
Cromwell Press, Melksham, Wiltshire

Contents

With warm affection and esteem, this book is dedicated by the editors to Dr. Ishwar Chandra Tiwari, Professor of Preventive and Social Medicine, Institute of Medical Sciences, Varanasi and Consultant, UNICEF, Delhi, India.

Fourth Decade of Professor Ishwar Chandra Tiwari's Contributions: An Insight

There are multiple reasons why authors dedicate their books to certain persons or personalities. Through dedication of the present book, *Meeting the Needs of Ethnic Minority Children*, Dr Kedar Nath Dwivedi and Dr. Ved Prakash Varma aim to emphasize the need for pragmatic approaches to community health problems which Professor Tiwari has shown during his professional work. Having been a very close associate of Professor Tiwari, as his teacher during early 1960s and a professional colleague subsequently, I can provide some insight to his achievements and their relevance to the present book. This insight might prove useful for channelling efforts for tackling community health problems, especially the pressing needs of ethnic minority children.

In facing any community health problem, one needs convictions, missionary zeal, perseverance and a sense of deep commitment to the needs of the community, particularly of those who have somehow been left out and who are incidently in need of care the most. And this Professor Tiwari has amply demonstrated during his four decades of ongoing professional contribution. Soon after his graduation in 1960, he started his career as a Medical Officer in a rural health centre in India then moved over to an academic career in 1965. The initial field exposure during early part of his professional life was instrumental in sensitizing him about and providing a deep insight into the health needs of the community at the grass roots as well as the essentials of primary health care. He spent a major part of his subsequent professional life during 1965 to 1990 in academic institutions as a lecturer, reader and Professor of Community Medicine, first in state medical schools and since 1966 at one of the country's premier institutions, the Institute of Medical Sciences, Banaras Hindu University, Varanasi.

A very popular teacher among his students, Professor Tiwari has inspired them, particularly his post-graduate students of whom the Dr. Kedar Nath Dwivedi is one, to think, act and advocate for the health of the community, specially those who are underprivileged.

Professor Tiwari has always maintained his links with the community, working in the field practice areas and pursuing community based research. This I believe is the secret of his pragmatism. A two year assignment during 1982–84 as Professor and Chairman of the Department of Community Medicine at the University of Jos, Nigeria, which provided him international experience, further strengthened his conviction about the essentiality of primary health care as the key instrument for meeting the health needs of the community in developing countries.

Research data are needed to provide the base and the basis for refining existing programmes and developing newer concepts and tools for the practice of community health. Professor Tiwari has headed a number of research projects funded by important national and international agencies mainly in the area of maternal and child health, family planning and environmental health. He has published more than seventy research papers and guided eight PhD and eighteen MD theses. His contributions have been acknowledged by professional bodies and institutions by conferring him the orations and honours. He has also served as the President of Indian Association of Preventive and Social Medicine and Indian Public Health Association of which he is an elected Fellow. He was also conferred the Honorary Fellowship of the Liverpool School of Tropical Medicine.

Subsequently Professor Tiwari worked as Advisor (Health and Family Planning), to The Planning Commission, Government of India (1991–93) and moved on as a Senior Consultant to Unicef, New Delhi where he is continuing.

Professor Tiwari has thus contributed in his own way to the principles and practice of community health. He has brought pragmatism, cultivated through practice of the discipline in the community and sharpened through field based research, and sensitivity for the issues concerning the health of the people, particularly those who have been denied access to the benefits of health care. Through dedication of this book to a personality's life time and still ongoing contribution to the practice of community medicine the editors illustrate the directions and strategies, comprehension of the issues, and the commitment and convictions needed for 'Meeting the Needs of Ethnic Minority Children'.

Professor Surendra Mohan Marwah MBBS, MD, FAMS, FCCM
Formerly, Head of the Department of Preventive and Social Medicine &
Dean of the Faculty of Medical Sciences, Institute of Medical Sciences,
Banaras Hindu University, Varanasi, India and
subsequently retired Professor, Community Medicine,
King Faisal University, Kingdom of Saudi Arabia.

Preface

There are now a considerable proportion of children living in this country and elsewhere who belong to minority ethnic groups. As the 'melting pot' concept of a single culture resulting from the blending of different ethnic groups has sensibly given way to a pluralistic view of recognising and accepting of differences amongst groups, the new Children Act emphasizes the need for sensitivity to children's cultural, ethnic and linguistic requirements. There is a huge variety of professionals involved in helping, caring, educating, looking after and advocating for children, such as solicitors, child care social workers, residential workers, educational therapists, child psychologists, teachers, probation officers, education welfare officers, child psychiatrists, paediatricians, school doctors, school nurses, health visitors, nursery nurses, community psychiatric nurses, child psychiatric nurses, art therapists, play therapists, family therapists, group therapists, child psychotherapists and so on. As we found these professionals working with the ethnic minority children looking for a practical, comprehensive and integrated book, we felt that this would be a worthwhile effort. Many professionals in fact, often find themselves at a loss as to how to understand and meet these children's different needs and we feel that this book will go a long way to help.

It has been a great pleasure to edit this book as we were extremely fortunate in receiving an excellent quality of contributions from each of the authors. It has also been a privilege to put together the work of such an extra ordinary group of multidisciplinary experts.

We are immensely grateful to Jessica Kingsley and the rest of the publishing team for their unique enthusiasm, unfailing support and in fact very hard work. We are equally most grateful to all the authors for producing such a quality material and for putting up with our so called 'gentle' reminders.

We are also very thankful to Jean Kurecki and Naina Sadrani for their secretarial help on various occasions and last but not the least to our readers for considering to make use of the material. We very much hope that the readership will find the book practically helpful in meeting the needs not only of ethnic minority children but all others as well.

Kedar Nath Dwivedi and
Ved Prakash Varma

CHAPTER 1

Introduction

Kedar Nath Dwivedi

Introduction

The professionals involved with children can be divided into two groups: those who the child meets in the normal course of life on a regular basis, such as teachers and representatives of the health services, and those who operate as a part of a specific referral service, such as police and social services. Thus almost all children growing up in this country come in contact with a variety of professionals, such as health visitors, general practitioners, school teachers, school nurses and school doctors. In addition, many children also come in contact with professionals such as youth workers, social workers, education welfare officers, educational psychologists and a variety of child health and child mental health specialists and other professionals. Professionals vary as regards how much professional contact they have with children. A school teacher and a child, for example, may get plenty of opportunities to get to know each other, their likes, dislikes, opinions and feelings. This has an enormous potential to influence and colour the other's perceptions such as that of the child's parents, culture, and many other aspects of the child's life. A general practitioner, on the other hand, may depend largely on the parents to understand their child. Thus, the relationships between the child, parents and the professionals (Figure 1.1) can vary a great deal from situation to situation.

The Attitudinal Balance in Triadic Relationships

Heider (1946, 1958) proposed a model to comprehend the process of attitudinal balance in such triadic relationships. Accordingly, in any triadic relationship the constellation is in a state of balance when (1) all the three parties are in a positive relationship with one another, (2) all the three parties are in a negative relationship with one another (although this is a vacuous balance), or (3) the relationship between any one dyad is positive and the other two dyads are negative.

However, when only one of the dyads is negative and the other two dyadic relationships are positive, the constellation is in a state of imbalance and there is a continuous pressure within the system to shift the relationships so that either the sole negative relationship becomes positive or one of the positive relationships becomes negative. However, a strongly negative relationship between any of the three dyads (e.g. parent–professional; professional–child; and child–parent) will exert a strong pressure on the other two positive dyads so that at least one of them (usually the weak one) will turn into a negative. The evolution of a professional's relationship with the child is thus greatly influenced by (and influences in turn) the parent–child and the professional–parent relationships.

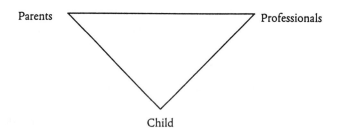

Figure 1.1 Triadic relationships

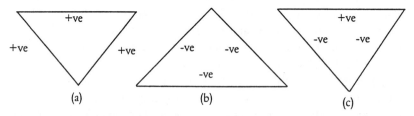

Figure 1.2. States of balance

A small proportion of children also get caught in legal proceedings and can come in contact with court welfare officers, social workers, Guardian Ad Litums, solicitors and so forth. The 1989 Children Act requires the court to find out and consider the wishes and feelings of the child giving due regard to the child's age and understanding. Sometimes a great deal of the court's time has to be spent in ascertaining how much of the child's apparent feelings and wishes in relation to individual parents are expressed as a result of the subtle pressures put upon the child by one or other of the parents and how much they are truly independent. More often than not one is really unsure.

Thus the attitudinal balancing process comes into sharp focus as the parental conflicts influence the parents' relationships with their child. In order to please one parent the child may develop a negative relationship with the other. For a child to love both parents when the parents hate each other (Figure 1.3), is to be in a state of attitudinal imbalance with constant systemic pressure attempting to shift the relationships in the direction of balance. A similar triadic dynamic can arise between the professional, the parents and the child (Figure 1.4).

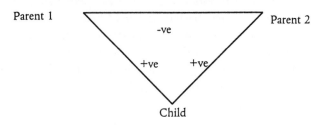

Figure 1.3. A state of imbalance

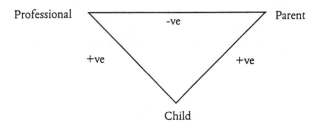

Figure 1.4. Another state of imbalance

Determinants of Professional Attitudes and Practices

The attitudes and practices of professionals are the product of a variety of factors. In addition to their psychological background and 'baggage', and their professional training and experiences, the concerns of the State and their cultural ideologies also exert a very important influence.

Concerns of the State

In western culture, ill treatment of children was not really recognized as a social problem until the end of the nineteenth century. There are numerous instances of barbarous treatment of children from medieval times including infanticide, mutilation, flogging, starvation and exploitation (Mause 1976). As the children were seen as the 'property' of their parents, parents had the full right to treat or punish their children as they saw fit. In 1880 Lord Shaftesbury tried to improve the conditions for children at work but left the parental ill treatment of children as beyond the reach of legislation. However, by 1889 the State took steps to intervene to protect children with the passage of the Protection of Cruelty to and Protection of Children Act 1889. The State intervention consisted primarily of physically removing the child, and this idea of 'rescue' remained the dominant ideology until after World War II. The 1933 Children and Young Persons Act was mainly concerned with preventing and controlling delinquency. As evacuation and the dislocation of families due to the war revealed that widespread deprivation and neglect were experienced by numerous children, the 1948 Children Act and the 1963 Children and Young Persons Act emphasized the strength and formative power of the family (Charles and Stevenson 1990). Then an increased awareness of incidents of child abuse led to the 1975 Children Act enabling local authorities to make legal application to free abused children for adoption. During the 1980s,

> Professionals working in child protection and hence representing the State, have been criticized on the one hand for too little intervention, too little attention to children's welfare and allowing children, such as Jasmine Beckford, Tyra Henry and Kimberly Carlile to die; whilst on the other hand, they have been accused of intervening unnecessarily in the families, with removing children without sufficient cause and with a lack of sensitivity to parent's rights, as was believed to have happened in Cleveland. (Charles and Stevenson 1990, p.5–6)

Cultural Ideology

The process is further compounded by the differences in values placed in the cultural ideologies on independence, autonomy, self-determination, separation, individuation and self-expression, Although social dependence had an honourable status in Europe until the fifteenth century it then began to be seen as a cause of grave social problems. However, the process of colonization created more dependency in the colonies. The American war of independence epitomized independence as the most cherished value and established dependency as a depicable state. The ideal of independence thus began to be held as the goal for personal growth in western culture and permeated all aspects of it.

Parents are therefore often at pains to make their children independent as quickly as possible, with an emphasis on early training (Roland 1980). Even the psychoanalytic literature conditioned by this preoccupation emphasizes the crucial place of separation, individuation and autonomy. Clear, open and direct expression of one's opinions, views and feelings is considered to be a manifestation of this process.

In such a cultural context, a professional's responses to the needs for guidance, advice and counsel can become rather awkward, indirect and disguised, taking on almost an art form. Even nonprofessional ordinary social interactions are often influenced by this ideology. Pande (1968) observed how requesting, telling, instructing or worse still ordering someone to do something even as trivial as closing a door requires camouflaging (e.g. 'do you want to close the door?') to make it appear as if motivation originated in the recipient of the request rather than the requester. In psychotherapy too, where one needs and seeks guidance and counsel from a mentor on life's difficult situations, the therapist, instead of telling the patient, has to offer 'interpretation' in which the therapist's own point of view is embedded. Thus the therapist gradually manages to influence the value system and major life themes of the patient in a culturally nourished mutual illusion that the decisions reached are that essentially of the patient.

> It is a commentary on deeper human needs that a society which above all prizes self direction and independence in life, and which is quite sensitive to the intrusion of personal belief systems of one individual upon another, has had to invent the institution of psychotherapy. Among other things, psychotherapy copes with needs that are perhaps more forthrightly met with by other societies that are oriented toward interdependence rather than toward independence. (Pande 1968, p.426)

Children, too, are often subject to similar disguised influences not only from the professionals around them but also their social network, media and their family members. The intensity of family relationships both financial and emotional makes it more conducive to organize each other's experiences and fantasies. The family members are in fact in an ideal position (just like the situation of hypnosis) to transmit suggestions to individuals within the family. Children can carry a playful and flexible boundary between the outer and the inner reality and can enjoy the company of playmates invisible to others. Their parents can easily join in the revivification of events complete with special smells, sights, laughters, sighs, tears and chills. Their words and sounds experienced during childhood can deeply reverberate within, ever after (Dwivedi 1993a; Ritterman 1983).

Influences on Children

The existence of such influences are seldom fully acknowledged as a great deal of such influence may take place outside conscious awareness and because of the cultural ideal of independent thinking. The professionals (such as teachers, social workers, counsellors and various health professionals) and the family members aim at fostering independent views and opinions along with skills in self-expression so that their children appear to have their own voices. When such a voice is separate, different and even opposite to their parents and other relatives, it creates a strong illusion of being really independent (Dwivedi 1995a). The rebellion of youth against institutions and their becoming non-conformist becomes understandable in such a cultural context. If a child or an adolescent does not express such independent views, it raises concerns and may lead to a professional's intervention, often with the assumption that the youngster's family may have been repressive and over restrictive, thus preventing self-expression. Many professionals may, therefore, feel passionate about 'rescuing' such children.

The professionals, because of their cultural conditioning tend to perceive their role as that of facilitators of individuality, self-expression and independence. Even if there is a genuine willingness to respect other cultural values of interdependence, heightened sensitivity to each other's feelings and the significance of mastering narcissistic individuality, it is difficult to do so without adequate preparation, development and training. It is only then that the resonance between the child and the parents as regards their feelings, views, attitudes and wishes is not automatically read as evidence of pathology. If a professional is unable to appreciate this fully, it will lead to distancing of the child either from the professional or from the parents, as outlined earlier.

Race, Racialization and Racism

'Race is an essentially biological concept based on those distinctive sets of hereditary phenotypical features that distinguish varieties of mankind' (Smith 1986, p.189). However, in fact, no race possesses a discrete package of genetic characteristics (Cooper 1984). Moreover, there is more genetic variation within than between races, and the genes responsible for morphological features such as skin colour, which are the usual basis of racial groupings, are very few and atypical (Hill 1989). The enumeration of races has depended upon the purpose of such classification and the classifications have left out several unclassified groups such as the Kalahari bushmen or pygmies (Mausner and Dramer 1985). Thus the concept of race as an objective category has very little credibility and is essentially incorrect. However, the process of categorization on racial lines does still continue.

In reality, 'race' is a social construction in which the variations between the groups said to be 'races' are emphasised more than the variations within the groups, in spite of the fact that these variations are continuous and not discrete (Thomas and Sillen 1979). Dalal (1993) describes this phenomenon in the following context:

> ...we live in a historical era that began in the sixteenth century, during which Imperial Europe colonized the rest of the world. The colonizer used various myths, phantasies and ideologies to maintain a division between the colonizer and the colonized. (p.277)

The World War II contained the most repugnant consequences of this process. The practices of racial discrimination, whether deliberate or unintentional, and the beliefs based on racial prejudice are referred to as 'racism'. Prejudice literally means pre-judging. A person who holds views about an individual, or group of people, which are not based on knowledge, and is unwilling to change these views even when presented with clear evidence that they are factually wrong, is a prejudiced person.

A larger proportion of coloured people than white suffer from social and economic disadvantages such as unemployment, poor jobs, poor housing and lesser opportunities for education and training in the UK. Government statistics show that black and minority people are twice as likely to be unemployed compared with white people. The media, particularly the popular press, are often biased in the way they report racial incidents and issues. The Home Office estimates that there are 130,000 racial attacks annually. There is also a tendency to suppress or dismiss minority cultures in the name of integration.

The racial frame of reference includes assumptions and myths about other cultures and can become an organizing principle of popular consciousness (Carter and Williams 1987). 'Racism affects black children – but it also affects white children, who may be growing up with a false sense of their own superiority and acquiring views based on unacceptable stereotypes if they are not shown alternative ways of thinking and behaving' (Pugh 1994, p.xi). It is this Eurocentric imperialistic cultural ideology through a process of *projective identification* that leads many young Asians, at times of distress, presenting to professionals with problems in a way that is more likely to elicit a sympathetic response (Ahmed, S. 1986). The concept of projective identification is extensively described and illustrated in the psychoanalytic literature (Ogden 1979; Cashdan 1988; see also Chapter 2 in this volume). It helps to comprehend the subtlety of interpersonal influences outside each other's conscious awareness and is believed to consist of three parts (1) a fantasy of some quality, attribute or emotion which is stripped off from oneself and, (2) projected onto someone else along with (3) considerable interpersonal pressure to comply with the projection. The mounting pressure makes the person onto whom the stripped off parts are projected, to unconsciously identify with what is projected and the recipient of the pressure is induced to think, feel and behave accordingly.

For example, the primitive, oppressive and other aspects of the Victorian extended family life from the cultural past can be stripped off and projected onto the family map of an ethnic minority group. Ethnic minority cultures are therefore described in a way which make them seem bizarre or backward or imply that their problems are somehow caused by the nature of their culture (Mares, Henley and Boxter 1985). The very fabric of the society appears to be permeated by such an attitude manifesting itself in education, media, history books, social work, counselling and psychotherapy literature, and children's story books. It is in such an atmosphere that youngsters, at times of distress and when needing help, end up identifying with such projections and present to the professionals with problems in a way that are more likely to elicit a sympathetic response, for example, a complaint of ill-treatment, fear of arranged marriage and so forth. (Ahmed, S. 1986). This marks the third component of projective identification. Goldberg and Hodes (1992) demonstrate how self-poisoning by a number of Asian adolescent girls symbolizes the acting out of the view of the dominant group that the minority is 'poisonous' or 'harmful'.

The ideological impositions illustrated above are clearly a kind of cultural imperialism and a form of institutional racism. This should be against the spirit of the 1989 Children Act which recommends giving full consideration to the racial origin and ethnic, cultural, religious and linguistic background of the child. Institutional racism is the way in which the society's institutions operate to the continued advantage of the majority either intentionally or unintentionally (Halstead 1988). Similarly, cultural racism

> seeks to justify racist attitudes and practices in cultural terms. The culture of minority groups is seen as deficient in social customs, manners, appropriate attitudes etc. and holding them back. If they refuse to turn their back on their own culture, then any 'discrimination' is their own fault. (Massey. 1991, p.34)

Ethnicity and Culture

The Kings Fund classes all disadvantaged people as 'black' believing that the experience of racism is most important (McKenzie and Crowcroft 1994). Dalal (1993) looks at its source.

> Colour was used as the primary visible signifier to distinguish 'us' from 'them'. In order to do this successfully it was necessary for the hallucinatory whitening of all the peoples of Europe including the Roman, the Greek, the Celt, and of course Jesus Christ, so that they could be distinguished from the 'coloured'. It was this that generated the political category 'black'. The categories 'black' and 'white' are hallucinations... (p.278)

The Commission for Racial Equality uses the term 'ethnic minorities', believing that cultural and religious differences are important. Thus there is now a tendency to use the notion of 'ethnicity' more than that of race, implying shared or common features such as social background or origin, language, culture, tradition and religion. McGoldrick (1982) describes the ethnic group as those who perceive themselves as alike by virtue of their common ancestry, real or fictitious, and who are so regarded by others. People from different ethnic groups also tend to experience and express their distress differently (Patel 1994). However, ethnic boundaries can also be very imprecise and fluid. The word 'ethnic' is often abused by referring to coloured populations as 'ethnic populations' or 'ethnic families', as if others do not have any ethnicity! It is also frequently confused with nationality or with migrant status.

In spite of the conceptual confusion, race and ethnicity are commonly used variables in research. Nearly 2500 papers just on medical research are indexed each year under the headings of 'ethnic groups' or 'racial stocks' on medline (National Library of Medicine 1994) but,

The categories of race or ethnic group are rarely defined, the use of
terms is inconsistent, and people are often allocated to racial or ethnic
groups, arbitrarily. Some researchers use the original Blumenbach
(1865) classification and class Asians as 'caucasian', though modern
definitions often class 'Asians' as 'black'. (McKenzie and Crowcroft
1994, p.286)

Ethnicity also includes *culture*. Culture was defined in the nineteenth century
as 'that complex whole which includes knowledge, belief, art, morals, law,
custom, and any other capabilities and habits acquired by man as a member of
society' (Tylor 1871). It contains the system of rules for governing behaviour,
and of beliefs or a web of meaning for making sense of experiences. Thus it
organizes our cognitive, emotional and behavioural functions in both subtle
and obvious ways, although the cultural values and assumptions may remain
outside our awareness (McGoldrick, Pearce and Giardano 1982).

Welfare

The Children Act 1989 emphasizes the concept of 'parental responsibility'
rather than that of 'parental rights' and requires the views of the children to be
actively sought. The Act also makes it unlawful to ignore the crucial aspects of
racial origin and cultural, ethnic, religious and linguistic background of the
child in the process of any decision making. However, the professional practices
and perceptions including the definitions of what is 'normal' or 'deviant' have
so far been largely white and eurocentric. If such professional perceptions and
practices continue the Act can easily work against the best interest and
protection of the ethnic minority child. The instrument of 'race, culture, religion
and language' can be easily abused to perpetuate the dominance of professional
control as a manifestation of their perception of ethnic minority families as
culturally deficient, dysfunctional or pathological from whom the children need
to be rescued on the one hand, to a justification of non-intervention even when
a child desperately needs intervention and protection, so that the professional
could appear to be culturally sensitive in case abuse is culturally acceptable!

> ...like the Race Relations Act 1976, the Children Act 1989 may end
> up with little or no impact in promoting the welfare and protecting the
> interest of the black child, if the interest and welfare of the black child
> are left to the rhetoric of the Act and not transferred into social work
> action. (Ahmed, B. 1991, p.III)

In Chapter 6 on 'Residential Care for ethnic minority children' Harish Mehra
through the moving case examples of Gurvinder highlights the above issues
for social work practice, particularly in residential child care. Professor Harry
Zeitlin in Chapter 5 on 'Adoption of children from minority groups' examines
the complex issues involved with the hope that this would help evolve practices

that are least damaging to the children but are conducive to their comprehensive growth. In Chapter 12 on 'Community and youth work with Asian women and girls' Radha Dwivedi provides an excellent account of a piece of community and youth work with Asian women and girls in a small town.

Education

The recent research looking at the experiences of young ethnic minority children in nursery and primary schools highlights that it is not only children who behave in racist manner but also some of their teachers (Wright 1992). They not only held negative stereotypes but were also aware of the racial harassment but reluctant to deal with it. The introduction of educational reforms has, therefore, produced a mixed feeling in the ethnic minority parents.

> Some black parents have welcomed the national curriculum and national testing as a guarantee that their children will not be fobbed off with a second rate curriculum or suffer discriminatory subjective assessments by prejudiced teachers. Others have seized on the possibilities of LMS for ensuring that black people's voices can no longer be disregarded by the schools. (Hatcher 1989, p.24)

It is the space between the policy and the classroom practices that provide the real opportunities for multicultural and anti-racist education (Smith 1989), although there is an enormous potential for improvement at the level of policy too. The decision of Cleveland Education Authority to allow a parent to exercise choice on racist grounds has arisen from the Education Reform Act. This in fact establishes the primacy of recent Education legislation over Race Relations legislation and opens the way for racial segregation in schools.

In Chapter 3, 'The immigrant (West Indian) child in school', Waverney Bushell looks at the stresses for the West Indian children and their families and Gerry German in Chapter 4 on 'Anti-racist strategies for educational perform-ance: Facilitating successful learning for all children' emphasizes the need for the actual implementation of anti racist strategies for educational performance and for creating a learning environment that could facilitate successful learning for all children.

Damage and Disturbance

For the ethnic minority families the impact of dislocation, loss of the extended family and that of other significant social network along with the experience of racism and the undermining of their value systems by the major institutions can produce serious consequences. The ethnic minority childrens emotional difficulties can be further exacerbated by professionals who unwittingly con-flate cultural differences with psychopathologies. The damage to self-identity of ethnic minority children in such a climate is often extremely deep and difficult to repair (Dwivedi 1993b, 1993c, 1993d, 1995b). The ethnic minority families have already embarked upon a process of ethnic redefinition. This has often meant loss of their traditional arrangements and the creation of new ones, but these new arrangements may still not fit in with their new context (Perelberg 1992).

A study in Tower Hamlets has shown that the Bangladeshi respondents experienced more serious life events and reported more symptoms than their indigenous neighbours (MacCarthy and Craissati 1989). Similarly, a recent survey by the Confederation of Indian Organisations revealed an alarmingly high rate of emotional distress within South Asian communities and little outlet for their expression (Beliappa 1991).

Health Needs

The Commission for Racial Equality (CRE) launched (1992) the Race Relations Code of Practice in Primary Health Care Services with the aim of facilitating fair access in provision of services. The Code was drawn up in consultation with the general practitioners, Family Health Service Authorities (FHSAs), Community Health Councils, Regional and District Health Authorities and a wide range of other related health bodies. However, when the FHSAs were contacted by the CRE in 1993, only 29 out of 600 contacted indicated that they were planning to implement the code. Similarly, a recent survey of the opinions of the ethnic minority populations in Buckinghamshire revealed that only 3.9 per cent correctly identified the purpose of the Patient's Charter, 40 per cent of the patients asked others to make their appointment to see the general practitioner and 65 per cent of patients who needed an interpreter were never offered one (Leisten and Richardson 1994). Chapter 7 on 'Health needs of children from ethnic minorities' by Carolyn Bailey examines the health needs of ethnic minority children and explores the ways of meeting them.

A recent outcome study of Bangladeshi families attending a child psychiatric service in London revealed that the congruence in problem definition between family and therapists was linked with good outcome as rated by the family (Hillier, Loshak, Rahman and Marks 1994). Chapter 8 on 'Psychiatric needs of ethnic minority children' by Surya and Soni Bhate looks particularly at their mental health, in the context of the stresses on ethnic minority families. They look at some of the childhood psychiatric disorders such as delinquency and conduct disorder, emotional disorder, drug abuse, eating disorders and so forth, the uptake of services and the way to improve the provisions.

Culture and Family Processes

Cultural ideologies have an impact on all aspects of life including one's purpose of life. Developing states of mind that are conducive to transcending narcissistic preoccupations and achieving enlightenment in this life or a future life time can be the most important purpose of life for a Hindu, Jain or Buddhist (Dwivedi 1990; 1994a; 1994b; 1994c).

Perelberg (1992) has explored the links between culture and the patterns of interactions between families with the help of the intervening concepts of social structure, social organization and family maps. Social structure and social organization are the form and processes respectively taken by the historical and sociological relationships. Family maps are a set of ideas that guide emotions and behaviour in everyday life... The patterns of interactions within the family between the individuals involve meaning, emotion and behaviour and contain within themselves an image of the whole expressing the family organization. Thus family maps link the family organization with the family interactions. The map can contain the conflicting ideas and expectations held by different generations.

Perelberg describes two models of nonpathological maps: hierarchical (segregated) and symmetrical (egalitarian). The term differentiated may be more appropriate than hierarchical to describe the family map characterized by differentiated or segregated roles, tasks and activities with a sociocentric view of individuals in a role relationship. At the other end of the continuum is the undifferentiated (symmetrical, egalitarian or democratic) family map with the egocentric emphasis on the autonomy of the individual. Thus cultural influences through the family processes and parenting have an enormous impact on the shaping of the personality and its disorders. This theme is further developed in Chapter 2, 'Culture and personality' (Dwivedi) utilizing the example of narcissism and narcissistic disorders in the context of eastern and western cultures.

Family Therapy

The helping professionals are also subject to the cultural conditioning of their own social group. It is difficult to step outside one's belief systems and to open to other cultural possibilities because such differences and ambiguities can be threatening and can lead to questioning of one's very methods of coping, treating or handling the situation. This is why Dayal (1990) points out that the emotional availability of many professionals to ethnic minority families is often very limited. Some fail to respond on the grounds that they cannot understand the cultural ways of ethnic minority families (Fernando 1988), while others look for and quickly find 'cultural conflict' type of explanation. Devereux (1953) called this 'culturalistic pseudo insight' whereby one attributes to the culture what is actually an explanation of the individual personality.

Similarly, many ethnic minority parents react to what they perceive and phantasize to be in the western culture in a way that leads to conflict. For example, many Asian parents, bombarded by the images of romantic courtships and of violent, drugged, excessively sexualized and senseless scenes of youngsters on the media, may feel panicky and overprotective towards their offspring. Youngsters' attempts to resist this can easily lead to the escalation of parental protectiveness. The triadic relationships between the child, parents and professionals can further compound the situation, culminating even into suicidal behaviours.

John Burnham and Queenie Harris in Chapter 10 on 'The emergence of ethnicity: a tale of three cultures' have utilized the framework offered by the Co-ordinated Management of Meaning from the social constructionist tradition. Through the case study of a Chinese family they explore some of the issues for children as they negotiate changes in family and cultural processes. In Chapter 9 on 'Children, families and therapists: Clinical considerations and ethnic minority cultures' Begum Maitra and Ann Miller examine the meeting between the psychological therapist and the ethnic minority families as a meeting between two cultures which may contain a conflict between potentially opposing, and possibly irreconcilable views of childhood and, with the help of a number of very informative case examples, highlight the significance of the process whereby this meeting is negotiated. Annie Lau in Chapter 11, on 'Family Therapy and ethnic minorities' highlights the cultural differences in family organizations, their knowledge, beliefs and rituals through family life cycles and offers some valuable guidelines for assessment and therapy along with a case example.

References

Ahmed, B. (1991) 'Setting the context: Race and the Children Act 1989.' In S Macdonald (ed) *All Equal Under the Act.* London: Race Equality Unit.

Ahmed, S. (1986) 'Cultural racism in work with Asian women and girls.' In S. Ahmed, J. Cheetham and J. Small (eds) *Social Work with Black Children and their Families.* London: Batsford.

Beliappa, J. (1991) *Illness or Distress: Alternative Models of Mental Health.* London: Confederation of Indian Organisations.

Carter, B. and Williams, J. (1987) 'Attacking racism in education.' In B. Troyna (ed) *Racial Inequality in Education.* London: Tavistock.

Cashdan, S. (1988) *Object Relations Therapy: Using the Relationship.* London: W.W. Norton.

Charles, M. and Stevenson, O. (1990) *Multidisciplinary is Different: Child Protection Working Together Part II: Sharing Perspectives.* Nottingham: The Nottingham University.

Cooper, R. (1984) 'A note on the biological concept of race and its application in epidemiological research.' *American Heart Journal 108,* 715–23.

Commission for Racial Equality (1992) *Race Relations Code of Practice in Primary Health Care Services.* London: CRE.

Dalal, F.N. (1993) '"Race" and racism: An attempt to organize difference.' *Group Analysis 26,* 277–293

Dayal, N. (1990) 'Psychotherapy services for minority ethnic communities in the NHS – a psychotherapist's view.' *Midland Journal of Psychotherapy 11*, 28–37.

Devereux, G. (1953) 'Cultural factors in psycho analytic therapy.' *Journal of American Psychoanalytic Association 1*, 629–55.

Dwivedi, K.N. (1990) 'Purification of mind by Vipassana meditation.' In J. Crook and D. Fontana (eds) *Space in Mind*. Shaftesbury: Element Books.

Dwivedi, K.N. (1993a) 'Confusion and underfunctioning in children.' In V.P. Varma (e) *How and Why Children Fail*. London: Jessica Kingsley Publishers.

Dwivedi, K.N. (1993b) 'Emotional development.' In K.N. Dwivedi (ed) *Groupwork with Children and Adolescents*. London: Jessica Kingsley Publishers.

Dwivedi, K.N. (1993c) 'Coping with unhappy children who are from ethnic minorities.' In V.P. Varma (ed) *Coping with Unhappy Children*. London: Cassell.

Dwivedi, K.N. (1993d) 'Child abuse and hatred.' In V.P. Varma (ed) *How and Why Children Hate*. London: Jessica Kingsley Publishers.

Dwivedi, K.N. (1994a) 'Mental cultivation (meditation) in Buddhism.' *Psychiatric Bulletin 18*, 503–4.

Dwivedi, K.N. (1994b) 'The Buddhist perspective in mental health.' *Open mind 70*, 20–22.

Dwivedi, K.N. (1994c) 'Social structures that support or undermine ethnic minority groups: eastern value systems.' *Context 20*, 11–12.

Dwivedi, K.N. (1995a) 'Race.' In G. Upton, R. Davie and V. P. Varma (eds) *The Voice of the Child: A Handbook for Professionals*. London: Falmer Press.

Dwivedi, K.N. (1995b) 'Stress in children from ethnic minorities.' In V.P. Varma (ed) *Coping with Stress in Children*. Aldershot: Arena.

Fernando, S. (1988) *Race and Culture in Psychiatry*. London: Croom Helm.

Goldberg, D. and Hodes, M. (1992) 'The poison of racism and the self poisoning of adolescents.' *Journal of Family Therapy 14*, 51:67

Halstead, M. (1988) *Education, Justice and Cultural Diversity: An examination of the Honeyford affair 1984–85*. London: Falmer Press.

Hatcher, R. (1989) 'Anti-racist education after the Act.' *Multicultural Teaching 7*, 3, 24–27.

Heider, F. (1946) 'Attitudes and cognitive organisation.' *Journal of Psychology 21*, 107–12

Heider, F. (1958) *The Psychology of Interpersonal Relations*. New York: John Wiley.

Hill, A.V.S. (1989) 'Molecular markers of ethnic groups.' In J.K. Cruickshank and D.G. Beevers (eds) *Ethnic Factors in Health and Disease*. London: Wright.

Hillier, S.A., Loshak, R., Rahman, S. and Marks, F (1994) 'An evaluation of child psychiatric services for Bangladeshi parents.' *Journal of Mental Health 3*, 327–337

Leisten, R. and Richardson, J. (1994) *Access to Health: A Minority Ethnic Perspective*. Northampton: Nene College.

MacCarthy, B. and Craissati, J. (1989) 'Ethnic differences in response to adversity: a community sample of Bangladeshis and their indigenous neighbours.' *Social Psychiatry and Psychiatric Epidemiology 24*,196–201.

Mares, P., Henley, A., and Baxter, C. (1985) *Healthcare in Multicultural Britain.* Cambridge: Health Education Council and National Extension College.

Massey, I. (1991) *More Than Skin Deep: Developing Anti Racist Multi Cultural Education in Schools.* London: Hodder Stoughton.

Mause, L. De (ed) (1976) *The History of Childhood.* New York: Souvenir.

Mausner, J.S. and Dramer, S. (1985) *Epidemiology: An Introductory Text.* Philadelphia: Saunders.

McGoldrick, M. (1982) 'Ethnicity and family therapy.' In M. McGoldrick, J.K. Pearce and J. Giardano (eds) *Ethnicity and Family Therapy.* New York: Guilford Press.

McGoldrick, M., Pearce, J. and Giardano, J. (eds) (1982) *Ethnicity and Family Therapy.* New York: Guilford Press.

McKenzie, K.J. and Crowcroft, N.S. (1994) 'Race, ethnicity, culture and science: researchers should understand and justify their use of ethnic groupings.' *British Medical Journal 309.* 6950, 286–7.

National Library of Medicine (1994) Medline Silver Plater 3.11 CDROM. *Medline Express 1989–1.* Bethseda, MD:NLM.

Ogden, T. (1979) 'On projective identification.' *International Journal of Psychoanalysis 60*, 357–73.

Pande, S.K. (1968) 'The mystique of western psychotherapy: an eastern interpretation.' *The Journal of Nervous and Mental Diseases 146*, 6, 425–32.

Patel, V. (1994) 'The cross-cultural assessment of depression.' *Focus on Depression 2*, 1, 5–8.

Perelberg, R.J. (1992) 'Familiar and unfamiliar types of family structure: towards a conceptual framework.' In J. Kareem and R. Littlewood (eds) *Intercultural Therapy: Themes, Interpretations and Practices.* Oxford: Blackwell Scientific Publications.

Pugh, G. (1994) 'Foreword.' In I. Siraj-Blatchford, *The Early Years: Laying the Foundations for Racial Equality.* Stoke on Trent: Trentham Books.

Ritterman, M. (1983) *Using Hypnosis in Family Therapy.* London: Jossey-Bass Publishers.

Roland, A. (1980) 'Psychoanalytic perspectives on personality development in India.' *International Review of Psychoanalysis 1*, 73–87.

Smith, J (1989) 'Anti-racist practice after the Act: What are the ways forward?' *Multicultural Teaching 7*, 3.

Smith, M.G. (1986) 'Pluralism, race and ethnicity in selected African countries.' In J. Rex and D. Mason (eds) *Theories of Race and Ethnic Relations.* Cambridge: Cambridge University Press.

Thomas, A. and Sillen, S. (1979) *Racism and Psychiatry*. New York: Citadel Press.

Tylor, E.B. (1871) *Primitive Culture*. London: John Murray.

Wright, C. (1992) 'Early education: Multiracial primary school classrooms.' In D. Gill *et al. Racism and Education*. London: Sage.

CHAPTER 2

Culture and Personality

Kedar Nath Dwivedi

> Every society reproduces its culture – its norms, its underlying assumptions, its mode of organising experience – in the individual, in the form of personality. (Lasch 1980, p.34)

Personality

Personality is 'that which characterizes an individual and determines his unique adaptation to the environment' (Harsh and Schrickel 1950). As studied by the modern western psychologist, it is conceptualized as an integrated whole which can be viewed from different directions; for example, temperament, attitudes, morphology, physiology, needs, interests, aptitudes and so on. However, in studying personality, the characteristics that affect an individual's ability to get along with other people and with oneself are given greater significance. Personality features (such as types, traits, dimensions) highlight some inner consistency over time, as well as some generality, so that predictions can be made of behaviour likely to occur in a variety of contexts (Guilford 1959).

A personality can be described by its position on a number of scales or dimensions, each of which represent a trait. A person can be characterized according to the profile of different traits. There have been a large number of studies to delineate different categories of traits or personality variables. Another approach has been to classify people into a few types by thinking in terms of some of the central themes or styles of life (such as extroversion versus introversion) that characterize some individuals so well. Such theories of personality types have been around from ancient times and persist even today in one form or another.

For example, the Buddhist meditation masters (since the sixth century B.C.) taught specific meditation techniques depending upon the particular personality of the trainee. Buddhism recognizes that there are three fundamental dimensions underlying the behaviour of all unenlightened human beings in varying degrees; craving versus faith, hatred versus intelligence, and confusion versus speculation. These factors condition almost everything that we do and the way we dress, relate, work, think and so on (Mann and Youd 1992). This approach resonated with the humoural theory of Ayurvedic medicine. Ayurveda has been the ancient and traditional system of medicine in India and still has an enormous influence on their day-to-day life (Rai and Dwivedi 1988). The golden period of Ayurveda corresponded with the rise of Buddhism in India (Dwivedi 1994a). In Ayurvedic medicine the humoural approach to diagnosis, treatment and health promotion is based upon three fundamental humours (Vaat, Pitt and Kaf) resonant with the Buddhist approach (Clifford 1984). Similarly in the Greek system of (Unani) medicine human temperaments were classified on the basis of the body humours: sanguine, phlegmatic, melancholic and choleric.

As there are a variety of approaches to comprehending the notion of personality today, there are also a variety of ways of assessing it (Vernon 1963). Suvh assessments can take the form of (1) unstructured or structured interviews, (2) self-report rating scales or personality inventories such as Minnesota Multiphasic Personality Inventory, Cattell's 16 PF Questionnaire, Eysenck Personality Inventory, Edwards Personal Preference Schedule, (3) projective tests such as Thematic Apperception Test, Rorschach Inkblot Test and (4) behavioural observations. In practice the personality inventories appear to be the most commonly used tools both for clinical and for occupational (such as the recruitment of managers with certain personality traits) purposes.

Personality Disorder

People can differ very widely as regards their profiles of personality traits but still be regarded as normal. However, in some individuals certain traits can be sufficiently maladaptive and abnormal as to constitute a 'Personality Disorder'. These traits can also cause enormous subjective distress.

As there are many ways of classifying personality, there are similarly many ways of classifying and assessing Personality Disorders. However, the classification systems based upon the International Classification of Diseases (World Health Organisation 1992) and the Diagnostic and Statistical Manual of Mental Disorders (American Psychiatric Association 1994) are the most commonly used.

The Structured Clinical Interview for DSM III (SCIDP), the Structured Interview for DSM III Personality Disorders (SIDP) and the Personality Disorders Examination (PDE) use the subject as the main source of information while in the Personality Assessment Schedule (PAS) both the subject and the informant may be interviewed and the final personality score determined by the combination of both results (Tyrer and Ferguson 1987).

The categories of Personality Disorders listed by the DSM-IV (American Psychiatric Association 1994, p.629) are as follows:

(1) *Paranoid Personality Disorder* is a pattern of distrust an suspiciousness such that others' motives are interpreted as malevolent.

(2) *Schizoid Personality Disorder* is a pattern of detachment from social relationships and a restricted range of emotional expression.

(3) *Schizotypal Personality Disorder* is a pattern of acute discomfort in close relationships, cognitive or perceptual distortions, and eccentricities of behaviour.

(4) *Antisocial Personality Disorder* is a pattern of disregard for, and violation of, the rights of others.

(5) *Borderline Personality Disorder* is a pattern of instability in interpersonal relationships, self-image, and affects, and marked impulsivity.

(6) *Histrionic Personality Disorder* is a pattern of excessive emotionality and attention seeking.

(7) *Narcissistic Personality Disorder* is a pattern of grandiosity, need for admiration, and lack of empathy.

(8) *Avoidant Personality Disorder* is a pattern of social inhibition, feelings of inadequacy, and hypersensitivity to negative evaluation.

(9) *Dependent Personality Disorder* is a pattern of submissive and clinging behaviour related to an excessive need to be taken care of.

(10) *Obsessive-Compulsive Personality Disorder* is a pattern of submissive and clinging behaviour related to an excessive need to be taken care of.

(11) *Personality Disorder* Not Otherwise Specified.

Cultural Influences on Personality and Personality Disorders

There has been a great deal written in the western anthropological literature about human differences. In the past this was heavily influenced by the tradition of 'environmental humouralism'. Such a theory assumed that different groups developed their characteristic inborn temperaments due to living for long periods in different geographical environments. Thus during the mid-eighteenth century Linnaeus divided mankind into four major races around an implicit geographical wheel of colour and other morphological features and temperament. These were: Americanus (rufus, cholericus, rectus) in the West;

Europaeus (albus, sanguineus, torosus) in the North; Asiaticus (luridus, melan-cholicus, rigidus) in the East; and Afer (niger, phlegmaticus, laxus) in the South! Although the concept of 'race' as an objective category is essentially incorrect and has very little credibility, racial categorization or the process of racialisation continued. 'The colonizer used various myths, phantasies and ideologies to maintain a division between the colonizer and the colonized' (Dalal 1993, p.277). This led to an explosive proliferation of anthropological studies. Ethnology became a branch of anthropology that studied racial characteristics. The science of determining the strength of the faculties by the size and shape of the skull was called Phrenology. Such pseudo-scientific speculations contin-ued throughout the nineteenth and even into the twentieth century.

In the twentieth century, however, an alternative explanation of human differences began to be put forward in terms of 'cultural determinism'. Thus in the aftermath of a world war, a 'Culture and Personality movement' was born in the context of a multi-ethnic make up of twentieth century American society. However, by the 1950s, it came under severe attack as the same racial prejudices had continued in the guise of cultural determinism. Vernon's (1969) survey of culture and intelligence is a typical example of such an Eurocentric approach. He concludes:

> Cultural groups and subgroups are exceedingly varied, and so also must be their effects on the intellectual growth of their members. A number of attempted classifications or typologies are examined, and it seems reasonable to regard the Puritan ethic of the western middle class as producing the greatest development of intelligence, in contrast, both to western lower class and to the 'less civilised' cultures. (Vernon 1969, p.219)

There has now been a revival of interest in culture, society, self, personhood and personality connections and a renaissance in cross cultural formulations of these relationships. The 'old culture and personality movement' (Stocking 1986) was essentially Eurocenteric, while the 'new culture and personality' approach aims to go beyond Eurocentrism by attempting to understand cultures and personality from indigenous ideological perspectives and explore the ways in which culturally contrasting people conceptualize their human nature.

'Culture' had been defined as 'that complex whole which includes knowl-edge, belief, art, law, custom, and any other capabilities and habits acquired by man as a member of society' (Tylor 1871 p.1). Now there is a greater emphasis on the cultural world view. Geertz (1973), in fact, conceptualizes culture as a 'web of meaning'.

> That people lose control over their lives, that people become depressed, unhappy and withdraw into a world of their own, unbounded by

constraints of time. space and reality, that people abandon their will to live, seek oblivion in alcohol, resort to uncontrollable and meaningless acts of cruelty and violence, that people are haunted by feelings of guilt, remorse, fear and shame, are all common human experiences which exist around us. The problem is not that these problems do not exist; they exist everywhere. The problem is *how* one construes them meaningfully. For it is the construing of an experience, its interpretation, and the meaning one assigns to the experience which involves making all sorts of assumptions. *It is those assumptions which often are culture-specific. Not the experience itself* as has been mistakenly assumed by the cultural relativists. (Laungani 1992, p.233, emphasis original)

Culture, Person and Self

Parsons (1964) pointed out that the bridge between personality and culture is the super ego acquired through the process of social interaction. Hsu (1985) emphasizes that ' the meaning of being human is found in interpersonal relationships, since no human being exists alone' (p.27) and criticizes the western concept of personality as rather restrictive. Such a concept, instead of seeing the individual in a web of interpersonal relationships, focuses on the individual's deep core of complexes and anxieties. In fact, the nature of the interpersonal relationships, in such a viewpoint, is seen merely as indicators of the expression of this core.

'In Western cultures, individuality is the prime value and relatedness is secondary in the sense that a person has the choice of whether to make certain relationships with other entities or not' (Tamura and Lau 1992, p.330). As it is essentially a 'work and activity centered' culture the relationships such as marital, family, friends colleagues and so on have to be developed by working for these on the basis of shared commanalities. Pande (1968) observes that one's performance at the table at a dinner party may influence whether one will be invited again, that a father has to take his son to a football game or some such activity in order to develop or prove a mutual trust, comradarie and intimacy. In a relationship centered eastern society on the other hand, no such hidden agenda (or excuse of shared commonality) is necessary for the cultivation of a relationship. From very early on one learns to regard the process of caring and mutual involvement, unfolding of emotional affinity and the relationship itself as the most important aspect of living.

> We might also view traditional Indian society as a therapeutic model of social organisation in that it attempts to alleviate dukha [existential suffering] by addressing itself to deep needs for connection and ·relationship to other human beings in an enduring and trustworthy fashion and for ongoing mentorship, guidance and help in getting through life and interpreting current experience with whatever has

gone before and with an anticipated future. In the relatively more activist and task oriented social organisation of western countries, these dependency needs of adults are generally seen as legitimate only in moments of acute crises or circumstances of sickness. (Kakar 1981, p.124–5)

In western culture, relationships of the individual to society are viewed from an 'egocentric' perspective, for example focusing on the reproduction of individuals rather than on the reproduction of relationships, with an emphasis on separateness, clear boundaries, individuality and autonomy within the relationships, while in eastern cultures there is a 'sociocentric' conception of these relationships and a person is seen as a part of the embedded interconnectedness of relationships (Shweder and Bourne 1982; Strathern 1992).

Self-control from the western point of view is seen to come from within the person, while the eastern perspective has a more ecological view, considering the individual in a wider system of cosmic (including both physical and social) relationships as evident in the humoural theory of Ayurvedic Medicine (Lutz 1988; Krause 1995). The eastern view of person is, therefore, essentially transactional and transformational:

> Persons – single actors – are not thought in South Asia to be 'individual', that is, indivisible, bounded units, as they are in much of western social and psychological theory as well as in common sense. Instead, it appears that persons are generally thought by South Asians to be 'dividual' or divisible. To exist, dividual persons absorb heterogeneous material influences. They must also give out from themselves particles of their own coded substances – essences, residues, or other active influences – that may then reproduce in others something of the nature of the persons in whom they have originated. (Marriott 1976, p.111)

The Indian concept of self, person or being can be traced back to the unique leap in the equation of *sat* (to be) = *sat* (being as an ontological entity) in the Rigveda, the oldest Indo-European text (Bharati 1985).

> I claim that Hindu notions of the self were generated and are being perpetuated from that metaphysical–speculative base just like western notions of self were generated and perpetuated by the empirical epistmologies created in ancient Greece on the secular side, as well as by the Judaeo–Christian (plus Islamic) doctrines of the soul as an ontological, self conscious entity. (pp.189–190)

Although the Buddhist concept of 'anatta' (that is lack of self) and the Hindu core – doctrine of 'atman' (that is, 'self' but not as identified with body, sense, mind) 'are mutually exclusive and polarized, *both of them together* radically contrast with any of the western perceptions of the self, from the Judaeo–Christian to the general systems and cybernatics-informed notions of self' (Bharati 1985, p.203, emphasis original).

Culture and Pathology

Cultural approach to self is also reflected in pathological processes. Littlewood (1995) points out that eating disorders were once identified exclusively with western societies but when these occur among in South Asian women including those living in the west, these arise as manifestations of self-renunciation rather than in the western ideal of self-cherishing and fear of fatness. Lasch (1980) commenting on the recent changes within the western culture writes:

> Every age develops its own peculiar forms of pathology, which express in exaggerated form its underlying character structure. In Freud's time, hysteria and obsessional neurosis carried to extremes the personality traits associated with the capitalist order at an earlier stage in its development – acquisitiveness, fanatical devotion to work, and a fierce repression of sexuality. In our time, the preschizophrenic, borderline, or personality disorders have attracted increasing attention, along with schizophrenia itself. (p.41)

For the purposes of further exploration, in this chapter we will take the example of *narcissism* as an aspect of personality and its disorders, in order to examine its cultural connections. It is not too difficult to comprehend the narcissistic character as there is so much written about it.

The DSM IV includes the following criteria from whom at least five criteria should be met for the diagnosis of Narcissistic Disorder (301.81) to be made:

(1) shows arrogant, haughty behaviours or attitudes

(2) is interpersonally exploitative: takes advantage of others to achieve his or her own ends

(3) has a grandiose sense of self-importance, e.g. exaggerates achievements and talents, expects to be recognised as superior without commensurate achievements

(4) believes that he or she is 'special' or unique and can only be understood by or should associate with other special or high status people.

(5) is preoccupied with fantasies of unlimited success, power, brilliance, beauty or ideal love

(6) has a sense of entitlement, for example unreasonable expectation of especially favourable treatment or automatic compliance with his or her expectations

(7) requires excessive admiration

(8) lacks empathy: is unable to recognize or identify with the feelings and needs of others

(9) is preoccupied with feelings of envy. (American Psychiatric Association 1994, p.661)

There appears to be a rising tide of narcissistic disorders in the western culture.

> We hear more and more that we live in a narcissistic society... 'Protect yourself from the demands of others and take care of yourself first'. Even where no pathological problem exists, narcissistic traits of grandiosity and idealisation are encouraged as behaviour norms... Faced with diminished sense of responsibility, more and more of us have turned inward, increasingly toward self-fulfilment... Now, however, important parts of our society regard narcissism as a goal, not a problem. Many who feel they are living according to the norms of society now end up in therapy confused over their feelings of emptiness, isolation, and desperation. (Solomon 1990, p.30–1)

> The narcissist comes to the attention of psychiatrists for some of the same reasons that he rises to positions of prominence not only in awareness movements and other cults but in business corporations, political organisations, and government bureaucracies. For all his inner suffering, the narcissist has many traits that make for success in bureaucratic institutions, which put a premium on the manipulation of interpersonal relations, discourage the formation of deep personal attachments, and at the same time provide the narcissist with the approval he needs in order to validate his self-esteem. (Lasch 1980, p.43–44)

Personality Disorders are often recognizable by adolescence or even earlier and tend to continue throughout most of the adult life. For example in Narcissistic Disorders the sense of grandiosity can be discerned even during childhood and is reflected in the child giving up putting effort in if there is no immediate success and therefore the child achieves either very good or very bad grades. Thus, despite their superior intelligence such children can fail their grades. Their school performance can be very erratic as they feel that nobody is entitled to tell them what to do. Though they may work for admiration, admiration does not actually touch the core of their selves. They may be very appealing and charismatic but may choose friends who are 'freaks' or ugly. They are often pre-occupied with self-image and spend a lot of time looking at themselves in the mirror, treating their body as their double self, providing sustenance. They get easily bored, may tend to avoid eye contact and have terrible temper tantrums when defeated in games. When frustrated they react with intense narcissistic rage (Kernberg 1989).

A narcissist is described like a foetus that receives everything but does not have to give anything in return (Grunberger 1975). Thus there is very little reciprocity in their relationships as they are always the receivers, while others are always givers. There is chronic and intense sense of entitlement, selfishness, mistrust, exploitativeness, coercion, possessiveness, demandingness and ruthlessness with very little empathic understanding of others. The parents of such children contribute to this situation by continually giving in to the child although in a covertly hostile way, appeasing the child's narcisstic rage. They may not enjoy caring for such a child and behave as if manipulated, coerced and emotionally flat. The child is thus caught in a parasitic relationship, devoid of warmth or respect.

Many parents because of their own pathological upbringing such as having been abused, neglected or made to perform beyond their ability in their childhood end up putting similar pressures on children. In our clinics we sometimes meet parents who feel pestered and tyranized by their toddlers or even their babies. They feel helpless and paralyzed when the child has a tantrum or becomes demanding (Dwivedi 1984). The unconscious needs and fantasies of the parents make their children become parts of themselves, especially those aspects that the parent did not dare express except vicariously through the child. This leads to a degree of individuation without enough separation, the condition of a pathologically pseudo-mature child.

The mechanisms leading to such a disorder in children of divorced, adoptive, narcissistic and abusive parents are outlined by Kernberg (1989). Narcissistic parents have a tendency to depersonification, that is, to treat the child as a surrogate figure (such as spouse, parent, sibling, infant). Children with anorexia nervosa tend to behave as though they are appendages of their parents. A sexually abused child may be functioning as a parent or an ideal self for the parents. Adopted children may distrust for having been rejected and may have a compensatory sense of entitlement to choose their parents. A divorced parent may coerce the child to become the offspring of the rejected parent.

Such interpersonal pressures tend to operate through projective identification and double bind communications. *Projective identification* is a way of influencing one another outside their conscious awareness. It involves stripping off some aspect of oneself and projecting it into another person. The person into whom this stripped-off part is projected can unconsciously identify with what is projected and is made to think, feel or behave accordingly (Ogden 1979). If different parents project different and conflicting aspects, this can become very confusing for the receiving child (Dwivedi 1993a).

In a *double bind* one is cornered from all the three sides. One is subjected to two contradictory negative injunctions and is prevented from escaping from either (Bateson, Jackson, Haley and Weakland 1956). For example, a mother may tell her child that she wouldn't like him if he didn't give her a cuddle, but when he tries to cuddle her she pushes him away. One of the double binding messages that a narcissistic child receives is, 'you may go through the motions of separating from me and appear accomplished and successful, but only if everything you achieve is ultimately in relation to me' (Rinsley 1989).

Because of excessive frustrations and disappointments in early childhood, especially due to the fact that the mothering person is not available to authenticate the child's experiences, there develops in the child the element of grandiosity as a self-defence against damaged self-concept. This defensive grandiosity is achieved by stripping off and externalizing all 'bad' parts. The person can develop chronic embitterment or addiction to hatred and even blind hatred towards certain people who may be assigned subhuman status. Child-hood abuse is an important cause of the rising tide of narcissistic disorder which in turn is an important factor in the epidemic of child abuse (Dwivedi 1993b).

Thus narcissistic pathology originates as a defence against feelings of helplessness due to the lack of adequate emotional and physical care in early life (Kohut 1972). As the child grows up an intense inner hunger grows within and continues throughout life. This leads to a great deal of emotional energy being used to avoid pervasive feelings of emptiness, lethargy and low self-worth. On the other hand, the individual is unable to develop a capacity to love or intimacy. Thus, what may sometimes appear to be independence and autonomy may actually be a narcissistic defence against anxieties aroused by intimacy and closeness.

Such a narcissistic pathology can influence different aspects of social life. For example, it may play the principal role in choosing one's marriage partner, to work through long neglected and damaged parts of the self by replaying the earlier trauma, 'since all objects (including the marriage partner) exist only to meet his or her principal emotional need – the never-ending quest to feel whole and safe' (Solomon 1990, p.32). And not only one's family life but also one's handling of career, work and organizations can be equally affected. In fact, the present management culture appears to be built upon narcissism and tends to breed it in turn. Thus culture and personality seem to be intricately interconnected in this respect.

> The manager's view of the world…is that of the narcissist, who sees the world as a mirror of himself and has no interest in external events except as they throw back a reflection of his own image. The dense interpersonal environment of modern bureaucracy, in which work assumes an abstract quantity almost wholly divorced from performance, by its very nature elicits and often rewards a narcissistic response. Bureaucracy, however is only one of a number of social influences that are bringing a narcissistic type of personality organisation into greater and greater prominence. Another such influence is the mechanical

reproduction of culture, the proliferation of visual and audual images in the 'society of spectacle'. (Lasch 1980, p.47)

Culture and Child Rearing Practices

'...child rearing is one area of life in which cultural, social, psychological and biological patterns converge and find simultaneous expression in single acts' (Trawick 1990, p.49). As childhood experiences do influence the shaping of personality and also determine the likelihood of the nature and extent of its disorders, and as the cultural and environmental factors influence the child rearing practices, culture has an enormous influence over personality through the child rearing practices. Minturn and Lambert (1964), emphasizing the role of environmental factors on child rearing, suggest that child training practices are based mainly upon conditions in the natural and social environment that make them necessary for survival. These practices are then rationalized and justified by a structure of beliefs and values designed to support them.

> It now appears that the pressures impinging upon the growing child are much more in the nature of by-products of the horde of apparently irrelevant considerations that impinge upon the parents. These considerations of household composition, size of family, work load etc., determine the time and energy that mothers have available to care for children. They determine the range and content of mother–child relations and the context in which these relations must take place. (Minturn and Lambert 1964, p.291)

Thus environmental factors can be responsible, at least to some extent, for shaping the cultural ideologies of the place, but the cultural ideologies can take on a life of their own and continue despite the changes in the environment and, in fact, can have an important influence on shaping the environment. To think of cultural ideologies only as a product of environmental factors would be extremely naive and an insult to the human capacity for considering and shaping one's social structures and human welfare. In fact, cultural ideologies greatly influence the way one interprets and responds to the environment and to personal experiences.

Cultural assumptions and ideologies have an enormous impact on child rearing practices and in any stable society there is also a reciprocity between the social structures of child rearing and that of other institutions governing adult lives. Child rearing practices are in a way the most important manifestations of cultural assumptions.

Roland (1980) highlights differences as regards early child rearing practices between the Western and Indian cultures. Since the Industrial Revolution in the Western culture, 'independence' is viewed as the cherished ideal and 'dependence' is seen as a despicable state. Although the process of colonization meant making others dependent, being dependent began to be seen as a stigma, a shameful state of being and the cause of a grave social problem. The parents are therefore often at pains to make their children independent as soon as possible. Similarly, professionals working with their clients consider fostering independence as the most important aspect of their work. Children are expected to have their own voices, preferably different from that of their parents (Dwivedi 1995b). For adolescents, leaving home is considered to be a very important developmental task (Lau 1990).

In contrast, the eastern cultures place more emphasis on 'dependability'. The parents are usually at pains to ensure that their children grow up in an atmosphere where parents are a model of dependability. Such a goal leads to an atmosphere of indulgence, physical closeness, common sleeping arrange-ments, immediate gratification of physical and emotional needs and a rather prolonged babyhood. From the western point of view this could be seen as a culture of spoilt children. However, it leads to the creation of very strong bonds and provides an inner sense of security and strength. As separation experiences for very young children are considered traumatic and therefore avoided, there is very little need for transitional objects. The care givers intend to be always there. Similarly, the commercial play materials are not seen as important as the purpose of play and interpersonal interactions of parenting is to create a feeling of contentment rather than achievement. The young ones are there to be loved just for 'being' there rather than 'doing' the right things. Kumar (1992), when visiting India, was most moved by their attitude towards children. 'Indians have a loving and tolerant attitude towards children even under the most trying circumstances' (p.1582).

> I once told the grandmother next door that in the West children sleep separately from their parents right from birth. Ammaji threw up her arms in horror. 'The poor little darlings! They must be so frightened, all by themselves. A child should sleep with his parents until he is at least five years old'... The practice of young children sharing the parents' bed is widespread in Eastern countries. Dr Spock would have been horrified. Dire consequences were predicted for children who sleep in the same bed with their parents. I've never observed any such consequences; in fact, Indian children are generally well adjusted and happy. Thumb sucking is rare, as are night terrors or sleep-walking. Indian toddlers never seem to need a favourite blanket or teddy bear to take to bed – why should they when they can cuddle up to their mothers at night? Perhaps the grandmother next door is right: children in Western countries *are* frightened of sleeping alone, and they try to tell us by thumb-sucking, teddy bears and sleepwalking. (Kumar 1992, -p.1582)

Similarly DeVos, describing the child rearing practices in the Japanese culture, writes:

> Mothers tend to 'suffer' their children rather than to forbid or inhibit their behaviour by using verbal chastisement or even physical punishment. The child, while this form of discipline is going on, learns gradually the vulnerability of the loved one and that control of an offender is exercised not by doing any thing to the offender but by self-control. (DeVos 1985, p.155)

Another manifestation of cultural embedding of interconnectedness of relationships is the value placed upon *extended family life*. For example, in India most people spend the formative years of their early childhood in an extended family setting. The cultural ideal of filial loyalty and fraternal solidarity stipulates common economic and social life, common residence, ritual activities and cooking arrangements. The joint celebration of religious festivals, family rituals and traditional ceremonies within the extended family circle helps further to consolidate the family ties. In the pure form of 'extended family' the brothers (along with their wives and children) live together with their parents. Nowadays, in practice, this pure form of extended family is not so common. However, its variants such as the 'joint family', where some of the brothers (with their wives and children) live together without their parents, and the 'intergenerational family', where the parents live together with one of their grown up children (and their spouse and children), are still very common. In any case, for the most children, one or the other form of extended family is the immediate 'society' which they encounter as they grow up and the indulgent attitude towards them is pervasive throughout the extended family circle.

> One might assume that this indulgent approach to child behaviour would result in very naughty children. Yet it doesn't, Indian children are generally well behaved. My theory is that Indian children get so much attention from a host of loving relatives that they do not need to act out for attention. (Kumar 1992, p.1582)

Proactive Training in Overcoming Narcissism

It is the cultural ideal of mastering narcissism that can be best achieved through growing up in an extended family system. On the other hand, it is impossible for an extended family system to be sustained without proactive training in mastering narcissism through extended family life. As the biggest danger to an extended family is the possibility of its fracturing along the boundaries around nuclear units because the natural tendency of love is to be concentrated towards one's own, an extra ideological effort is required to redirect it across the nuclear family boundaries.

> For the strength and cohesion of the extended family depend upon certain psycho-social diffusion; it is essential that nuclear cells do not build up within the family, or at the very least, that these cells do not involve intense emotional loyalties that potentially exclude other family members and their interest. Thus, the principles of Indian family life demand that a father be restrained in the presence of his own son and divide his interest and support equally among his own and his brother's sons. (Kakar 1981, p.131)

Trawick (1990) describes how in a Tamil extended family that she studied, the mother first fed all the other children while her own son whimpered. Only when others had been served did she serve her own son. She (Trawick) also noticed how repeated efforts had to be made to encourage children to share food and play materials in order to foster love between them across nuclear units.

> Annan would often seat the two boys opposite each other on his two knees with a single toy between them, that he tried to make them share. When the two boys went out with their mothers, each woman would carry the other's son. the mothers themselves shared the kind of love that they hoped their sons would share... All of them, including my own, were 'our children', and if I needed to distinguish between them, I should refer to them by name. In the extreme, this mixture of yours and mine into ours became reversal again – mine were called yours, and yours mine. So when I wrote to Ayya's sister Porutcelvi that my second child had been born, she wrote back, 'I can't wait to see my new son'. (Trawick 1990, p.52–58)

One of the cultural forces that also helps prevent fracturing of extended families along nuclear lines is the strongly held ideology in the Indian culture that '*love grows in hiding*'. Therefore, in order to make true love grow properly, it must be kept hidden. Thus, a mother's love for her child (the strongest and the most highly valued of all loves in the Indian culture) must be kept hidden and contained. Many women, therefore, show great affection for other's children but avoid (at least in public), expressing intense love for their own children. Some may even spurn their own children, forcing their affection outward. Sometimes it can take the form of downgrading the loved one, especially a very precious child, for example, may be given a very ugly name, or the mother may pretend not to care for the child. Similarly in the marital relationship there is a mutual avoidance between spouses at least in public including the avoidance of mentioning the spouse's name.

Another important aspect of the child rearing practices in such a culture is the training in dealings with one's own feelings and also the training in becoming sensitive to other's feelings. DeVos (1980,1985), describing the Japanese culture, emphasises their 'field independent' cognitive style on the one hand and a strong evidence of conforming behaviour in school and elsewhere, and a refinement of interpersonal concerns with acute sensitivity to what others are thinking, on the other.

As the toddlers mature and receive training in urinary and faecal continence, they are also expected to develop emotional continence and a capacity gradually to self-regulate their affect (Dwivedi 1993d). Unlike the western ideal of self-expression, the eastern cultures aim to express feelings in such a way that it is not harmful either to oneself or to others. This, therefore, influences the style of communication, placing more value on indirect and metaphorical communication rather than direct and clear communication as emphasized in the western culture. In fact, one of the most important aspects of religious training is in better handling of one's feelings through expanding one's consciousness, getting in touch with one's emotions at the subtlest levels, accepting them, discerning their transitory nature and transmuting them by harnessing their energy to one's advantage, sometimes described metaphorically as 'tiger taming' (Rimpoche 1987).

It is not only the boundaries around the nuclear units that are subjected to cultural editing but also those in gender relationships and in intergenerational hierarchical structures that are transformed by the cultural influences in a paradoxical manner. Although the wife of a family patriarch pays:

> a formal, and often perfunctory deference to her husband, especially in front of strangers, she may exercise considerable domestic power, not merely among the other women of the household, but with her husband, and she often makes many of the vital decisions affecting the family's interests. (Kakar 1981, p.118)

Similarly, the intergenerationally hierarchical relationships are no exceptions to this paradoxical reality. Trawick (1990, p.42) writes, 'When I told her it was an American custom to let people lead their own lives, she said simply, 'Tappu' (that is a mistake). After some time I learned that if you cared about people, you would interfere'. In fact, the most important qualitiy of the 'head' or the superior of the family is that of acting in a nurturing way so that the 'subordinates' either anticipate his or her wishes or accept them without questioning. It is emancipation and renunciation through which the individuals within the family establish the superiority of their love and express it in the form of *metta* or loving kindness, *mudita* or empathic joy, *karuna* or compassion and *upekkha* or equanimity (Dwivedi 1990, 1992, 1994c). The paradox of love turns the acts of humility into pride, of servitude into respect, and the master into a slave.

> Thus, although family relationships are generally hierarchical in structure, the mode of the relationship is characterised by an almost maternal nurturing on the part of the superior, by filial respect and compliance on the part of the subordinate and by a mutual sense of highly personal attachment. (Kakar 1981, p.119)

The other social institutions too, in such a culture, reflect the hierarchial structure of the extended family system sustained by the complementary mode of nurturing. Child rearing practices aimed at fostering dependability rather than independence, attempt to create an atmosphere whereby children can model upon their parents and grow up to become model dependable parents themselves for their children and also to look after their elderly parents. The 12th blessing of the Mangala Sutta, in Buddhism, is about passing on one's wealth to one's children and the 11th blessing is about taking care of one's parents (Jureegate 1993).

> The concept of long term intergenerational reciprocity is communicated to children at an early age, in a very direct and explicit manner. ...The idea that parent–child reciprocity involves a life-span calculus was prominent in these people's thoughts about old age. To make one's home with adult children was not associated with emotions like shame or guilt, such as have been reported for American elderly people unable to conform to our cultural ideal of self-reliance and independent living in the later years of life. On the contrary, these Indian elders typically displayed pride in having offspring who could and did support them in comfort with grace and loving concern. (Vatuk 1990, pp.66–68)

In western culture, the ideal is that of self-reliance and independent living even during the later years of life. The parents don't want to be a burden on their children's independence in their old age. An elderly person usually thinks that the most important thing in their life is that they do not become a burden on anyone as becoming dependent has acquired a rather pejorative connotation. To make home with one's grown up children is therefore associated with intense shame and guilt. The '...fear of dependency in old age is rooted in a deeply inculcated need for self-reliance and self-sufficiency, not only to retain the respect of others but, most important, to retain respect for oneself' (Vatuk 1990, p.84). Children too don't think of looking after their parents in their old age because they don't see their parents looking after their own parents. When the social values dictate that the children should not be expected to look after their parents in their old age, they should not come asking for money either.

Thus in summary, the various cultural components such as the emphasis on dependability, extended family life, indirect communication, interdependence and so on, mutually support each other. However, in day-to-day life, the cultural ideals described and contrasted above may appear to be rather far from the actual reality. In fact, in real life there are enormous variations, although the cultural ideals do influence the overall picture.

Due to global communications and influences of other cultures and their media, it is now becoming hard for the cultural transmission of these traditional values (designed to transcend narcissistic tendencies) to take place smoothly even within the society where these values actually originated in the past. Their transmission to the ethnic minority children growing up in the west is, therefore, much harder, as it can very easily be undermined by the emphasis on autonomy and independence in western culture (Dwivedi 1993c, 1994b, 1995a).

> The sad truth is that no one can simply construct for themselves 'an identity'. Culture is both inherited and has to be recreated through experience so that it may reside within the individual in memory and feeling. It is the product of experience and history represented in individuals through our internalised parents and by the values and traditions they have passed on to us. Ethnic minority children are born into a society which often differs markedly in its social and family organisation and they themselves may experience different types of care and upbringing. (Andreou 1992, pp.147–8)

Acknowledgement

I am very grateful to Mrs. Sue Cook and Naina Sadrani for word processing this chapter.

References

American Psychiatric Association (1994) *Diagnostic and Statistical Manual. Fourth Edition.* Washington. D.C.: American Psychiatric Association.

Andreou, C. (1992) 'Inner and outer reality in children and adolescents.' In J. Kareem and R. Littlewood (eds) *Intercultural Therapy.* Oxford: Blackwell Scientific Publications.

Bateson, G., Jackson, D.D., Haley, J. and Weakland, J. (1956) 'Toward a theory of schizophrenia.' *Behavioural Science 1*, 251–64.

Bharati, A. (1985) 'The self in Hindu thought and action.' In A.J. Marsella, G. DeVos and F.L.K. Hsu (eds) *Culture and Self: Asian and Western Perspectives.* London: Tavistock Publications.

Clifford, T. (1984) *Tibetan Buddhist Medicine and Psychiatry.* Wellingborough: The Aquarian Press.

Dalal, F.N. (1993) 'Race and racism: an attempt to organise difference.' *Group Analysis 26*, 277–293.

DeVos, G.A. (1980) 'Ethnic adaptation and minority status.' *Journal of Cross-Cultural Psychology 11*, 1, 101–24.

DeVos, G.A. (1985) 'Dimensions of the self in Japanese culture.' In A.J. Marsella, G. DeVos and F.L.K. Hsu (eds) *Culture and Self: Asian and Western Perspectives.* London: Tavistock Publications.

Dwivedi, K.N. (1984) 'Mother–Baby Psychotherapy.' *Health Visitor 57*, 10, 306–7.

Dwivedi, K.N. (1990) 'Purification of mind by Vipassana meditation.' In J, Crook and D. Fontana (eds) *Space in Mind.* Shaftesbury: Elements Books, Ch. 7:86–91.

Dwivedi, K.N. (1992) 'Eastern approaches to mental health.' In T. Ahmed, B. Naidu and A. Webb-Johnson (eds) *Concepts of Mental Health in the Asian Community.* London: Confederation of Indian Organisations (UK), pp 24–30.

Dwivedi, K.N. (1993a) 'Confusion and under-functioning in children.' In V.P. Varma (ed) *How and Why Children Fail.* London: Jessica Kingsley Publishers.

Dwivedi, K.N. (1993b) 'Child abuse and hatred.' In V.P. Varma (ed) *How and Why Children Hate.* London: Jessica Kingsley Publishers.

Dwivedi, K.N. (1993c) 'Coping with unhappy children who are from ethnic minorities.' In V.P. Varma (ed) *Coping with Unhappy Children.* London: Cassell, Ch 11: 134–151.

Dwivedi, K.N. (1993d) 'Emotional development.' In K.N. Dwivedi (ed) *Group Work with Children and Adolescents: A Handbook.* London: Jessica Kingsley Publishers.

Dwivedi, K.N. (1994a) 'The Buddhist perspective in mental health.' *Open Mind 70,* 20–21.

Dwivedi, K.N. (1994b) 'Social structures that support or undermine families from ethnic minority groups: Eastern value systems.' *Context 20,* 11–12.

Dwivedi, K.N. (1994c) 'Mental cultivation (meditation) in Buddhism.' *Psychiatric Bulletin 18,* 503–504.

Dwivedi, K.N. (1995a) 'Stress in children from ethnic minorities.' In V.P. Varma (ed) *Coping with Stress in Children.* Aldershot: Arena Publishers.

Dwivedi, K.N. (1995b) 'Race and the child's perspective.' In G. Upton, R. Davie and V.P. Varma (eds) *The Voice of the Child: A Handbook for Professionals.* London: Falmer Press.

Geertz, C. (19730 *The Interpretation of Cultures.* New York: Basic Books.

Grunberger, B. (1975) *Narcissism: Psychoanalysis Essays.* New York: International University Press.

Guilford, J.P. (1959) *Personality.* New York: McGraw-Hill.

Harsh, C.M. and Schrickel, H.G. (1950) *Personality Development and Assessment.* New York: Ronald Press.

Hsu, F.L.K. (1985) 'The self in cross cultural perspective.' In A.J. Marsella, G. DeVos and F.L.K. Hsu (eds) *Culture and Self: Asian and Western Perspectives.* London: Tavistock Publications.

Jureegate, S. (1993) 'Where there's a will.' *The Light of Peace 5,* 2, 30–31

Kakar, S. (1981) *The Inner World: A Psychoanalytic study of Childhood and Society in India.* Delhi: Oxford University Press (2nd Edition).

Kernberg, P.F. (1989) 'Narcissistic personality disorder in childhood.' *Psychiatric Clinics of North America 12,* 3, 671–94.

Kohut, H. (1972) 'Thoughts on narcissism and narcissistic rage.' *Psychoanalytic Study and Child 27,* 360–400.

Krause, I-B. (1995) 'Personhood, culture and family therapy.' *Journal of Family Therapy 17*, 4, 363–382.

Kumar, K.T. (1992) 'To children with love.' *British Medical Journal 305*, 1582–3.

Lau, A. (1990) 'Psychological problems in adolescents from ethnic minorities.' *British Journal of Hospital Medicine 44*, 201–205.

Lasch, C. (1980) *The Culture of Narcissism*. London: Norton (Abacus).

Laungani, P. (1992) 'Cultural variations in the understanding and treatment of psychiatric disorders: India and England.' *Counselling Psychology Quarterly 5*, 3, 231–44.

Littlewood, R. (1995) 'Psychopathology and personal agency: Modernity, culture change and eating disorders in South Asian societies.' *British Journal of Medical Psychology 68*, 45–63.

Lutz, C. (1988) *Unnatural Emotions: Everyday Sentiments on a Micronesian Atoll and their Challenge to Western Theory*. Cambridge: Cambridge University Press.

Mann, R. and Youd, R. (1992) *Buddhist Character Analysis*. Bradford on Avon: Aukana.

Marriott, McK. (1976) 'Hindu transactions: Diversity without dualism.' In B. Kapferer (ed) *Transaction and Meaning, Directions in the Anthropology of Exchange and Symbolic Behaviour*. Philadelphia: Institute for the Study of Human Issues.

Minturn, L. and Lambert, W.W. (1964) *Mothers of Six Cultures: Antecedants of Child Rearing*. New York: John Wiley.

Ogden, T. (1979) 'On projective identification.' *International Journal of Psychoanalysis 60*, 357–73.

Pande, S.K. (1968) 'The mystique of Western psychotherapy. An Eastern interpretation.' *Journal of Nervous and Mental Disease 46*, 425–32.

Parsons, T. (1964) *Social Structure and Personality*. Glencoe, IU: Free Press.

Rai, P.H. and Dwivedi, K.N. (1988) 'The value of Parhej and sick role in Indian culture.' *Journal of the Institute of Health Education 16*, 2, 56–61.

Rimpoche, D.A. (1987) *Taming the Tiger*. Eskdalemuir: Dzalendra Publishing.

Rinsley, D.B. (1989) 'Notes on the developmental pathologies of narcissistic personality disorder.' *Psychiatric Clinics of North America 12*, 3, 695–707.

Roland, A. (1980) 'Psychoanalytic perspectives on personality development in India.' *International Review of Psychoanalysis 1*, 73–87.

Shweder, R.A. and Bourne, E.J. (1982) 'Does the concept of the person vary cross-culturally?' In A.J. Marsella and G.M. White (eds) *Cultural Conceptions of Mental Health and Therapy*. Dordrecht: D. Reidel Publishing Company.

Solomon, M.F. (1990) 'Narcissistic vulnerability in marriage.' *Journal of Couples Therapy 1*, 3/4, 25–38

Stocking, G.W. (ed) (1986) *Malinowski, Rivers, Benedict and Others: Essays on Culture and Personality*. Wisconson: The University of Winconson Press.

Strathern, M. (1992) *After Nature: English Kinship in the Late Twentieth Century.* Cambridge: Cambridge University Press.

Tamura, T. and Lau, A (1992) 'Connectedness versus separations: Applicability of family therapy to Japanese families.' *Family Process 31,* 4, 319–40

Trawick, M. (1990) 'The ideology of love in a Tamil family.' In O.M. Lynch (ed) *Divine Passions: The Social Construction of Emotion in India.* Berkeley: University of California Press.

Tylor, E.B. (1871) *Primitive Culture.* London: John Murray.

Tyrer, P. and Ferguson, B. (1987) 'Problems in the classification of personality disorder.' *Psychological Medicine 17,* 15–20.

Vatuk, S. (1990) 'To be a burden on others: Dependency anxiety among the elderly in India.' In O.M. Lynch (ed) *Divine Passions: The Social Construction of Emotion in India.* Berkeley: University of California Press.

Vernon, P.E. (1963) *Personality Assessment.* London: Methuen.

Vernon, P.E. (1969) *Intelligence and Cultural Environment.* London: Methuen.

World Health Organisation (1992) *The ICD-10 Classification of Mental and Behavioural Disorders: Clinical Descriptions and Diagnostic Guidelines.* Geneva: World Health Organisation.

CHAPTER 3

The Immigrant (West Indian) Child in School

Waveney Bushell

Since the mid-1950s there has been a steady increase in the number of West Indian children attending English schools. A few of these children came with their parents from their native lands; many others joined one or both parents already settled here; some were born here. Today, children of West Indian parents are easily identified throughout the English school; for some, adjustment has been easy, others have shown signs of considerable stress, particularly when first introduced to school; with others, stress signals become evident during the adolescent years.

Historical and Sociological Background of West Indians

The West Indies are small groups of islands scattered along a great arc of more than 2000 miles in the Caribbean Archipelago. These islands, Jamaica, Trinidad, Tobago, Barbados, and the Leeward and Windward Islands, share, with the rest of the Caribbean, the experience of colonialism, slavery and the plantation. The term 'West Indian' therefore extends beyond the frontiers of the islands; it denotes an underlying similarity, a characteristic way of life, which has grown out of historical events. For the three and a half million English-speaking West Indians these events have linked them with Britain, and because of this relationship social and legal institutions are essentially British.

The West Indian society comprises an upper and middle class with a family structure based on formal marriage, and the mass of the population with a family unit based on the matrifocal household group, resulting from unstable or 'visiting' relationships and common law marriages. Such a household is mother-centred, with a close bond existing between mother, daughter and granddaughter, the man's status depending largely on his ability to provide financial support. The foundations for this type of organization seem to have been laid during slavery. As a slave, the man was forbidden to marry, although he was free to mate, and this freedom lent itself easily to the establishment of unstable relationships. The children of such relationships were the lawful property of the owner of the slave mother, who with her child could be disposed of at will by her master. It is easy to see how, under these circumstances, the woman acted as the sole permanent element of the slave family, a position existing in many West Indian households today.

Education

The colonial policy of education, when this was provided, was that for the masses education should be limited to the elementary stage. As secondary education had to be paid for, it was available for a small elite only. Education became, therefore, a divisive instrument, keeping rigid barriers between primary and secondary levels, at the same time providing on the one hand an inferior type of education up to the elementary stage for the masses, and on the other an education oriented to the English public school system existing through the secondary school years for the elite.

For the masses, therefore, the educational system, though following the English pattern, seemed never to have been revised during the colonial days. The pupil–teacher system which ensured the provision of cheap labour has been replaced in recent years by a local teachers' training system, under which teachers are exposed to and trained in modern teaching methods, although often after training they are faced with the difficulty of adjusting to existing classroom situations.

Classes are very large, averaging about 60 or 70; schools are usually overcrowded, particularly those controlled by religious bodies, although those more recently built compare favourable with the modern type in the UK. The older schools are generally housed in the dormitory type buildings, which permit children of one class to see, hear and even touch those of another. It is easy to appreciate why in this type of environment children are encouraged to speak in class only when spoken to. Teaching usually takes the form of group instruction, with the whole class representing the group, often repeating in unison as required by the teacher.

Few classes have access to more than one reader a year. This text is bought by the parent, and it is not unusual for some children to go without the text book for the school year in any one class, because of the parents' inability to buy this book. The absence of supplementary readers implies that:

(1) The class moves ahead methodically as a group from lesson 1 to the end of the book, no consideration being given to the individual differences. This method could create boredom for the child whose reading ability and rate of progress exceed that of the rest of the class.

(2) The child's vocabulary is limited to that provided by the one book used in class.

(3) Reading can hardly take place for pleasure.

Teaching of reading is therefore rather formally carried out, and often the main method used is repetition by the children of the teacher's example in class. Very little use is made of the phonic method but the alphabet method is popular as a means of facilitating spelling; the use of this method has no doubt been noticed by teachers of recently arrived West Indian children.

In these large schools education depends largely on reproduction of examples set by the teacher to her class, rather than encouragement of thinking or the production of ideas on the part of the child. Reproduction of work is encouraged by parents at home, where often the child is required to repeat an example of the day's work for their approval. Educational standards vary from territory to territory.

Language

In addition to the standard English spoken by the upper and middle classes, each island has its own creole language; the word 'creole' being used to denote belonging to the island. The particular type of creole spoken on an island depends largely on the country of origin of the earliest colonists and slave owners. In Trinidad, for example, the creole language is strongly influenced by Spanish and French, the popular creole construction 'It have a shop down the road' being reminiscent of the French construction.

Many old English words survive in the creole language, for example 'fowl' for 'chicken', 'beast' for 'mule' or 'horse', 'breadkind' for 'food', 'to carry one along the way' for 'to accompany'. Other words not in modern usage are retained as well. The West Indian child would mean 'tap' instead of 'knock'.

The other main influence on the structure of the creole language was African, but this influence seems to have varied with the size and physical features of the island. For example, in small compact Barbados, in which there was a relatively large group of white servants who came into contact with the African slave, the influence of African on the creole language was not as pronounced as in Jamaica. In this larger mountainous island contact between the black and the relatively small number of poor whites was less easy, and the influence of the African language on the spoken creole was much stronger. In addition to the vocabulary, the African language affected pronunciation and grammar, and influenced the character and mood of the creole language, sound playing an integral part, and gesture concretizing thought as well as supplementing a limited vocabulary.

For these reasons, for the child recently arrived from a rural area of any of the West Indian Islands where creole is the most common and sometimes only means of verbal communication, comprehension of the English spoken in the classroom here as a means of instruction would at first be difficult. Gradually, as time passes and the child grows accustomed to this new speech pattern, it becomes easier for him to follow instruction and so assimilate knowledge.

Stresses of the Newly Arrived Child

Stresses related mainly to school

Perhaps of greater concern to a teacher of West Indian children is the boy or girl of about nine or ten years of age who arrives in England to begin or continue his schooling here. Given the difference in educational systems the child who has attended school regularly and shown steady progress in the West Indies should, all things being equal, be able to apply himself intelligently to mechanical problems in arithmetic, and to read and spell adequately; however, he would find it difficult to express his thoughts freely in written form, because this particular area is often neglected in the West Indies. For such a child the transition period at school varies according to his ability to adapt to the new situation and unfamiliar requirements; adjustment to the new educational system slowly takes place. But the child who had been previously exposed to little or not formal education in the West Indies, who has come from a rural area where the creole language is the most common and perhaps the only means of communication, would experience extreme difficulty in understanding the English spoken at school and great anxiety in trying to cope with this new means of communication. In this situation learning is intimately related to and highly dependent on the ability to interpret what is heard, think about it and then translate his own answer from the creole to the formal English required in the classroom. The sudden change from thinking in terms of the creole language to thinking in terms of formal English makes this process slower and creates for the child the type of anxieties which could affect his own communication.

Teachers of West Indian children will no doubt call to mind the child who, soon after joining the class, spoke very little or not at all. An example of such a case was Elaine, who came to join her mother in England after an absence of about nine years. She had very little previous schooling when she first attended school here, was placed with a group of six weak readers every morning in the care of a sympathetic teacher. For months her reaction to school was one of complete silence, even though she seemed more relaxed in the small group. In the parent class she was seen not to smile or talk to anyone. Gradually Elaine began to whisper to her friends in the small group, and finally spoke to her teacher after months of silence. She described in detail her experience on arriving in England, how she was told that she was coming to join her mother here, how utterly confused she felt when she could not identify her mother when two women approached her. It is significant that the first time Elaine spoke to her teacher, she mentioned what had bothered her from the time of her arrival here. What seems even more significant is the fact that, although she needed to talk about her anxieties to someone she saw as a friend, she dared not speak until she was sure that her attempts would be acceptable. However, once this venture was made Elaine gained more confidence and was seen to speak not only in the small group, but in the larger class as well.

Stresses related mainly to the home environment

Although adjusting to school may in most cases be stressful, the newly arrived child can also experience many anxieties relating to the home situation. No two children's situations are the same, but a common factor among West Indian children is overcrowding. Parents tend to live in multiple-occupied houses where some facilities have to be shared. If the families occupying these houses are on very friendly terms, the child has to adjust to the behaviour of this 'extended family' within a new setting. If the families are not friendly, the effects of adjustment to the negative attitudes of his immediate neighbours could be damaging, and affect his work and relationships at school.

Many children come to join a mother whom they have not seen for years, or rather have never known (some were sent photographs). In many cases adjustment to reality could be stressful, expectations having been idealistic and totally different. Situations like these could be further complicated by the presence of a new father who is seen as a powerful stranger, unlike the indulgent grandfather left in the West Indies. The greatest threat to the newcomer, however, could be the younger children who are usually more secure in their relationship with their parents and whose very self-assurance and security arouse jealousy and dislike in the newcomer.

An example of the struggle for adjustment was seen in the behaviour of Michael. He joined his mother after an absence of about eight years, during which time he lived with his grandmother in Jamaica. His mother, now married, had four younger lively boys; Michael, having joined the family whose varying roles had already been established, felt a misfit when at home, where he gave no indication of his feelings until he disappeared one Saturday afternoon, later being returned home by the police. His relationship with his mother quickly deteriorated because of this behaviour and gradually the effects of his unhappiness at home were seen at school, where hitherto he had shown signs of settling down. In contrast to his silent withdrawn behaviour at home, Michael now displayed at school unsolicited anger which later gave way to violent temper tantrums. Eventually, as the tantrums became more frequent, Michael was withdrawn from school and placed in a small unit for maladjusted children, where after a year he returned to normal school.

Poor adjustment to the home does not involve only the newcomers' attitude to the established family: that of the family to the child just arrived is of equal importance. Parents who are unaware of the importance of the child's emotional needs could do much damage, and we shall see later how the West Indian mother, quite unwittingly, gives the impression of depriving the growing child of the affection he grew accustomed to accepting as a matter of course. For the newcomer, the home, and more often the school, becomes the focal point for the release of tensions which result from the combination and interaction of frustrating experiences – disorientation, absence of those he loves, loneliness and loss of friends, change of climate, bewilderment at being in a new school with its strange language sounds, fear of the future. All these considerations crowd the mind and in his total confusion the child seems unable to talk of his feelings.

Let us now consider the child who does not overtly show signs of emotional stress, but who nevertheless must experience extreme stress in the classroom because of his gross retardation. Many West Indian children join the English school at the junior school age having had little or no previous schooling in the West Indies. Unlike his more literate counterpart, who would be required merely to accommodate to a different educational system, he would have no academic foundation on which to build; reading particularly would be very poor. Most local authorities now run reception centres where newcomers attend classes for a given period of time, but unless the function of such a class is clearly thought out, the newcomer gains little or no help academically. Such classes should aim at bridging the gap created by the child's loss of schooling over the years, as well as fitting him to take up his position in his own age group at school; failure to achieve this merely helps to create pockets of semi-literate West Indian children throughout the English school. Ideally, language classes should be set up to run concurrently with the child's parent class, children being withdrawn at certain intervals for individual help, and at the same time being able to participate in class activities such as games, music, singing, painting, and so forth. Tape recorders would be of great help in pointing to the difference in intonation and speech pattern of the new arrivals. For the teacher who has to help such a child within the classroom it is important to remember that the new word taught should always be reinforced with a drawing or picture of the object representing the word. The writer found that even with children who have lived here for some years the word 'coal' is almost always misunderstood as 'cold'. This is because in the West Indies 'coal' is a plural noun (coal(s)) and again 'd' at the end of the word is not often sounded.

Stress of the Infant School Child

Stress related to the cultural background of the parent

The West Indian family arriving in Britain is usually received by relatives and friends who tend to live in twilight areas; families move about from one such area to another, often because of opportunities for employment, sometimes in search of better accommodation and cheaper rents. Children, especially the newly arrived, could be exposed to stress as a result of frequent movement from the area to another; in many cases previous adjustment to school achieved over a long period could be affected by such a move, causing a regression in behaviour. Children seem to experience the same effects of disorientation in moving from one area of a large city to another, as from the West Indies to England.

West Indians tend to be unaware of the importance of the emotional needs of the growing child. Children are fondled and fussed over while they remain babies; as the child makes his first step across the room or utters his first word the entire family rejoices with him, and he is the recipient of love and affection. But as he leaves the stage of babyhood behind and approaches his school age, the affection he had hitherto accepted as part of his right is seen to be suddenly withdrawn and bestowed on the new-born baby. It seems, therefore, that with the West Indian mother the degree of affection shown to her child varies with the amount of physical care the child requires, the fast growing child pushed out from the inner circle of love which includes mother and baby only. In the West Indies the matrifocal family organization caters for this dilution of relationship, some of the growing child's emotional needs being met by another member of the extended family, particularly the maternal grandmother and an aunt.

In England, in the nuclear family organization, children are made more aware of what may appear to them a reduction of their mother's affection and even before starting school tend to make more demands for her attention and love. The mother's inability to understand the need for these demands could lead to a breakdown in relationship between herself and the growing child, whose behaviour therefore reflects that of the emotionally deprived child. Conditions of living tend to accentuate what would be regarded by the mother as bad behaviour, and slapping becomes the only form of correction. One calls to mind the case of Winston, born in London to West Indian parents; he started school after his mother had given birth to her second child. At school, he was immediately seen to be a source of trouble, unable to cope with the free activity in the classroom. He tended to snatch toys away from the other children, rush about disturbing others, and generally disrupted the class. A visit to Winston's home revealed that he was expected to accept replacement by the young baby without question and that he had spent all of his life in conditions which did not permit him to learn to pay without arousing anxiety in the household. After some months he settled at school, a change in his behaviour coinciding with removal from the flat his family occupied to better accommodation.

How could the teacher meet the needs of a child coming from such a home environment?

In some infant schools there is more opportunity for teachers to discuss difficult cases with health visitors who visit the homes. Children who come from homes where the value of play is unknown to parents could be introduced to school gradually, spending one or two afternoons only during the first week in which they start school. Parents should be encouraged to attend with their children on these days; in this way they could be helped towards changing their attitude towards play.

Stresses related directly to baby-minding conditions

The research by Pless and Hood (1967) pointed to the fact that a higher proportion of West Indians relied on substitute care for their children from an early age. The Gregory study in Paddington, 1967–1968, found that West Indian mothers tended to make use of both registered and unregistered baby-minders for their children; that generally the latter were more poorly housed and had more domestic commitments, although a number of the former lived in more crowded and unsatisfactory circumstances. Few of the unregistered minders provided stimulating care and some of the registered minders provided no toys and had nowhere for the children to play. Generally the impression gained was that quite a large number of children were confined to the one room used by the minder.

The West Indian mother's reasons for using substitute care for her child at an early age are closely related to her own home circumstances; if she is the sole supporter of the home it is necessary for her to earn: if there is a father in the home, she must try to add to his contribution if better living accommodation is to be obtained. Her choice of a minder is determined largely by proximity to her own home, the price charged and willingness to fit in with her long working hours. Very little importance is attached to the number of children the baby-minder has in her care, and all that this implies; reliability and personal cleanliness are her main considerations. Because she herself is unaware of the importance of stimulation, derived verbally and through the use of toys, she does not regard this as part of the function of a baby-minder.

Baby-minding conditions therefore have far-reaching results on the child's future progress at school; poor verbal stimulation limits the child's vocabulary and lack of play leaves a gap in the child's imaginative experience. The passivity encouraged during the pre-school years by the baby-minder of the many children in her care does not prepare the child for the spontaneous investigation of ideas and acquisition of concepts in the classroom at the age of five. The West Indian child who spends his pre-school years under these conditions represents the culturally deprived children mentioned by Pringle (1969) who 'have lost the educational race long before starting school'. Often these children find themselves at a loss to comprehend what is taking place in the classroom.

But if inadequate intellectual pre-school stimulation places the child at a disadvantage when he starts school, lack of emotional stimulation is an even greater hazard for children of West Indian parents. A report by Dr Prince at a conference held in London, organized by the World Organisation for Early Childhood Education, drew attention to the fact that an increasing number of immigrant children, mostly of West Indian parents, were referred to the psychiatry department of Kings College Hospital and other child guidance clinics, suffering from a condition which at first sign resembles autism. Further investigation of the condition showed, however, that the symptoms of aloofness, apathy and little or no speech reflected maternal deprivation and lack of emotional and intellectual stimulation. What was common among the cases was the fact that the children lived with mothers who felt homesick for their own country as they felt depressed and isolated in their neighbourhood and disillusioned about life in this country. In many cases children were separated from an early age for varying lengths of time during the day from their mothers who worked long hours and who, on returning home, were too exhausted, depressed or busy to give some emotional support to their children. Often parents supported other children left in the West Indies, and so problems of finance were severe.

Keith's case is a classic example of the effects of maternal deprivation and limited early stimulation. He was minded out on a daily basis from an early age as his father was a full-time student so his mother had to go out to work. By the time he started school at the age of five it was evident that he was 'different'; he merely sat in class, saying nothing to the other children, not wishing to participate in the classroom activity, verbally or otherwise. On referral to the school psychological service for assessment the possibility of autism or even mental defectiveness was raised. However, he was given a place in a small diagnostic unit where he spent more than three years. During this period Keith gradually became less withdrawn and more aware of his surroundings, and at last began talking to his peers and taking a great interest in books and started responding to reading sessions with his teacher. By the time he was eight he was able to take his place in a class for normal children, laughing and talking as children do, an achievement which three years previously one would not have dared hope for. Keith's mother did experience at about the time he was born a feeling of intense loneliness and depression, having had to spend most of her free time alone at home while her husband attended lectures. It seems that during his period she was unable to give adequate emotional stimulation to her child, this deprivation being closely followed by separation, as he as minded out on a daily basis from a very early age.

The behaviour of children who are handicapped because of limited pre-school intellectual stimulation seems to represent one end of a continuum, the other end representing that described by Dr Prince of the child who, because of an absence of emotional stimulation as well, is aloof, almost unable to speak, apathetic, reflecting perhaps the emotional climate in which he lives. Teachers, health visitors and other social workers could assist greatly if they were able to detect this type of behaviour as a reaction to the stress to which the child is exposed, and help not only the child by referral to the local clinics, but the mother or guardian.

Stresses of the Adolescent Related to Continuous Retardation in School and a Breakdown of Relationship with Parents

Many West Indian children now attending secondary school are grossly retarded educationally, and are experiencing the effects of continuous retardation at school. Generally they are those who, having joined their parents when of junior school age with little or no previous formal education, have coped with the painful period of adjustment to a previously unknown parent and a new family, while trying at the same time to become a member of the school community. Few children who find difficulty in settling at home are able to show progress at school at the same time and, given the educational gap between them and their contemporaries at school, and the lack of facilities existing in schools for coping with the educational problem that they present, they tend, by and large, to occupy positions at the bottom end of the class. Most of these children are lively, intelligent youngsters, who would be capable of learning at the same rate as their English counterparts, but for the fact that they lack the basic skills in reading and numbers. By the time they reach secondary school and become aware of their continuous failure, they begin to doubt their own ability to improve, and so lose the will to attempt anything new. In some cases school becomes a place they would prefer not to attend.

In most cases realization of their failure at school is combined with an awareness of their parents' disappointment in their lack of progress. Many West Indian parents send for their children mainly because of the educational opportunities, and so find it difficult to hid their feelings of disappointment and even their criticism as the child's performance at school falls below expectation. In this way they show little or no insight into the difficulties which the child must overcome before he becomes adjusted to school.

The case of Frank comes to mind. His uncle, having lived here for some years, felt that he could be of some help to his sister in the West Indies by sending for one of her sons. Frank was chosen to attend school in England, to avail himself of the educational opportunities. Unfortunately, no thought had been given to the fact that Frank would have had to adjust to the life in England, one which was far removed from that to which he was accustomed, and one which involved the absence of all his loved ones. Frank had had little previous schooling, and was attending a secondary school when I saw him; attendance at the remedial class in school had helped to raise his reading age to about eight years, but he showed no desire to participate in school activities. His uncle was extremely critical of the fact that he had shown little progress after nearly two years at school and seemed to place little importance in the fact that in strong contrast to the West Indian situation, Frank now lived an extremely lonely life, often returning home to an empty flat in the evenings, and sometimes retiring at night without seeing his uncle or communicating with anyone else in the house.

Lack of parents' awareness of the need for adolescents to conform to the group norm would lead to disapproval on the part of the West Indian parent, and even a breakdown of relationship between parent and child. Parents tend to remain West Indian in outlook, particularly with regard to the authority they seek to exercise over their children and the standards of behaviour expected of them. Relationship between parent and child could sometimes be reminiscent of the Victorian era, with the former giving the impression that the latter should 'love, honour and obey' a severe and chastising parent. In the West Indies this type of upbringing, although regarded by the adolescent as harsh, is accepted as part of growing up; but in this society the adolescent, realizing that his English counterpart is not subject to such treatment, objects strenuously, and a clash of personality follows. The West Indian adolescent seems to be caught between identifying with a world belonging to his parents and with one which he regards his own. Most adolescents, in their bid to assert their independence, experience a period of poor relationship with their parents, but with the West Indian in England this experience is made more crucial by the clash of the two worlds of which he is a part, particularly since he is aware that as a West Indian acceptance by the group with which he identifies is limited to a few rather than the wider more general adolescent world.

The stresses of the West Indian child are closely related to the conditions under which he lives, his parents' cultural background, and his own attempts to come to terms with these, first within the framework of the English educational system, and later as one of a minority group within the wider adult community. Any attempt to help the child to make full use of his potential at school should take this socio-cultural background into consideration. There is no doubt that for the child of three to four years, we should think in terms of offering him an opportunity to enquire more of his immediate environment, to acquire concepts, and to learn to enjoy play experience without arousing anxiety in himself and others around him; in this way we could help to prepare him for the type of education to which he would be exposed at the age of five. This immediately suggests the need for more nursery classes in the twilight areas. For the newcomers there should be a more positive attempt on the part of local authorities to integrate children into the school system; this could only be achieved through the establishment of well-planned language units with facilities for providing for children for at least a year, and opportunity for them to continue to attend after this period if necessary, while attending ordinary school. Without such an establishment we run the risk of exposing children to complete bewilderment throughout their school life, or of effecting a hasty and often unnecessary transfer to a school for the educationally subnormal and creating maladjustment in this way.

We also need to think in terms of planning, for the children now in the lowest stream at secondary school, the type of curriculum which would aim at exploiting their particular interests, with emphasis on subjects such as wood-work, metalwork, handicraft, art, so that through these subjects the basic skills in reading, writing and numbers could be acquired. For this group particularly we would need a reorganization of the traditional remedial class within the school, if we hope to sustain their interest in class, and reduce the degree of difficult behaviour seen at school. If we accept unreservedly that the West Indian child is capable of good intellectual functioning, in spite of his sometimes seemingly gross retardation, we could help him to overcome his feelings of intellectual inadequacy which he must experience after long-standing retardation at school. Unless we plan in this way, and aim to succeed, we run the risk of sending out of school into the adult world adolescents whose limited education may well make it more difficult for them to bear the frustration that they could experience as a result of living in a society in which they are not wholly accepted.

CHAPTER 4

Anti-Racist Strategies for Educational Performance
Facilitating Successful Learning for all Children

Gerry German

In what ways are your programmes going to benefit the oppressed – working class pupils and their communities the world over; girls the world over; black pupils in white societies; children with disabilities and learning difficulties the world over; ethnic and cultural minorities the world over? In what ways, that is to say, are your programmes going to close gaps, reduce inequalities, remove discriminations, in particular discriminations which are covertly, indeed invisibly institutionalised? And how are you going to win the trust of the oppressed? Which is to say, what risks – real risks to your material well-being, your career prospects, your reputation, your livelihood – are you taking? What boundaries of convention and courtesy are you prepared to transgress, what conferences, forums and arenas are you prepared to subvert, what comforts and friends are you prepared to lose? (Richardson 1990, p.53)

All children, black and white, want to succeed at whatever they do. They want to work, play and make friends to the best of their ability. Parents, too, black and white, have the highest hopes for their children. They want them to succeed at school. They want them to get a good job. And they want them to lead happy lives as responsible citizens worthy of respect on the one hand and capable of respecting others and co-operating with them on the other.

Teachers, too, would like the children in their schools to succeed, and they have obvious reasons for aiming at a high success rate. It would enhance public relations as well as job satisfaction and status. It would redound to the credit of the school, and there would be a growing and gratifying demand for appointment as teacher or governor and admission as pupil. Some people might deny that such an interest exists but they would be hard pressed to produce children, parents or teachers who would express a greater concern with failure than with success. On the other hand, one needs to recognize that there are children and parents, as well as teachers, whose experiences have made them cynical about the future.

If there is such an apparent general unanimity of outlook with regard to academic success, why is it that so many children fail and why is it that so many of the failures come from identifiable groups such as the working class, or travellers, or certain black communities?

The quotation at the head of this chapter is aimed at the transformation of individuals and structures in order to make society less unequal and less unjust and to ensure that individuals have the energy and skill to develop structures and procedures that are a permanent guarantee of justice (Richardson 1990, p.45)

The problem is that schools and other educational institutions as they now exist are so structured and organized that they seem inherently incapable of ensuring the success of all the children and young people in their care?

One recalls the response of the then Secretary of State for Education, John Patten, at the announcement of the record-breaking number of GCSE passes in the summer of 1993 when he expressed the opinion that it must have been due to easier marking and lower standards than in the past (Education Guardian, London 1993).

If academic performance is related to a particular view of intelligence, and if intelligence is hierarchically distributed along a success–failure continuum, the so-called bell curve of the distribution of ability, we should not be surprised that examinations, tests and standard assessment tests produce failures as well as successes. Nor should we be surprised by the obsession of some people in authority with the need for the educational process to identify failures!

It can be no surprise, therefore, when the system of selection and ranking seems to favour certain groups rather than others. In a system characterized by perceptions and practices based on concepts of social class status – male superiority and white supremacy, for example – it is inevitable that those who are seen to attain the highest academic standards are generally white, male and middle-class. The exceptions only serve to prove the rule, and those who emerge from the ranks of the otherwise disadvantaged very often do so as a result of embracing establishment values. This serves in turn to confirm the validity of those values.

With the introduction of league tables to identify institutional excellence or otherwise, teachers in poor performing schools have been calling for the inclusion of value-added criteria to indicate the nature of the problems of social deprivation in their schools; for example, to show how much they have managed to achieve with such disadvantaged children compared with other schools enjoying social privilege, parental support and pupil motivation.

Children and their parents – and possibly teachers – are hardly likely to be encouraged by a finely tuned statistical account of unemployment, poor housing, ill health, crime and delinquency, and one-parent families to rational-ize and explain away low standards of literacy and numeracy as well as the absence of success in external examinations. If career prospects and life chances are so closely tied to examination success, it is no consolation for people to be told that while they have no academic qualifications to take them up the next rung of the ladder, they have done very well bearing in mind social background and family circumstances. Such a record is unlikely to impress either the college admissions tutor or the employer when it comes to seeking a place in further or higher education or something better than casual, low paid jobs.

What happens, however, if the value-added exercise shows a downward spiral – as well it might – rather than progress of one sort or another? A recent study of 6000 children of five years old by the Birmingham local education authority (Birmingham Metropolitan Council 1994) has shattered the conven-tional belief that African-Caribbean children are trapped by under-achievement and low aspirations almost from birth. On the contrary, the study shows that they start school with the best grasp of the basic skills and that they maintain their lead until at least seven years of age. African-Caribbean children were shown to be almost twice as likely as five-year-olds from other ethnic groups to be classed as above average, against national norms, in numeracy tests that included tasks such as counting up to 20 and identifying shapes. White and Indian pupils came next, followed by Bangladeshis and Pakistanis.

Almost one in twenty (4.6%) black pupils were about a year or more ahead of what would be expected of five-year-olds in the English national curriculum, compared with one in twenty-eight (3.6%) white pupils. About a third (32.1%) of the African-Caribbean pupils were average or above for their age, against 30 per cent for all Birmingham pupils. Similar results were revealed in national curriculum tests for seven-year-olds in English and mathematics.

By the time they reach 16 years of age, African-Caribbean pupils are among the least successful ethnic groups. They are four times more likely to be excluded from secondary school and considerably less likely to get five or more GCSE passes at grades A to C. What happens to deny their early promise of academic success?

This is a question that many black parents have been asking for a long time. Why were their children unhappy at school? Why were they punished, apparently frequently and unfairly? Why were they suspended from class or from school? Why were they under-achieving? These were matters that they were at first reluctant to take up with teachers because of an initial combination of faith in schooling and respect for the authority of teachers. When at last they felt constrained to make representations on behalf of their children, they felt that they were not getting the answers they sought, and in addition many of them became alienated by their humiliating treatment when they visited the school. They felt even more humiliated when they had to attend the school in response to a summons for them to discuss their children's alleged misdemeanours.

In 1971 Bernard Coard's book *How the West Indian Child is Made Educationally Sub-Normal in the British School System* articulated what many African-Caribbean parents felt about the inferior education their children were receiving and the threat of the white establishment to their children's identity. He urged parents to cooperate in creating a black educational environment with a curriculum of black studies taught by people who could provide black professional role models (Coard 1971, p.38–9).

This gave a further fillip to the black voluntary school movement where weekend teaching attended not only to the basic skills but to other aspects of the curriculum that children and parents felt were being neglected in the mainstream schools. However, it is still only a small number of children who attend these schools, and it is unfortunate that mainstream teachers fail to avail themselves of the opportunity to learn from their experiences in enhancing both self-discipline and academic progress even among otherwise disillusioned and disaffected black children. The enrolment record shows keen, well-motivated children for the most part, strongly supported by their parents (Chevannes and Reeves 1987, pp.147–169).

Such schools exist also for children from other black communities. There are language classes for children of African, Chinese and Asian origin. Many are initiated into their culture through dance and festivals, for example. Children whose parents originate from Muslim countries are brought together to study the Koran and learn Arabic as well as practice their mother tongue.

Here are interesting examples of vigorous self-help on the part of communities whose parents are often criticized by teachers as either lacking any interest in their children's education or being over-ambitious for them and therefore impractical. What greater practical commitment to children can there be than long-term efforts to raise funds, hire premises, provide equipment, books and other resources, recruit teachers on a voluntary basis, arrange a timetable and encourage children to attend in their own time?

In addition to the black voluntary schools' implicit criticisms of racist attitudes and practices in mainstream schools, they are also affirming the arguments of the advocates of alternative educational provision and community education. They want curriculum relevance, service to and participation by the community, and democratic accountability within and outside the learning community. In alternative education, the emphasis is on schools as communities rather than institutions.

As Clark (1971, p.122–3) states, it is counter-productive to pursue policies and practices that fail to develop the vast potential of human beings while at the same time criticizing children and parents – and even teachers – who are the product of such an inefficient system. On the other hand, his demand for alternatives to what he terms the state monopoly are hardly likely to be satisfied by the growth of grant-maintained schools and City Technology Colleges, for example, which give an illusion of parental choice but still deny democratic participation in terms of governance, parental involvement, pupil participation and real accountability.

It would be wrong to conclude from the discussion about identity that black under-achievement is the result of a widespread problem of poor self-image or low self-esteem. There is no doubt that a positive sense of identity is enhanced by the presence of role models, relevant curriculum content and resources that provide positive images of black children, but one needs to remember that racial violence and discrimination do not avoid choosing as their victims black children and adults who are self-aware, self-confident and assertive. The trigger to racial violence and discrimination is skin colour, not one's ranking on a quickly applied, primitive ready reckoner of self-esteem.

Milner's (1983) work on the black–white orientation of black children led him to assert that 'Black consciousness has grown, Black social and political organisations have flourished, and Black culture has evolved a specifically British variant, all of which has given Black children and youth an alternative, acceptable image of their group with which to identify' (p.161).

People cannot have it both ways. On the one hand, poor academic perform-ance may be attributed to a poor sense of identity, among other things. But then self-assertive, articulate black children may be punished for expressing their reservations and criticisms and even challenging curriculum content, resources and teacher–pupil relationships.

For example, a 13-year-old African-Caribbean girl was excluded from a London school after a series of carefully logged allegations of misbehaviour. One of the charges against her was that she had refused to collect the books from her class when asked to do so by her teacher, a white woman of Australian origin. Instead she refused to do so and added 'Slavery finish'. The confronta-tion continued and the girl challenged her teacher about the mistreatment of the aboriginal peoples of Australia. She was told to go to the Year Head and the incident was logged as another example of her rudeness and indiscipline (WGARCR 1994a).

How much better it would have been if the teacher had put her pupil's sense of self and history to good account in getting her to present her views as part of the process of developing debating skills, for example. Instead, an opportu-nity was lost because of a stereotypical knee-jerk reaction to a situation perceived as a challenge to constituted authority rather than the occasion for dialogue and exploring relationships. In the end, the school lost a good human resource which could have added to its fund of wisdom. It may well be that both the teacher and pupil were reacting to each other on the basis of stereotypes. Here was a good opportunity to examine the issue within the curriculum in a way that would have enhanced understanding and relationships as well as the function of schooling.

But what happens even when such open confrontations do not occur? Wright (1992) carried out an ethnographic study in a small number of inner-city nursery, first and middle schools in the north of England which had equal opportunities policies and training programmes and support structures for staff who were described as caring and committed to quality education.

Despite that, both Asian and African-Caribbean children experienced negative but different interactions with the teachers in the classrooms. Asian children were seen as weak in the English language, social skills generally and their ability to socialize with other groups in the classroom. On the other hand, they were also perceived as tractable, hard-working and eager to learn, with stable and supportive family backgrounds where educational success was highly valued.

African-Caribbean children, on the other hand, especially boys, were regarded as disruptive and in need of frequent reprimanding. Wright observed that they were singled out even when other children from different ethnic groups were engaged in the same behaviour. While African-Caribbean children experienced conflict with auxiliary staff outside the classroom, Asian pupils suffered from peer-group racial harassment in the playground which was a further extension of the racist name-calling initiated by white pupils in the classroom. Staff were observed as unwilling to intervene despite the self-evident intimidation and fear of the Asian pupils.

While Asian parents were generally satisfied with the quality of teaching, they were critical of the school's tokenistic approach to cultural diversity and its failure to tackle the racial harassment of their children. Muslim parents were concerned about the failure of the schools to accommodate religious and cultural demands and the frequent occasions when teaching the curriculum caused conflict between school and family values. African-Caribbean parents were among the most dissatisfied, especially with what they felt was the unjust treatment of their children by teachers. White parents were generally satisfied, although some had reservations about teaching methods and discipline while others objected to a curriculum they saw as favouring black children.

But despite conflict and dissatisfaction, an analysis of standardized tests scores showed African-Caribbean children to be performing better, especially in reading, than other groups. Asian children's performance in the tests was marginally lower. The latter were evidently not helped by the teacher's perceptions of them as tractable and hard-working. Obviously, one of the key problems was how the teachers viewed their language skills: bilingual strengths were overshadowed by English language weaknesses, and the former was not used as an opportunity to enhance the latter by paying tribute at least to the ability to speak more than one language.

Wright's findings in 1992 echoed the findings of a previous ethnographic study by her at secondary level between 1982 and 1984 (Wright 1987). Teachers were generally seen to hold adverse attitudes and expectations regarding African-Caribbean pupils. The pupils described how unfortunate encounters with teachers they perceived as hostile were fixed in their minds and the extent to which these then influenced their perceptions of schooling. African-Caribbean boys and girls were often perceived as trouble-makers and reprimanded and punished accordingly. A higher proportion of them – despite being the smallest ethnic group in the schools studied – were suspended and even excluded permanently without alternative educational provision. Little wonder that they became academic failures as a result of their experiences.

The influence of stereotyping and the breakdown in relationships was so strong, however, that behaviour criteria outweighed cognitive criteria in assessing African-Caribbean pupils. Consequently, they were likely to be placed in ability bands and examination sets below their actual academic ability, even as demonstrated in tests devised and conducted by the teachers who, in the event, failed to exercise objective, professional judgements in their allocation to bands and sets.

Under-achievement is not a neutral term. It is particularly loaded as far as black pupils are concerned. For them schools are not a purely meritocratic arena where they are assured of equal opportunities in teaching and assessment in order to develop their potential to the full. On the contrary, the generally lowly outcome is the result of a complexity of school process based on a combination of negative prejudice, destructive stereo-typing and low expectations.

Take, for example, the treatment of four nine-year-old black children at a largely white rural primary school in eastern England. They were children of mixed parentage whose parents wanted them to be fully aware of their black identity. Their parents were members of the same support group who had originally come together to share their concerns about the harassment of their children and the absence of curriculum content and play and learning resources that presented positive images of black children. Parents and children had much in common and they had personal experiences of the workings of racism in relation to the everyday treatment of themselves as black and white spouses and their off-spring. The children drew strength and inspiration from their solidarity as a group where they could share experiences and work out coping and survival strategies. Some of the teachers saw this as a threat and wanted to separate them. The parents sought advice from a national organization, courteously but firmly stood their ground, advised against such a negative response and diplomatically offered in-service training to the staff by the national group to which they belonged. The advice and the offer were accepted. The children, the parents and the teachers have all learned a valuable lesson from the experience. From all accounts, there has been some improvement already in school relationships and in the position and performance of the black children whom the parents see as potential high achievers anyway (WGARCR 1994b)

But still opportunities are missed. In one of the London boroughs, the mother of a five-year-old child asked the head of his new school to change his name from Kieron, under which he had been registered for admission some months previously, to his African name. The head refused on the grounds that the labels had already been prepared for the school's opening the next day. The mother offered to prepare the new ones on her Word Processor. The head still refused. The mother sought advice from the national children's organization to which she belonged. Her rights with regard to name-changes were explained and tactics for a new approach discussed, especially since, as she explained, she had been so humiliated by her encounter with the head in a matter of such significance for her and her child. In the event, she wrote a carefully worded letter to the head, with a copy to her child's teacher, firmly reiterating her request and enclosing a number of new labels to replace those prepared by the school. She succeeded, and she believes that the child now has the opportunity to learn in congenial circumstances which she has helped to create (WGARCR 1994c).

The point to be made is that *nothing succeeds like success*. It is not only the parents and children at the rural school who have gained but the school itself. Similarly, the London infant school has made progress. Significantly, it is the children's confidence that has developed while witnessing their parents' struggle on their behalf resulting in the school's acceptance of their position on their terms. What both sides have learned is that there is no need for conflict. Agreement can be negotiated, and through acceptance the performance of both individuals and community can be enhanced.

Unfortunately, despite the work of the past, despite the inquiries that have been initiated, despite the recommendations, despite the adoption of policies, the provision of training and the availability of positive learning resources, the same struggle is being waged and the same battles fought by countless black families who feel that their children are being disadvantaged by the schools they attend and by teacher attitudes and classroom practices.

This means that much of the energy that should be available for learning has to be expended on overcoming and compensating for the racial discrimination that threatens the welfare and progress of black children, even those who emerge with a clutch of examination successes guaranteeing a place in higher education. If circumstances are uncongenial for learning, they are also bad for effective teaching and teacher self-fulfilment and the promotion of mutual respect and co-operation among pupils and teachers.

What about the absence of effective bilingual teaching and progress towards multilingual provision in schools? There are obvious situations where such provision is desirable in order to facilitate the effective learning of skills and concepts as well as to promote the ability of black children more closely to identify with their schools as officially recognized speakers of other languages. White monolingual children will benefit from their opportunities to recognize and appreciate linguistic diversity, not only on a continental but a global scale

– and through that the richness and variety of spoken English by themselves and others, nationally, regionally and locally.

Gurnah (1989) sees multilingual studies as the natural and necessary development of bilingual support for black pupils with first languages other than English. He describes multilingual studies as 'a new subject for a new generation' (pp.176–198). His priorities are black children's community languages and the various forms of English and Creole because of the obvious neglect of those children's potential as well as their special needs. To be meaningful and relevant, European languages can eventually or even simultaneously be included in the same framework.

For Gurnah, multilingual studies are

> neither merely the learning of Standard or second-language English, nor…simply the maintenance of the parents' language – whether written or spoken. It denotes a complex new dynamic that forges languages and cultures, politics and philosophies for a new generation of keen, young, British, working-class, black people, who will make liars of those who accuse them of being caught *between* two cultures, implying confusion and lack of fulfilment in their lives. What these young people are in fact doing is existentially forging a new culture for their own benefit, which will integrate their parents and enrich the British community as a whole by also addressing the neglect of regional and working class English. (p.191, emphasis original)

Gurnah envisages a holistic dynamic approach for black and white children that will include not only providing an induction to linguistic rules and conventions but the range of issues, concerns and aspirations expressed in those languages through literature, philosophy and religion as well as through social and political organisation and economic and cultural choices. 'An important aspect of that curriculum must follow up the historical and political *relationship between* the said languages and cultures and their resolution in contemporary society' (pp.191–192). Bilingual provision, for example, would enable children to inhabit the two worlds where English and their first language were spoken. *It would* promote an understanding by *all* children that 'British culture is now more multifaceted' (p.192, emphasis original).

Gurnah says that such a framework is essential to eradicate the impoverishment of most bilingual support, the low status of bilingual teachers and the marginalization of working class black children. He is talking not just about an adjustment of the curriculum but its fundamental reorientation, and he concludes with a challenge to providers and practitioners:

> Language is a symbolic expression of individual and community life. If that life reflects a multiplicity of backgrounds, experiences and languages, our education system must learn to recognize their worth, create ways of absorbing them in the curriculum, and promote sharing them with everybody else. (p.197)

It is that kind of recognition of individuals as valued and respected that enhances self-esteem along with feelings of security and well-being as well as a range of good social and working relationships within which children and young people will feel encouraged both to learn and be themselves. It is in such circumstances that they can make optimum use of their energies to develop all aspects of their lives freely without having to struggle against attitudes and practices that constantly question their presence and threaten the space that they occupy.

Jane Lane (1989, pp.75–101) stresses the importance of understanding that attention must be paid to early years provision in the lives of children if they are to develop their full range of intellectual, emotional, physical and social skills. She deals with the low priority accorded to meeting the needs of young children and their carers as well as with the myths about childhood innocence and minimal social influences in the early years. While adults pay lip-service to equality, she says, they fail to appreciate that their commitment has implications for organization, management and practice in early years play and learning provision. She states that

> The struggle for equality starts in the earliest years and is about breaking down practices, customs and procedures that result in some people having poorer life chances, poorer job opportunities, poorer housing and poorer education than others and having little influence on the political and economic decisions that affect their lives. (p.78)

She deals with the muddle and inadequacy of national provision, and she exposes the labelling and stereotyping that can follow allocation to particular types of provision. For example, children in Social Services day nurseries may be stigmatized as having (or being) a problem because of the admission criteria based on 'social and physical need'. This in turn can lead to the pathologizing of families and communities, with unfortunate effects on future educational progress.

In addition to exposing inadequacy and myth, she stresses the importance of recognizing both the diversity and value of the range of different practices of child-rearing, for example, and in making provision for the children and parents accordingly. She looks critically at language and how it is used about and in relation to the children. She deals with resources as a means of conveying positive messages about children, and she details the activities that might be pursued in the quest for genuine equality of opportunity. She makes practical suggestions about how adults can deal with ignorance, prejudice, harassment and inequality in discussion with children. Her conclusion is clear:

> If children in their earliest years are not given a chance to be equally valued, there is even less hope that they will be accorded equal treatment as they grow up. Providing a framework where young children can think for themselves, evaluate information and respect and

value difference may give them a chance of justice and equality that is the fundamental right of all children. It is a right that adults (under-fives workers and families) must support. (p.100)

Lane's exhortations are strongly supported by the Working Group Against Racism in Children's Resources who urge not only the provision of good anti-racist resources in domestic, caring and learning situations but their use by properly trained adults who are equally convinced about equal respect and provision for *all* children. It is not just black children who benefit from the ready availability of resources that present positive images of black children. White children must also be enabled to correct the distorted vision of the world imposed by adults choosing to restrict their experiences to things that flow from the myth of white supremacy (WGARCR 1990, p.6)

Successful academic performance depends on good teaching and honest assessment. In a paper delivered by Dr Julia Dreyden to the National Foundation For Educational Research (Dreyden 1989) there is a thought-provoking examination of the effect on assessment procedures of a body of knowledge arising out of a particular world view held by white people. People from groups that have been excluded from contributing to that world view are therefore likely to have their talents under-measured by the assessment procedures. To counter the anachronisms of such a view, Dr Dreyden suggests infusing curricula with the 'histories and cultures of under-represented groups' in largely white as well as multi-ethnic areas. The so-called sub-cultures should be presented, she says, in ways illustrating their importance as 'ballast' to the predominant culture, thus enhancing its chances of survival in facing the increasingly complex challenges of the modern world. As far as test results are concerned, she says, they should be used with 'a healthy dash of professional scepticism', especially since 'they have a limited validity in predicting real world success'. In support of her last claim, she quotes the findings of the US Office of Employment in relation to the equally good performance of black employees appointed under the positive discrimination quota system.

She also deals with the stresses and strains imposed on black people by hostile learning environments. She contrasts them with the way in which members of majority groups can use their reservoirs of energy simply for playing the game of life by the rules enunciated to ensure their participation in the first place and ultimately their success or victory. She says 'A normal intelligence may be said to have at its disposal limited resources to expend for self-preservation, then more disinterested motives'. But, she adds

> Members of the society devalued by the tradition are in the position of...having to spend limited resources on a hierarchy of priorities .beginning with diffusing hostility to obtain physical security; to transforming the environment to one that is sympathetic to

non-traditional experience; to establishing and extending one's own traditions (p.12)

Mac an Ghaill (1992) describes a two-year ethnographic study which illustrates further how young black Asian and African-Caribbean people in Britain have, in response to their alienating experiences of schooling, '...collectively and individually, creatively developed coping and survival strategies'. The young people are placed at the centre of the research, and it is their experiences of school, teachers, friends and family that enable Mac an Ghaill to conclude that

> Their adoption of a variety of coping and survival strategies that are linked to the wider black community illustrates that, more than any other fraction of the working class, they are consciously creating their own material culture. (Mac an Ghaill 1988, p.56)

In so doing, they are rejecting the model of white society presented by teachers and are resisting institutional incorporation into white cultural identities (Hall *et al.* 1978, p.341).

One of the important things to come out of this research and one of the things that needs to be repeated for teachers and other people in authority who often pontificate on the problem of inter-generational conflict in the black communities – between the parents' 'traditional rural culture' and the young peoples' 'modern urban life-style' – is the fact that without exception all these students explicitly identified with their parents and saw them as their main support and source of inspiration.

Here is yet another important resource as yet inadequately recognized by teachers. There is a tendency for the professionals to disregard the experiences and views of parents because they see them as unqualified and amateur instead of being prepared to learn from their knowledge of their children, gained in the closest encounters over many years in a variety of settings. Likewise, their classroom organization limits the opportunities that could supply them with honest feed-back about the effectiveness of teaching, relationships, discipline and extra-curricular activities in their schools, insights just as valuable, if indeed not more valuable, than the views exchanged in staff meetings. Their work could be enhanced if their protestations of an interest in community outreach were matched by an interest in how individuals, families and communities actually lived in their catchment area.

When asked many years ago about the relevance and significance of Latin and Greek, the Quaker Professor of Education, E. B. Castle, replied that it was the relevance of teachers to life that made their subject relevant and of significance in the lives of children and young people. Unless teachers are seen to be passionately interested in the subjects they teach and unless they can be seen to want relationships with young people that are based on respect for them as individuals and to require similar respect in return, they will be perceived as irrelevant to the successful all-round performance of children and young people in their schools and colleges. As Richardson says, unless they are willing to be involved in the real, everyday struggle for justice for all, unless black children can see them as challenging racist attitudes and procedures, they and what they have to offer in education will be seen as ultimately irrelevant as far as their lives are concerned.

As far as black people in Britain are concerned, one of the biggest obstacles to their children's success and security is racism. What they would like to see is teachers and schools availing themselves of every opportunity to eradicate the effects of racist attitudes and practices in all aspects of school life so that they can enjoy their full share of equality with regard to educational access, treatment and outcome.

References

Birmingham Metropolitan Council (1994) *Report to the Birmingham Education Services and Special Needs Sub-Committee 28 June 1994 – Baseline Assessment for the Primary Phase Autumn 1993 Analysis of Results.*

Chevannes, M. and Reeves, F. (1987) 'The black voluntary school movement.' In B. Troyna (ed) *Racial Equality in Education.* London: Tavistock.

Clark, K. (1971) 'Alternative public school systems.' In B. Gross and R. Gross (eds) *Radical School Reform.* London: Victor Gollancz.

Coard, B. (1971) H*ow the West Indian Child is Made Educationally Sub-normal in the British School System.* London: New Beacon Books.

Dreyden, J. (1989) *Multiculturalism and the Structure of Knowledge: A Discussion of Standardised Tests. A paper given at the National Foundation for Educational Research.*

Guardian (1993) *Education Guardian,* September 7th.

Gurnah, A. (1989) 'After bilingual support?' in M. Cole (ed) *Education For Equality Some Guidelines for Good Practice.* London: Routledge.

Hall, S., Critcher, C., Jefferson, T., Clarke, J. and Roberts, B. (1978) *Policing the Crisis: Mugging the State and Law and Order.* London: Macmillan.

Lane, J. (1989) 'The playgroup/nursery.' In M. Cole (ed) *Education For Equality Some Guidelines for Good Practice.* London: Routledge.

Mac an Ghaill, M. (1988) *Young, Gifted and Black: Student-Teacher Relations in the Schooling of Black Youths.* Milton Keynes: Open University Press.

Mac an Ghaill, M. (1992) 'Coming of age in 1980s England: reconceptualising black students' schooling experience.' In D. Gill, B. Mayor and M. Blair (ed) *Racism and Education Structures and Strategies.* London: Sage Publications.

Milner, D. (1983) *Children and Race, Ten Years On.* London: Ward Lock.

Richardson, R. (1990) *Daring to be a Teacher Essays, Stories and Memoranda.* Stoke-on-Trent: Trentham Books.

Working Group Against Racism in Children's Resources (1990) *Guidelines for the Evaluation and Selection of Toys and other Resources for Children.* WGARCR, 460 Wandsworth Road, London, SW8 3LX.

Working Group Against Racism in Children's Resources (1994a) Exclusions File – London Boroughs. Confidential document.

Working Group Against Racism in Children's Resources (1994b) Racial Harassment File – Eastern region. Confidential Document.

Working Group Against Racism in Children's Resources (1994c) Discrimination File – Infant/Primary Schools. Confidential Document.

Wright, C. (1987) 'Black students – white teachers.' In B,. Troyna (ed) *Racial Inequality in Education.* London: Tavistock.

Wright, C. (1992) *Race Relations in the Primary School.* London. David Fulton.

CHAPTER 5

Adoption of Children from Minority Groups

Harry Zeitlin

Introduction

Meera was born in Southern India and is very dark skinned. She was adopted by an affluent white Anglo Saxon Church of England family at six weeks. The mother had other natural children and though the girl bonded to the mother, the mother did not bond to her. They never discussed with Meera her origins, culture of heritage, religion or difference in appearance from the rest of the family. The rejection progressively affected her behaviour, giving reason to place her further and further from the heart of the family unit. At twelve she came into the care of the local authority. She was placed with a woman of Afro-Caribbean origin, who was a Jehovah witness, of low income and a single mother. She was kind and caring but frequently took supportive comment as a criticism of her based on prejudice against black people. After a suicidal attempt by the girl a proposal was made to place her with a recently immigrated Indian Muslim family.

This case history raises nearly all of the issues relevant to adoption and fostering of children from minority groups, but it is almost impossible to examine them without immediately entering into controversy. The whole subject has become one of emotional debate, partly because of the media sensation seeking and partly because of understandable feelings of resentment against prejudice and 'racism'.

Same race placement has been put forward as the determining principle in adoption. Thoburn (1988) stated that 'Although babies should be placed as early as possible, there is reason to be hopeful that they will settle in with a new family when a suitable family is found, if care is taken over the introductory period...it is preferable, even for babies, for a same race placement to be made after some delay, than to make a transracial placement' (p.78). No evidence is offered either to support the bad outcome for transracial adoption or the lack of effect of delay in placement and ignores current research on attachment. There is also a tendency to a simple polarized argument for and against placement of black children with white families. This policy is often taken further so that any 'black' child must be placed in a 'black' family, if unable to live with his birth parents. Children of 'mixed' parentage are usually considered as black for the purpose of placement decisions.

One of the greatest problems is confusion over terminology. Such fostering and adoption has variously been referred to as transracial, transcultural and mixed ethnic. Unfortunately, there is a lack of consistency in the use of the terms – Race, Ethnicity and Culture each being used with variable meaning but also interchangeably. Although for some the problems seems quite clear with regard to themselves, for example about being black in a majority white community, or about specific religious persecution, the same problems arise with regard to wide variety of other people of different national origins and cultures. Those would include among many others, Turks, Chinese, American Indian and, depending on the majority community, nearly every religion.

These issues matter greatly when considering placement for a child. The phrase 'same race placement' is easy to say but exactly what is meant is obscure and it is a term born more in response to social prejudice than anything else. In view of the confusion it is valuable to review briefly the meaning of the terms and then to consider the impact of the relevant factors on placement.

Race and Racial

The word 'race' is freely used and often without regard to meaning. Dictionary definitions give various meanings from 'a group of persons, animals or plants connected by common descent or origin' to 'a genus, species'. Much of the present social usage derives from nineteenth century ethnologists and Pritchard in 1845 wrote 'The principle object of the following work (The Natural History of Man) may then be described as an attempt to point out the most important diversities by which mankind, or the genus of man, is distinguished and separated into different races, and to determine whether these races constitute separate species or are merely varieties of one species' (p.10). Strictly speaking as noted by Darwin (1871, p.214) racial difference really implies genetic incompatibility, a different species. As there are no two human groups where cross mating produces diminished fertility in this sense there is only one human race.

Tizard and Phoenix (1989) comment that the term 'race' is 'socially constructed and contentious', but found 'no alternative for its use in a society where it has deep political and psychological meaning'. For the most part it seems that the term is used to imply reference to people with a common national heritage and who share certain physical characteristics, but with very uncertain implication as to associated cultures. As far as possible here reference instead will be made to physical characteristics, culture, country of heritage, culture of heritage and where possible the use of the race and ethnic will be interpreted in these terms.

Ethnicity

Dictionary definitions give **Ethnic:** Pertaining to nations, gentile, heathen. **Ethnology:** Science of human races, their relations and characteristics. Not a great deal of help, except perhaps in the reference to nations. Unfortunately, when this is applied to the British nation we immediately run into a total lack of consistency with physical characteristics. The British origins were Nordic, Saxon, Roman and so forth. with a range of appearance from flaxen haired to swarthy Mediterranean. Today a significant proportion of the British population take their origins in Africa or Asia and much of the open debate centres on being black or white. However, there is no agreed definition of what being black constitutes, except as non-white. What is more important is that such categorization is based on xenophobic hostility, is neither logical nor exact, and is not a helpful basis on which to examine the best interests of children unable to stay with their natural parents. Certainly many people see themselves as being black and would be so described by others. However, many others in this society would neither be able to decide whether they are black or white nor wish to so categorize themselves. There is no evidence to support the suggestion that there is a 'black race' compared with white other than politically and in discussing placement of a child, if the importance of being black in this society is because it identifies a section of society for hostility and prejudice, then the real issue is to help children cope with prejudice.

Apart from skin colour there is a wide variety of genetically determined physical characteristics which are related to 'ethnic' or 'racial' groups, including aspects of stature and physiognomy and to which social stereotypes are applied. Stereotyping of this nature is made by well meaning professionals as well as more hostile members of society, with assumptions about cultural practice and experience. It would be incorrect to assume that all Semites are of the same religion or that black Asians share a common culture with black Afro-Caribbeans. In any case, as soon as a family migrates to a different majority culture the children will have a different experience from that of their parents, even if they adhere strictly to their culture of heritage.

Culture

Both Pritchard and Darwin mixed issues of physical status with those of culture. Culture refers to 'improvement or refinement by education and training'. It usually applies to patterns of behaviour that are linked to national and religious customs. The cultural experience of children should be distinguished from the cultural associations linked to 'National' characteristics or heritage as these have different implications for the children. The former, being part of a child's personal experience, is more relevant to learned coping styles and the latter to a sense of historical identity. In the case example quoted, Meera's heritage was of Indian culture, although across India that differs greatly. Her religion of heritage might have been Muslim or Christian but statistically more probably Hindu. In reality no-one knew and false assumptions were made. Her experience was of Christian culture, but that was Church of England and very different from Jehovah witness. However, talking to Meera it was apparent that there were many other areas of culture that were important to her, not the least being that she had become poor and missed celebrating Christmas.

The policy of black with black assumes not only a black race but a single black culture, another stereotype as there is no unifying 'black culture' but a wide and rich range of very different cultures. An appreciation of the particular child's experience becomes more relevant than a blanket policy. It is also hazardous to generalize about the ways that children react to differences between their culture of origin and majority culture as, for example, Weinreich (1983) found that there were not only differences between Asian and West Indian groups but also between male and female within those groups.

Confusion of Issues

Closer examination of the use of these terms indicates that there is considerable confusion of the issues relating to placement of a child. Each of the items needs to be considered separately to avoid transferring that confusion to the child (Alstein *et al.* 1994). Alstein and colleagues noted that there were dangers of making assumptions that became self-fulfilling and stressed the need for self-awareness among social workers involved in adoption placement.

It even remains difficult to find a terminology to deal with the problems. Transracial/ethnic/cultural adoption is somewhat cumbersome and perhaps the terms Euharmonic and Euharmony for those matching in every respect is preferable, otherwise specifying the mismatch condition relevant.

> *As food for thought the reader might at this point consider the following question. If the choice is between a black Christian family or a white Muslim family, with which would you place a black Muslim child?*

This chapter will address the problem from a general point of view, although with particular focus on 'black' children. With regard to adoption and fostering the issues that are entangled can be summarized by the list in Chart 1 and we can proceed to examine what evidence there is to prioritize each in importance when planning placement.

Fostering and Adoption

It is essential to stress that the most important approach to fostering and adoption is to address the root causes that result in parents being unable to care for their children.

Chart 1: Confusion of Issues	
Race	Unhelpful ambiguous term now linked with prejudice
Ethnic	Too varied in usage
Physical appearance	Does not indicate important areas of culture
Culture	Culture of Heritage may differ from that experienced
Identity	Normally based on various factors not usually mainly appearance
	Differences between personal and assigned
Reasons for adoption	Relate to special needs of the child
Attachment/ stability/consistency	Where in prioritization of matching?

However, children do and will continue to need alternative care and three factors make it necessary to address the problems of 'mixed race adoption'. First, there is a shortage of suitable minority group families compared with the numbers of children needing alternative care. Second, at present there is greater risk for some minority group children to need alternative care compared with the rest of the community (Jenkins and Diamond 1985). That means that the biggest pool of families is majority group whereas a relatively greater proportion of minority group children need alternative families. Third, the increasing variations of heritage and culture from mixed parentage make placement into families that are dissimilar difficult to avoid.

If children do have to be in alternative care there are aspects of placement that need to be considered before looking at the question of match. Although it would not be appropriate here to review all issues relevant to adoptions, there are some generally accepted principles. The younger the child the lower the rate of placement breakdown. The more problems within the natural home that the child has been subject to, the more the impact of separation and uncertainty. Children who have spent some time in institutional care are more likely to be over affectionate but also later to have difficulty in forming close relationships. From personal clinical experience children who either spend prolonged periods in temporary care or move through a series of short term carers become increasingly rigid, untrusting and emotionally distant. Some of the aspects of adoption common to all placements are listed in Chart 2.

Chart 2	
Reason for placement	**Need to be taken into account**
Bereavement	
Parental illness/incapacity	
Abuse/neglect	
Beyond parental control	
Special needs	
Age of child	Adoption outcome better when placement before age three.
	After age five not likely to make too much difference between fostering or adoption
Number of previous placements	More placements less trust
Period of time in temporary care	Longer time gives more relationship problems
Emotional or behavioural disorder	Special demands on alternative parents

What Might go Wrong for Minority Group Children

Tizard and Phoenix (1989) considered the anxieties relating to black children in white families

(1) Black children living in white families fail to develop a positive black identity. Instead they suffer from identity confusion and develop a negative self concept, believing or wishing they were white.

(2) Unless they are carefully trained, white families cannot provide black children with survival skills that they need for coping with racial prejudice in society.

(3) The children will grow up unable to relate to black people and at the same time will experience rejection by white society.

Identity·

Issues of identity and its development are of great importance in any adoption but how central is racial or ethnic identity and should it be the main means of personal identification? Erikson in the 1950s (1968) laid the foundation for conceptualization and research on identity formation. He saw identity formation as part of the developmental process by which choices could be made by the individual.

> The young person in order to experience wholeness must feel a progressive continuity between that which he has come to be during the long years of childhood and that which he promises to become in the anticipated future; between that which he conceives himself to be and that which he perceives others to see in him and to expect of him.

Marcia (1968) further developed Erikson's ideas and construed identity as

> an internal, self constructed organisation of drives, abilities, beliefs, and individual history. The better developed this structure is, the more aware the individual appears to be of their own uniqueness...the less developed this structure is, the more confused individuals seem to be about their own distinctiveness from others and the more they have to rely on external sources to evaluate themselves. (p.159–187)

Ideas have progressed in some aspects pushed by the issues concerning 'ethnic identity'. The idea of a single composite identity is replaced by one with several components or domains. If we look at the available means by which children, individuals, gain their identity, they include gender role, family values, social grouping, occupation, religion, political ideology, relationships and personal values. The various components of identity are not developed or fixed at the same time. Gender identity is, for example, set very early in life, whereas career-based identity evolves much later, at least for most. Fairly fundamental to identity formation are rather diffuse feelings of being valuable, and of having desirable personal characteristics. Most children in this society are not primarily identified by their appearance but by being good at reading, skilled at football or kind and loving. Some, of course, by being aggressive or violent. Early reinforcement of those same types of quality enables children to evaluate more constructively characteristics that might be seen as negative by others (Jacobs 1978).

Tizard and Phoenix (1989) challenged the value of the concept of 'positive black identity' as being too simplistic with regard to the way in which children identify themselves. Early research based on forced choice between seeing self as black or white lead to some incorrect conclusions. When children were given a range of appearances to match themselves with they had from an early age quite accurate independent awareness of their skin colour that was more precise and different from a black white categorization (Jacobs 1978). Spencer (1984) from a study of 130 black pre-school children found that the children were able to conceptualize and compartmentalize a view of self that is independent of attitudes surrounding the evaluation of their racial group, and strong personal identity rather than group identity is associated with good outcome in terms of low rates of disturbance (Scott 1986).

Children of mixed marriages, 'black' and 'white', are of special concern. Currently there is a pressure that they should be classified as black and that they should see themselves as so. The argument is that society sees them as black and they will be better off if that is their self perceived identity. Eleven out of twenty-eight interracial children studied by Arnold (1984) rated themselves as black, but twelve saw themselves as interracial and five as white. As a whole, the children expressed an uncertainty about their racial identification but those who saw themselves as interracial showed greater emotional and psychiatric stability. They also scored higher on self-concept.

Identity and Self-Esteem

Self-esteem is related to identity in a very uncertain manner. A simple model is that strong positive identity leads to high self-esteem but it does not always seem to work like that. Although black children are not particularly of low self-esteem (Gill and Jackson 1983) and Rasheed (1981) found little correlation between ethnic identity and self-esteem, strong identification with a minority group has been found to have an adverse effect (Casey 1986). This is not confined to groups identified by skin colour and Casey's data, for example, refers to Italian and Polish second and third generation immigrants in America. Stein (1984) compared 91 adoptees at age 15–18 with matched non-adopted children using self-rating scales for identity and self-image. It was the quality of family relationships in both groups that was predictive of positive identity outcome rather than the adoptive status.

The political writers correctly noted that people with black skin will be classified according to that skin colour by at least a proportion of society. They argue that a black identity should be encouraged as the primary means of identification. However, such identity is an assigned one and difficult to separate from stereotypes and prejudices. The danger is that central identification in that manner results in the individual being controlled by the assigned identity rather than owning and being proud of the attributes that had been used to classify them.

Negative Identity

Erikson (1968) wrote also about choice of a negative identity. 'They choose instead a negative identity i.e. based perversely on all those identifications and roles which, at critical stages of development, had been presented to them as most undesirable or dangerous and yet also as most real' (p.174). However, that is based largely on the supposition that identity formation is based on a series of choices. In this case it is not so much a negative identity as a negative connotation of the identity assigned. How then can children achieve a positive identification with those characteristics used as a source of prejudice. How can strong ethnic/cultural identity be developed as an asset rather than something that isolates the individual from other parts of society and restricts individual exploration and growth?

First, the child should be secure within a safe environment. It is for secure individuals with clearly identified assets in a safe environment, that ongoing exploration of identity is safe and effective. Those individuals can cope with the uncertainty involved. Second, for many, early positive identity formation is protective particularly from adverse assigned identity. That identification should be with a range of individual positive characteristics as well as with the culture of heritage (rather than race or those physical characteristics that have been used for prejudice). Third, failure to form elements of personal identity, based on positive attributes, early in the process of independence, leaves children vulnerable to a range of emotional and behavioural disturbances including aggressive behaviour, drug abuse and depression. Fourth ethnic and cultural domains of identity become important valuable personal assets against this background. Finally, if care professionals assign identity because society uses that identification for prejudice, children receive a very mixed message about the value of that aspect of personal identity.

The issue of identity can become circular. Identifying because of assigned identity based on prejudice will lead to angry defensiveness which in turn leads to segregation and then back to seeking to impose a segregated identity. In this way a group of angry people unable to deal with prejudice and or participate in a dialogue is developed.

Outcome Studies for Fostering and Adoption

There is relatively little good systematic data on long term outcome for 'crossed adoption', most still confusing culture, heritage appearance and so on. What there is, though, has a remarkable consistency, showing no major differences in outcome for matched and non-matched 'race' adoptions on a variety of measures (Womak and Fulton 1981; Moore 1986; Wrobel 1990). Overall it appears that some 80 per cent of such adoption are satisfactory in term of adult adjustment, although obviously what is meant by that is open to debate. Womak and Fulton (1981) studied 28 'transracially' adopted black children, comparing them with 13 non-adopted black children. They found no significant differences on measures of development or of racial attitude. Wrobel (1990) reported that all 78 transracially adopted adolescents in his study rated themselves positively, males more strongly so than females and good communication with the mother was central to positive self-esteem. Berridge and Cleaver (1987) from a study of foster home breakdown concluded that ethnicity (referring to black or 'mixed race') was not strongly related to outcome, although there was a small excess of foster breakdown for transracial placement. They noted that the rates of disturbance in adopted children were actually quite low and that the majority did well. This seems to be a common factor in what studies have been reported, even those that anticipate later problems.

In adoption some children become 'searchers' for their family and culture of origin, but these tend to be those who have experience of instability and difficulty in developing individual identity (Stein 1984). The associated psychological disturbance is best dealt with by minimizing periods of uncertainty and instability and promoting identification with the family of adoption. Kim (1980) reporting on problems with three Korean children adopted by white American families noted that the children had experienced major cultural change which, though usually ignored, could well explain the children's disturbance. Given the wide range of cultural, ethnic and social factors associated with people of any one skin colour or national origin, the stereotyped associations that ignore the real experience of the child are hazardous. However, more research is needed on the effects of 'cultural dissonance' as well as physical dissimilarity.

Chart 3: Summary of Outcome studies	
Womack and Fulton 1981	Comparison of TRA and non adopted black children:
	No significant difference in development of racial attitudes.
	Early placement and open social attitudes relate to good outcome.
Cleaver 1987	Ethnicity not strongly related to foster breakdown.
	Rates of disturbance low. Most (80%+) do well.
Wrobel 1990	TRA black children rated themselves positively.
	Communication with mother important.
Stein 1984	Search behaviour greater with physical mismatch but mainly linked to family relationship difficulty. Less with early placement, stability and open social attitudes.

Good Adjustment in Transracial Adoption

Womak and Fulton (1981) proposed that the good outcome in their study was largely due to the stability given to the adopted children by early placement. They noted that the adopters that they studied were of higher than average socio-economic status and thought that they also showed relatively more open social attitudes.

Physical match does have relevance. Stein (1984) compared 91 adoptees at age 15–18 with matched non-adopted children using self-rating scales for identity and self-image. It was the quality of family relationships in both groups that was predictive of positive identity outcome rather than the adoptive status. Stein did find that search behaviour (looking for the family of origin) among adoptees was more likely where there was a heightened sense of physical dissimilarity from the family. That occurred, however, when there was also unsatisfactory family relationship and tended to be those who had experience of instability and difficulty in developing individual identity. The associated psychological disturbance is best dealt with by minimizing periods of uncertainty and instability and promoting identification with the family of adoption. Early placement, stability, and open social attitudes were also important factors for good adjustment.

Jacobs (1978) studied interracial black/white and found that there were a number of factors that were supportive of positive interracial self-concept formation. These had three main elements: a good relationship with the adoptive mother, early strong reinforcement of the child's skills and character and a policy of open discussion of the child's origins and of ethnic and racial issues.

Chart 4: Summary of factors linked to good adjustment

Good communication with mother

Early ego enhancing treatment

Assistance in verbalizing racial material

Supportive interest in expression of racial ambivalence

Multiracial Associations

Interracial label for the child

Early age of adoption

Coping with Racism

It is assumed that it is best to place a child who may experience prejudice with a family who have been subjected to prejudice. Whilst racism is common and highly distressing to those subjected to it, there has been little systematic study of the effects of racism on children or on the best means of psychological defence. A number of studies have concerned ethnic identity and its effect on racial attitudes (Branch 1982; Heavan 1978; Jahoda and Harrison 1975), but not the well being of the child. Some effects have been noted within the educational system with impairment of teacher relationship, peer group environment and educational achievement (Comer 1989; Stephen and Rosenfield 1978). Racism has also been linked to antisocial behaviour, with the suggestion that unfairness of opportunity resulted in 'displacement' behaviour directed against social rules (Simons and Gray 1989). Children subjected to intense racial animosity in concentration camps during World War II also showed marked behavioural effects (Kestenberg and Breener 1986; Roseman 1984). For both of these it is difficult to separate the components of social deprivation, separation and loss, although these themselves are indirect effects of racism.

What indications there are suggest, not surprisingly, that the same factors that are linked to successful adoption placement also are related to dealing with racism. It is important for children to feel valued in their own right and not primarily because they are part of a minority group. The children should know that they are adopted from an early age and should be taught to be proud of their appearance, culture and heritage. There should be open discussion that racism occurs in society but also help to distinguish adversity that is not due to racism or prejudice – a task easier said than done. Membership of mixed social groups based on interests other than ethnicity can help. This form of approach has been criticized as bringing children up to be 'human beings' and denying that they are black. It must be quite clear that that is unequivocally not what is proposed – rather that 'the parents convey to their child that they, themselves, do not judge and relate to people on the basis of their skin colour, but they should tell the child that many people in the society do' (Jones and Else 1979).

Placements that do Break-Down

Whilst the rate of breakdown is not significantly greater than for 'euharmonious' adoption there are some possible markers for special reasons. In two transracial adoptions that broke down a principle factor was the reason for adoption being an altruistic wish to do good (Cassel and Zeitlin 1995). Choulot and Brodier (1993) report four cases of failed adoption of foreign children. They found that older age adopting parents and lack of counselling were related factors.

Apart from breakdown of placement, some children become 'searchers' for their biological parents. Search behaviour is slightly more common where there is a physical dissimilarity between adopters and adoptee. However it seems that the search behaviour within this group was more linked to poor relationship with the adoptive mother' (Stein 1984, p.2908).

Education for Practice in a Multi-Ethnic Society

One approach to practice is to employ professionals who are representative of minority sections of the population served. To some extent that can be helpful where there is a large and relatively uniform recent immigrant population. Special knowledge of the language and culture can aid communication and understanding. It may also help in recruiting substitute families from minority groups. There are, however, hazards in such an approach. It assumes a relevance of the professional's own cultural experience although there may be major differences between the culture of a successful professional social worker and an immigrant family of similar heritage. There are also many communities with immigrants from several source countries. Most important, professionals should be selected for their professionals skills first and additional linguistic and special cultural knowledge second.

It is more appropriate that training should include an approach to evaluating and understanding the special needs of children from 'ethnic groups'. That would include an analysis of the issues, access to relevant literature, skills to listen to the child, awareness of personal feelings about the situation and a preparedness to enlist the help of those who do have special knowledge. The aim should be as much to prepare practitioners raised in minority groups to work with 'the majority' as the reverse.

Recommendations for Practice

- Training should be available for professionals relevant to the special problems of minority groups.
- Training should include the means of helping people deal with prejudice.
- Professional advice should be based on research and empirical evidence and not on political attitude.
- Assessments for fostering or adoption should consider separately the relevance of physical match (including skin colour), 'racial' identification, culture of origin and the social and cultural experience of the child.
- The closer the match between the child and alternative family the better.
- Placement with a caring stable family is of prime importance.
- Wherever possible a match with the child's experienced culture should be made.

- If possible without undue delay in placement a physical match with the adoptive family is helpful.

- Significant delay in placement whilst seeking a 'same race' family is not justified.

- Fostered and adopted children should be encouraged and helped to take pride in their national and cultural origins.

- Adoptive and foster parents should be counselled to help children develop a positive identity based on personal skills and attributes rather than one that is based solely on appearance or identification with a minority group. Children should be helped to proud of personal characteristics including skin colour.

- Parents of children from minority groups should be counselled to help their children be aware of social prejudice.

(Adapted from Zeitlin, Harris, Garralda and Sein 1991)

Conclusions

If a child can be matched on physique and culture with a family who are stable, loving and consistent and who will accept guidance on helping the child deal with being adopted and with prejudice that they might experience, then that is best of all. The closer the match, the more 'Euharmonic', the easier the task for the child and parents.

The pessimism over placement of children with physically dissimilar families, 'transracial' adoption is unjustified and the majority do well. There is a shortage of families of Asian or African origin, 'black families', and certainly every effort should be made to recruit more families from 'minorities'. However, until there is a sufficient pool of minority group families able to foster or adopt, it is better to make the best match for culture and to avoid undue delay trying to match race.

Once a child has been placed with a family then the task commences of helping that child cope with being adopted (or fostered), with the differences between his or her self and the adoptive family, and with such issues as prejudice in society. That applies no matter how close the match between the child and family and it cannot though be assumed that experiencing prejudice trains a person to cope with that prejudice. There are guidelines that can help and professional support should be available to all families.

Children in minority groups should first be helped to identify themselves by the same type of criteria as all other children and then to use their heritage and 'racial' characteristics as part of their developing and maturing identity. They will then be more able to own and be proud of those characteristics that are used by others as a source of prejudice. Whilst we are far from it at present, we should not lose sight of the goal of all members of society being proud of their individual heritage but not separated from others by it.

References

Alstein, H., Coster, M., First Hartling, L., Ford, C., Glascoe, B., Hariston, S., Kasoff, J. and Grier A.W. (1994) 'Clinical observations of adult intercountry adoptees and their adoptive parents.' *Child Welfare 73*, 3. 261–9.

Arnold, M.C. (1984) 'The effects of racial identity on self concept in interracial children.' *Dissertation-Abstracts-International 45*, 9A, 3000.

Berridge, D. and Cleaver, H. (1987) *Foster Home Breakdown.* Blackwell: Oxford.

Branch, C.W. (1982) 'A cross sectional longitudinal study of the development of racial attitudes among black children as a function of parental attitudes.' *Dissertation-Abstracts-International 43*, 3-B, 846.

Casey, C. (1986) 'Ethnic identity and self esteem in second and third generation Polish and Italian sixth grade children.' *Dissertation-Abstracts-International 46*, 11A, 3273.

Cassel, D. and Zeitlin, H. (1995) Two cases of placement breakdown in transcultural adoption. Unpublished report.

Choulot, J.J. and Brodier, J.M. (1993) 'Risk of failure in uncontrolled adoption of foreign children.' *Ann. Paediatr.* Paris. 40, 10, 635–638.

Comer, J.P. (1989) Racism and the Education of Young Children. *Teachers College Record 90*, 3.

Darwin, C. (1871) *The Descent of Man.* London: John Murray.

Erikson, E.H. (1968) *Identity, Youth and Crisis.* New York: Norton.

Gill, O, and Jackson B. (1983) *Adoption and Race: Black, Asian and Mixed Race Children in White Families.* London: Batsford Academic and Educational.

Grotevant, H. (1992) 'Assigned and chosen identity components; process perspective on their integration. In G.R. Adams, T.P. Gullotta and R. Montemayor (eds) *Adolescent Identity Formation. Advances in Adolescent Development.* Newbury Park, CA: Sage publications.

Heavan, P.C. (1978) 'The social attitudes of a group of South African children.' *S.African J.Psychol. 8*, 30–34.

Isaacs-Giraldi, G.J. (1980) 'Influences of the frequency of visitation by the divorced natural father on the self-concept and sexual identity of the male child.' *Dissertation-Abstracts-International 41*, 3B, 1111–1112.

Jacobs, J.H. (1978) 'Black/white interracial families: marital process and identity development in young children.' *Dissertation-Abstracts-International 38*, 10B, 5023.

Jahoda, D. and Harrison, S. (1975) 'Belfast children: some effects of a conflict environment.' *Irish J. Psychol. 3*, 1, 1–19.

Jenkins, S. and Diamond B. (1985) 'Ethnicity and foster care. Census data as predictors of placement variables.' *Amer. J.Orthopsychiatry 55*, 2, 267–276.

Jones, C.E. and Else, J.F. (1979) 'Racial and cultural issues in adoption.' *Child Welfare LVIII*, 6, 373–382.

Kestenberg, J.S. and Breener, I. (1986) 'Children who survived the holocaust.' *Int. J. Psychoanal 67*, 3, 309–316.

Kim, S.P. (1980) 'Behaviour symptoms in three transracially adopted Asian children: diagnosis dilemma.' *Child-Welfare* Apr, 59, 4, 213–24.

Marcia, J.E. (1980) Identity in Adolescence. In J. Adolson (ed) *Handbook of Adolescent Psychology*. New York: John Wilson.

Moore, E.G.J. (1986) 'Family socialisation and the IQ test performance of traditionally and transracially adopted black children.' *Developmental Psychology 22*, 317–326.

Pritchard. J.C., (1845) *The Natural History of Man*. 2nd edition. London: Hippolyte Balliere.

Rasheed, S.Y. (1981) 'Self esteem and ethnicity in African American third grade children.' *Dissertation-Abstracts-International 42*, 6B, 2604.

Roseman, S. (1984) 'Out of the holocaust.' *J.Psychohistory. II*, 4, 555–567.

Scott, S.L. (1986) 'Personality correlates of personal identity in black children.' *Dissertation-Abstracts-International 46*, 8-B, 2823–2824.

Simons, R.L, and Gray, P.A. (1989) 'Perceived blocked opportunity as an explanation of delinquency among lower-class black males: a research note.' *J. Research In Crime And Delinquency 26*, 1, 90–101.

Spencer, M.B. (1984) 'Black children's race awareness, racial attitudes and self-concept: a re-interpretation.' *J.Child Psychol. Psychiat. 25*, 433–441.

Stephen, W.G. and Rosenfeld, D. (1978) 'Effects of desegregation on race relations and self esteem.' *J.Educ. Psychol. 70*, 5, 670–679.

Stein, L.M., (1984) 'A study of identity formation in the adopted.' *Dissertation-Abstracts-International 44*, 9B, 2908.

Thoburn, J. (1988) *Child Placement: Principles and Practice*. Community Care Practice Handbooks. Aldershot: Wildwood House.

Tizard, B. And Phoenix, A. (1989) 'Black identity and transracial adoption.' *New Community 15*, 3, 427–437.

Weinreich, P. (1983) 'Emerging from threatened identities: ethnicity and gender in redefinitions of ethnic identity.' In G.M. Breakwell *Threatened Identities*. Chichester: John Wiley and Sons.

Wrobel, G.E.M. (1990) 'The self esteem of transracially adopted adolescents.' *Diss-Abstr-Int. 51*, 8, 4093–B.

Womack, W.M. and Fulton,W. (1981) 'Transracial adoption and the black preschool child.' *J-Am-Acad-Child-Psychiatry* Autumn, 20, 4, 712–24,

Zeitlin, H. Harris-Hendricks, J. Garralda, E. and Sein, E. (1991) Child Psychiatry in a Multi-Ethnic Society: Principles of Good Practice in Fostering and Adoption. From the Report of the Working Party of the Child and Adolescent Section of the Royal College of Psychiatrists.

CHAPTER 6

Residential Care for Ethnic Minorities Children

Harish Mehra

In this chapter, the term 'black' is used to describe people who share similar experiences of belonging to ethnic minority groups in the UK and being easily recognizable as such. Therefore in this sense 'black' is used as a political term. Similarly the term 'mixed parentage' is preferred to the more often used term 'mixed race'

In the 1976 Race Relations Act (Section 71) there is a duty placed on local authorities.

> To make appropriate arrangements with a view to securing that various functions are carried out with due regard to the need to eliminate unlawful discrimination and to promote equality of opportunity and good relations between persons of different racial groups. (HMSO 1976)

Since the Race Relations Act 1976, the quality of service delivery to black clients has not dramatically changed; rather, the national picture is, as Roys (1988, p.224) highlights, 'one of piecemeal activity or no serious activity at all'. Anti-racism is essential for all children's sake.

> An anti-racism strategy is an ongoing process. It needs constantly to be reviewed and challenged by all who profess to care about the well-being of children and their families. Such a strategy needs to be integrated into all aspects of provision, play, staffing, admissions, discipline, and assessment. If we fail to do so, we fail all of children and continue to contribute to the pain that racism causes. (Durrant 1986, p.135).

Furthermore, Social Services Inspectorate (1980) issued a letter [c(90) 2] to all the directorates of Social Services stating

> Social Services must address and seek to meet the needs of children and families from all groups in the community. Society is made up of

people of many different ethnic and racial origins and of different religious affiliations. The provision of services which will reach all members of the community calls for the development within Social Services Departments of awareness, sensitivity and understanding of the different cultures of groups in the local community, and an understanding of the effects of racial discrimination on these groups. These principles apply to services to help children to remain within their own families as well as to services for children in care and their families, so that children are not admitted to care through lack of appropriate and effective Social Work support for the family. This is especially important in the light of indicators that children from certain minority ethnic groups are over-represented among children in care. (pp.1–2)

With the Children Act 1989 (HMSO 1989) agencies are required, in all decisions in respect of a child they are looking after, to have regard to the child's religious persuasion, cultural and linguistic background and racial origin, and to the wishes and feeling of parents and other adults who have played a significant part in the child's life, as well as to the wishes and feelings of the child (section 22/5/c).

For the ethnic minority child, the care which is provided needs to recognize the different cultural content of both physical and social needs of food, hair and skin care, clothing, religion, education and history. Overall, the child's emotional, psychological, religious, physical and social needs require to be met in a way which enables the child:

(1) To develop a positive identity for him/herself as an ethnic minority child.

(2) To develop the necessary linguistic, cultural, religious and social skills to function effectively as an adult in a multiracial multicultural society.

(3) To acquire skills to cope as both child and adult in a society in which the child is likely to encounter racism, prejudice and disadvantage.

(4) To enable the child to come to terms with living apart from its birth family.

Any child in care has a particular need to build and sustain a *positive self-identity*, and, if they are placed in an environment where people of their kind are held in low esteem or rarely encountered at all, the outcome will be a marginalized identity. Rejection by many white peers, so frequently encountered at the stage of adolescence or young adulthood, is most likely to lead to an identity confusion. Also, children may try to resist the negative projections of the ethnic majority both in relation to their colour and as regards their being in care, by determinedly defiant behaviours that puts them at risk of serious sanctions and/or of exploitation by others.

> A central issue facing most black families (regardless of class and health), is how to prepare their children to deal with their devalued racial status in a way which will be most beneficial to their overall emotional and social growth and development. Socialisation of children is now doubly challenging for the black family for now it must teach its young members not only to be human and not dislike white people (the dominant group) but also how to be black with pride. (Ahmed 1985, p.17)

In order to meet the needs of and help the development of any child, black or white, it is essential that the service operates with adequate knowledge, understanding, sensitivity, intelligence and most importantly the ability to empathize.

> It is doubtful that the majority of well intentioned white care-takers, be they residential staff, foster or adoptive parents, can understand the pain of apparently small hurts that come through racially prejudiced behaviour towards the child of others, and offer comfort, 'the ultimate survival tool', rather than tension or rage. Not having internalised these survival mechanisms, the child grows up without needed defences or learned coping behaviours. (Small 1984, p.171)

Inequalities, of provision at the institutional level and inequalities of treatment in the world outside the residential care, combine to give black children their perception of themselves which itself becomes a hindrance in the way of racial equality. Very few of them have been able to grasp that their positions are socially constructed and do not just happen. There is not only a need for appreciating the fact that the ethnic minority consumers in such institutions often become objects of racism but, it is also necessary to recognize that the racism in the wider society is reflected in, and reinforced by racism in social services institutions.

It is important to emphasize the need for proportionate matching of staff to children, otherwise it would disproportionately disadvantages the black child in care who would lose the capacity to identify, feel with and communicate readily with members of their community of origin. This would also reduce the strangeness felt on first arrival in care. There is also a need for specific training in the care of ethnic minority children to ensure competence at the basic level of physical care. Otherwise the staff may not be aware even of the matters of day-to-day importance such as the need to avoid dry skin by the use of moisture creams or oils. They may not be able to carry out specialized hair care for younger children or to produce enjoyable food. It may also be more difficult for them to act as role models for the children. Similarly, young people who are of mixed parentage cannot push aside the white side of them but knowing you are black can be positive. To stop this identity problem, the teaching and learning has to come from the social workers whether they are black or white, as well as themselves. There is already a vast body of knowledge regarding the issues surrounding mixed parentage and its difficulties which need to be assimilated by the worker in order to meet the needs appropriately (see also Bhate and Bhate in this volume).

Ethnic minority children in care may also be disproportionately disadvantaged by the location of residential provision, which is often outside of areas of black settlement in the suburbs or in the country. This is relevant to 'matching' difficulties but may also geographically distance the child from other black people. It is important for the child's feelings of well-being as well as for their behaviour that they are afforded relief from the pressure of pervasive whiteness.

A Case Example

The following case history, which is not atypical of an Asian family on social workers' case loads, highlights the issues discussed above:

> When Gurvinder's case was allocated to me, he had already been in local authority care for the last four years. Now he was 13 years old. He was not living with foster parents but had been placed in a local authority residential home. He liked to call himself Gary and strongly objected to his original name, Gurvinder. He hardly had any contact with his father, stepmother or his siblings. His father, younger brother and sister had all been feeling very desperate to meet him regularly. In actual fact, the family really wanted him to return home and live with them.

> It was revealed that Gurvinder was taken into care when his father had a divorce and Gurvinder started displaying disruptive behaviour in the school. Gurvinder's mother did not contest the custody. She refused to have to do any thing with him or have access to him. Following this decision, she tried to avoid the label of being a divorcee which made her path easier for re-marriage in her cultural context. When Gurvinder had started exhibiting some behavioural difficulties, there were no extended family members from his father's side residing in this country. If they were, they would have supported and helped in looking after Gurvinder. After the divorce, father re-married but Gurvinder and his stepmother did not develop a good relationship.

> When this case was referred to the social services department a social worker of white ethnic background, who had very little knowledge of racial and cultural issues, was allocated to deal with it. Instead of exploring the possibility of any in depth work in terms of building up relationships even with the help of any Asian social

worker or a consultant on race and cultural issues, Gurvinder was taken into local authority care. Again no real efforts were made to find an Asian foster family for him. This must have been an easy and convenient solution for the social worker but, for Gurvinder, this was the beginning of his alienation and loss of his family, language, religion, food, culture and ethnic identity.

During the last four years of being in care, he did not have any input of Asian culture and there were no provisions or opportunities in the residential home or the programmes organized for him, to expose him to Sikh religion, Asian food or to maintain any contact with the Asian community or his own family. All the children in the residential home were white and Gurvinder was living an excluded life. To be accepted by his co-residents and social workers involved he was doing his utmost to become a white child. He started to develop friendship with white children and their parents who sometimes used to visit them. Eventually, he was successful in strengthening his relationship with one white parent whose child was also residing with Gurvinder in the local authority residential home which was located in a all white community. Gurvinder was now allowed to visit this white family and spend weekends with them. Gurvinder started to call these white parents, Mummy and Daddy. He refused to meet his father who tried several times to contact him on the telephone and in person. Social workers (both residential and from the area office) did not feel the need to alter this development.

On my first visit to Gurvinder, he refused to see me. He informed his residential social worker and the manager of the residential home that he would like to have a white social worker. I did not insist at this point but informed the residential social worker and Gurvinder that I would discuss this issue with my line manager. In discussion with my line manager, we agreed that I should continue to work with Gurvinder but with acute sensitivity and care. This decision was communicated to the concerned manager, residential social worker and Gurvinder.

On my second visit I had a general discussion with Gurvinder and also made a strong recommendation to the manager of the home to arrange for an Asian residential social worker to work with me jointly. I then had several meetings with this new residential Asian social worker and developed a number of strategies.

During my subsequent visits, I started to explore Gurvinder's feelings about his identity. He was outrightly stating, '*I am British. My name is Gary. I don't like Pakis. All Asians are Pakis*'. I kept calm and asked Gurvinder '*if all Asians are Pakis then what about your father? Is he a Paki too?*' He could not answer me. I did not force him to reply. The other question I posed to him, '*Gurvinder, I accept you were born in Britain and you have a British passport and you call yourself British. Suppose, you are walking alone down the road and confront a gang of National Front Youths. How would you convince them that you are British and not Asian? In addition how would you hide your skin colour and your features?*' Once again he did not answer. At this stage I left him and made an appointment to see him in the next couple of weeks. During this period, the residential social worker was kept informed of all the developments and was advised to assist and counsel Gurvinder so he could also understand and remain in touch with some of these important issues being discussed.

While this was proceeding Gurvinder's new-found white parents telephoned me several times to say that Gurvinder was upset since I had been allocated to his case and threatened to make an official complaint against me. In discussion with my line manager we felt it was essential to pursue our plan in spite of this resistance and obstruction. Our extensive efforts and negotiations between different parties were successful in holding a meeting between Gurvinder and his father. Gurvinder's father, younger brother and sister were overjoyed to see him. Gurvinder's father was anxious to have Gurvinder back home immediately but we insisted that any reintegration of Gurvinder with his family had to be a slow and well worked out process for it to be successful. The frequency of meetings between Gurvinder and his family were therefore gradually increased; first it was at three weekly intervals, then at two weekly and eventually at weekly intervals before he started spending weekends with his family.

His father disclosed to him that since he (Gurvinder) was the eldest son in the family, he (father) had already bought a house for him (Gurvinder) as a wedding gift. He (father) also shared as to how he (father) had felt lost without him (Gurvinder) and that if Gurvinder wished to start a business, he (father) would be delighted to help him financially to set up a business or if Gurvinder wished to continue his studies, he (father) would be equally delighted to finance this. For us it took a year before Gurvinder was successfully rehabilitated with his family. He and his family at the final reunion were extremely delighted and we were happy to close our files.

Nearly six months later I met Gurvinder and his father while shopping. Father emphasized that they had no problems whatsoever now, with Gurvinder planning to pursue his further studies. He spoke Panjabi at home, enjoyed eating Asian food and

attended the Sikh Temple every Sunday without fail. Gurvinde
father pressed my hand and said, '*I am indebted to you, you brou*
my son back to me. I can never forget this in my life'.

Matters of Policy

Child care social workers and their managers can only break the process of
racism by acknowledging that it exists, deciding that it is wrong and making
a commitment to change. To refuse to do so negates ethnic minority children
and contradicts the caring role which the work demands. Most of the local
authorities in Britain have an equal opportunity policy which is applicable to
all its departments including social services. The Commission for Racial
Equality (1978) suggested that an equal opportunity policy is aimed at developing positive measures to eliminate overt discrimination, as well as conditions,
requirements or practices which are discriminatory in operation. It has the
legislation support of the Race Relations Act 1976 (section 71) which makes
racial discrimination unlawful and establishes the basis on which equal opportunities may be pursued.

Unless there is a common core of values which underpin social work practice
informed by equal opportunity, the social workers, I think, are likely to operate
in idiosyncratic ways. It is essential that such values become central to social
work practice and not 'added on' or marginalized. It is also important to be
clear about what is meant by equal opportunity. Mason and Jewson (1989) make
the distinction between liberal and radical conceptions of equal opportunity.
The latter focuses on equality of outcome and understands fairness to exist
when numbers of different groups are distributed in proportion to their
presence in the wider population.

There is a need to focus on what the equal opportunity outcomes are of
working with ethnic minority children in residential care. Jenkins (1989) points
out that the pursuit of equal opportunity as a formal statement only has symbolic
value creating an image of success. It is important that the policy statement is
combined with strategies of implementation. He emphasizes that although a
voluntarist approach (i.e. organisations and agencies etc. taking steps themselves
to adopt equal opportunity policy) is vital, it has severe limitations. He argued
that equal opportunities can only be solved by recognizing that it is a political
problem. For example, we need to look outside the boundaries of individual
organizations since individuals within organizations are influenced by popular
racism and the way equal opportunity and anti-racism are portrayed as something that will disadvantage whites.

Social workers and their managers may have internalized negative perceptions about anti-racism. The media portrayal of anti-racism as being associated
with the so-called labour 'loony left' and attempts by right wing intellectuals
to discredit it by referring to anti-racism as indoctrination have become part of
'common sense'. (Honeyford 1982; Flew 1984; Lewis 1988).

Many social services departments may even have anti-racist policies. The question is whether these departments actually draw on anti-racism concepts, implement it and closely monitor it. Also, who does the monitoring? Do the people who monitor it have adequate knowledge and understanding of racism? Brandt (1986) has explored the way in which these concepts are concerned with power, justice, gender, equal human rights, oppression, structural inequalities, racist ideologies, institutionalized racism, equality, liberation and emancipation. Many black people and practitioners believe, as Dominelli (1988) argues, that white social workers should not work with black or ethnic minorities families until they have demonstrated their ability to practice anti-racist social work. The implementation of policies and Acts become more important as the racist ideologies may be in operation which may have led to ethnic minority children in residential care feeling powerless and experiencing a deep sense of injustice.

Jane Lane (1990) emphasizes:

> Issues of child care/education are high on the national agenda. There are many national and local organisations in the field that are in the process of adopting or having adopted equality of opportunity policies. Local Authorities are in likely positions to monitor what is happening in their own areas, to make information widely available and to ensure that, together with other organisations which are committed to racial equality, both the latter and the spirit of both pieces of legislation are enacted... Despite the lack of resources the extra requirements put on staff as a result of legislation, Authorities can make the task easier at the outset, defining the task to be done within the framework of the law. Such definitions, rather than ad hoc responses, will make it possible both to see what needs to be done and to take appropriate measures and permanent steps to eliminate discrimination and provide a service based on principles of equality. (p.49)

Some Guidelines

If social care practice is to meet the needs of a multi-racial society, the development of an anti-racist practice is essential. Following are some of the dimensions of crucial importance in developing such practices.

(1) The implementation and monitoring of anti-racist policies and Acts along with anti-racist training to all the employers of the department, including senior managers with the emphasis on the credibility of minority ethnic community's norms and life styles.

(2) Where need be, the talking through of emotional and cultural issues, valuing and acknowledging of cultural identities, heritage and histories of ethnic minority people.

(3) Meeting the cultural, religious, linguistic, skin care, hair care and dietary needs of the ethnic minority children in care.

(4) The enabling of ethnic minority children in care to take pride in their race, skin colour, physical features, religious, linguistic and cultural identity.

(5) Acknowledging and understanding the implications of discriminations and racism upon ethnic minority children in residential care; for example, lack of personal growth, dignity, worth and power.

(6) To examine the use of language, personal norms and values, which may be degrading and stereotyping to ethnic minority children and people. Promotion of positive images of ethnic minority people and supporting those who take stand against any kind of discrimination and racism.

(7) Declaring anti-racist policies to the liaising statutory and voluntary agencies, ensuring that the child's environment is in line with the departmental policy. It needs to be acknowledged that one central fact is that the accumulative and persistent effects of racial prejudice in society is the psychic assault on ethnic minority people. These attacks take many forms; for example name calling, spitting, beating, shouting, and can sometimes include torturing, maiming and killing.

(8) Committed social workers and their managers whether from the white majority or the ethnic minority need to be able to have a network of support within the department, in other local authorities and from people and organizations in the society.

References

Ahmed, S. (1985) 'Black children in day nursery – some issues of practice.' *Focus 33*, 17–20.

Brandt, G. (1986) *The Realisation of Anti-Racist Teaching*. London: The Falmer Press.

Commission for Racial Equality (1978) *A Home from Home: Some Policy Considerations on Black Children in Residential care*. London: CRE.

Dominelli, L. (1988) *Anti-Racist Social Work*. Basingstoke: Macmillan Education.

Durrant, J. (1986) 'Racism and the under fives.' In V. Coombe and A. Little (eds) *Race and Social Work*. London: Tavistock Publications.

Flew, A. (1984) *Education, Race and Revolution*. London: Centre for Policy Studies

Honeyford, R (1982) 'The end of anti-racism.' *Salisbury Review 1*.

HMSO (1976) *Race Relations Act*. London: HMSO.

HMSO (1989) *Children Act*. London: HMSO.

Jenkins, R. (1989) 'Equal opportunity in the private sector: the limits of voluntarism.' In R. Jenkins and J. Solomos (eds) *Racism and Equal Opportunity Policies in 1980s.* Cambridge: Cambridge University Press.

Lane, J. (1990) 'Sticks and carrots.' *Local Government Policy Making 17*, 3, 40–49.

Lewis, R. (1988) *Anti-Racism – A Mania Exposed.* London: Quartet.

Mason, D. and Jewson, N. (1989) 'Monitoring equal opportunities policies, principles and practice.' In R. Jenkins and J. Solomos (eds) *Racism and Equal Opportunity Policies in 1980s.* Cambridge: Cambridge University Press.

Roys, P. (1988) 'Social services.' In A. Bhat, R. Carr-Hill and S. Ohri (eds) *Britain's Black Population.* Aldershot: Gower.

Small, J. (1984) 'The crisis in adoption.' *International Journal of Social Psychiatry 30*, (1&2, Spring).

Social Services Inspectorate (1980) *Letter Issued to Directors of Social Services* [c.1(90)2] Dept of Health. Richmond House. 79 White Hall London. SW1A 2NS. pp. 1–5.

CHAPTER 7

The Health Needs of Children from Ethnic Minorities

Carolyn Bailey

The term 'Ethnic Minority' is much debated but includes a wide variety of races and culture both white and black. For the purposes of this chapter, I am considering those populations from the so-called 'black' communities, such as Asians, African-Caribbean, Chinese, Vietnamese, and so forth. It should not, however, be forgotten the Britain also hosts a variety of communities that originated from parts of Europe, such as Polish, Italian, Bosnian, Latvian and so on, as well as the Travelling Communities, all of whom are categorized as ethnic minorities. Many of the health issues that will be discussed also apply to these latter communities but some are culture or race-specific. This chapter, therefore, is specifically looking at the former groups.

The 1991 Census gives the national statistic of Ethnic Minorities as 5.9 per cent of the population. The greatest numbers have their origins in their Indian sub-continent, Africa and the Caribbean Islands. Their numbers have grown quite rapidly and we are therefore looking at a substantial part of our population who may have specific needs.

When looking at the needs of these communities, however, we must be aware of the possibility of reinforcing stereotypes. A number of sections of the population are deemed to have special needs and, in health terms, ethnic minorities need specific provision to facilitate both access to health care and for race-specific conditions. But there is a fine line between making provision for communities with 'special needs' and discrimination, albeit positive, or 'victim-blaming'. Nevertheless, certain aspects of ethnic minority cultures do indicate a real need for extra provision. This is further indicated by findings that show a positive correlation between ethnicity, socio-economic group and disadvantage. Mares, Henley and Baxter (1985) confirm the finding of the Black Report (Townsend and Davidson 1982) that inequalities in health care are class-related, but also state:

Poor housing, high unemployment and poverty are problems of class disadvantage that black people share with white people living in the same area. But ethnic minority communities face additional disadvantages that are not shared by the white population...

A growing number of research studies confirm that the position of black people in British society is largely due to the racial discrimination they experience in many areas of life. (Mares *et al.* 1985, p.9)

Racial discrimination may be overt or covert but will affect accessibility of service provision. Language and cultural barriers often cause or compound poorer provision of health care and other services, together with lower expectations or lack of knowledge of services on the part of the ethnic communities themselves.

In considering the needs of children from these communities, we have to recognize that they are, by the fact of age-minority, dependent on adults for the provision of these needs. If these adults are ignorant of the needs and the services available, it stands to reason that the health status of the children will be jeopardized. Many of the adults are still new or first generation immigrants to this country and may not therefore be aware of health information, care and services. Generationally, of course, this will change as the communities become more integrated into this society. This has happened within the communities that have been in Britain longer. Initially, language can form the greatest barrier to gaining information on health services so health professionals themselves should be aware that social provision should be made.

In many parts of Britain, Link worker, interpreter or advocacy posts and projects have been established to facilitate better communication and take up of services. However, this is not the case in all areas, especially where the ethnic population is smaller. It is also too simplistic to provide leaflets or information in translated form. Within these communities, many of the older people and women read little or not at all. In a study, published by the Health Education Authority in 1994, of 3500 South Asian, 24 per cent of Indians, 37 per cent of Pakistanis and 48 per cent of Bangladeshis were unable to read English, the figures rising through the age groups, especially amongst women, up to 93 per cent of Pakistani and 96 per cent of Bangladeshi women in the 50–74 age bracket not reading English. Among the same groups, only 15 per cent and 10 per cent respectively spoke English, and 42 per cent and 21 per cent of women in the 30–49 age bracket from these communities (HEA 1994). Indeed, for the Bangladeshi communities, the issue is compounded by the fact that their first language is in fact a dialect, Sylheti, as almost all the Bangladeshis in Britain originate from a district called Sylhet. Sylheti is only a spoken dialect, there is no written form. If people have been educated to read Bengali, the 'official' language of Bangladesh, they will, generally speaking, have been educated in English and able to both read and write in both. This is not the case for everyone and especially women. It is, of course the women who have the responsibility for the care of the children and health information must be provided in an appropriate form or else is missed by, possibly, the families who most need it.

What are the health needs of these children? It has been the case that ethnic minorities have been all grouped together, especially the Asian communities. But the groups are very different in many ways. Each group has its own culture, language, religion, diet, status. It is obviously important that health care providers and those involved in health education and promotion are aware of these cultural differences and the needs of these groups, and individuals and families within them. Only then can they respond or be proactive in health promotion in a positive way. Cultural awareness should be a part of every health professional's training at either basic, undergraduate or post qualification level so that at least a degree of knowledge and understanding is gained.

In many ways, the health needs of children from ethnic communities are much the same as those of the host populations, in terms of immunisation, correct diet, dental care and physical and mental health. But cultural and language differences will and do have a bearing on the appropriateness of services and information. Health professionals must know their own ethnic communities in order to adapt service provision to them.

When immigration from the Indian sub-continent occurred during the 1950s to 1980s, health ministers and professionals became aware of two areas of concern in particular – Asian mothers and children, and the higher incidence of Rickets and Vitamin D deficiency. These concerns gave rise to two major campaigns, the 'Asian Mother and Baby Campaign' and the 'Stop Rickets Campaign'. The former was particularly focused on the provision of link workers to encourage mothers to attend ante-natal classes and setting up of support groups for mothers and children, to produce health promotion resources on nutrition and 'healthy pregnancy' and so on. The campaign ran from 1984 to 1987 and, by its own admission was a pilot scheme and experienced a number of problems. However, it did highlight a number of issues facing pregnant and new mothers and raised these issues with health professionals.

The 'Stop Rickets Campaign' had similar effects, in that it raised awareness of the potential nutritional deficiencies of traditional Asian diets. These diets contain much that is healthy, but may be lacking in Vitamin D, iron and protein, particularly in the vegetarian diets and also because of the low exposure to sunlight. Schemes were introduced to reinforce Chapatti flour with Vitamin D and, again, videos and leaflets were produced to educate and inform the communities. The campaigns produced much that was worthwhile but both had problems and were, like all campaigns, limited in effect if only by time.

Some ethnic groups are susceptible to specific disorders or Haemoglobi-nopathies. African Caribbean children and some Asian and Mediterraneans are at risk from iron-deficiency and sickle-cell anaemia and Thalassaemia. Screening programmes and counselling services are being established in some areas for these groups. The incidence of these conditions is not high but for sufferers they are painful and debilitating and every support should be given to the families of these children. These Haemoglobinopathies are congenital blood disorders resulting in extreme pain, anaemia and related disorders. Early screening in pregnancy can indicate the presence of such conditions. For children who suffer with these diseases and their families, health care and support should be of highest standard to maintain quality of life.

Children from the black and ethnic minorities are generally felt to be at greater risk from conditions stemming from the typical childhood diseases, not only because immunization rates have, in the past, been lower in some of the groups, but also because many of the mothers have themselves not been immunized against, for instance, Rubella. The incidence, therefore of abnormalities and serious side effects of these diseases has tended to be greater. The take-up of immunisation has, and may still be, lower than the indigenous population for a number of reasons. The main one is a lack of knowledge and understanding, partly because of language barriers and partly because of low expectation and information. As the family and family life is so important to these communities, the English speaking members, often the fathers, will generally be more aware and insistent on the children being immunised, and, of course, over the generations the awareness will grow.

Health protection generally, in terms of screening, immunisation and health promotion has, until now, been poorly understood; hence the uptake of these services has been low. Attendance to GPs and nurses for treatment of illness and ailments has always been high, but to attend when there is no illness has not been understood by many members of the communities, especially those most recently arrived in Britain.

The incidence of both perinatal mortality and congenital abnormalities is considerably higher amongst Pakistani families than either other Asian, black or white groups. The rate of perinatal mortality among Pakistani babies is, in fact, almost double that of those born to mothers from the United Kingdom (Balarajan and Soni Raleight 1993). This is believed to be because of the high number of inter-family marriages, particularly between first cousins. This pattern is continuing among the Pakistani communities in Britain and it is felt that advice and counselling should be made more available to this group to reduce significantly this particular inequality. It should be remembered, however, that this is an accepted cultural practice and, if there is to be any change, albeit for the good of the community and families, it must come from within, and the process of cultural change is slow. Here is a classic case of avoiding the 'victim-blaming' approach, which can be so easily occur, however well-meaning health and social care professionals may be.

In 1992 the Government published the White Paper 'The Health of the Nation', identifying five specific areas of health concern for the country as a whole. These were coronary heart disease and stroke, cancers, mental health, sexual health and accidents. Among the black and ethnic minorities, certain of these are known to have a lower incidence, particularly cancers such as those of breast and skin, but some have a markedly higher incidence. Of particular note is the high propensity for coronary heart disease among Asians and stroke among African-Caribbeans. There have been a number of saturated fats in the diets, low levels of activity and exercise, central body-mass, rather than even distribution, and high levels of diabetes found in these communities. Diabetes is a particular problem and is though to impact on the circulatory diseases.

How is this of particular relevance to the health of the children from these groups? As with any health risk the earlier it is known, understood and acted upon, the more likely will be the reduction of those risk factors in later life. Diet has already been mentioned in terms of possible nutritional deficiencies, but good dietary practice can be laid down in childhood, such as the replacement of ghee (high fat butter used for cooking) with sunflower or other low fat oils. All of the nutritional advice available to reduce the risks of CHD are equally applicable to the ethnic minority communities. The same applies to increasing levels of activity. Exercise has not formed an important part of life for many of us, including and perhaps especially the South Asian communities. It has even been seen to be a sign of affluence to be overweight, indicating that the individual does not have to do their own work. But exercise can be encouraged, and again, the earlier the better. For some communities, notably the African, Caribbean and Indian, dancing is part of the way of life, although, for Muslims, it is often felt to be inappropriate, particularly in public. Dancing is a good way of exercising, so if it is more acceptable than 'Keep-fit' type of activity, this should be encouraged. A number of Asian groups have produced videos and so on to encourage exercising and childhood again is the best time to establish these good practices.

The other 'Health of the Nation' Key Area that has particular significance for the ethnic minorities is mental health. It would appear that African-Caribbeans are over-represented within mental health care whilst Asians are under-represented. There continues to be considerable debate about whether this is a true picture and what could be done about it. There appears to be a higher incidence of enduring mental illness such as schizophrenia among the African and Caribbean populations in relation to other groups, whether white or Asian, but it is unclear whether this is the effect of social deprivation and racism, or indeed other factors. South Asians appear to be far less likely to present and be admitted to hospital for psychiatric disorders. Again, whether this is due to other factors such as inability or reluctance to present with symptoms, is unclear.

What is known, however, is that young Asian women and girls have a three-fold risk of suicide from the national average. Cultural conflict may play a part in this, as do the implications of arranged marriages, living with extended families, psychosocial and racial factors. Racism can cause great distress for young people from the ethnic minority communities, and low educational achievement is also frequently associated with these children: all of these factors impact on their mental health and emotional well-being.

Children with learning difficulties, however, are often treated as 'special' and revered rather than pitied. Their families are highly protective of them. However, when being assessed, the difficulties of learning or physical disability may be further compounded by language and cultural barriers. With any aspect of mental health, language can form an inadvertent barrier to communicating feelings. If the first language is different from that of the health professional, the true feelings will not be able to be expressed. Language forms so much of our conceptual skills and, whereas we can express physical illness or pain with limited language skills, our feelings must be articulated in a familiar tongue.

Children are often used as interpreters for other members of their families and this can also cause considerable stress. To discuss with a parents an professional issues of a person or delicate nature can be a source of considerable embarrassment. Although this is common practice in medical settings, it is far from ideal and a properly trained interpreter service should be made available. Furthermore, consideration should be given when children are prescribed medication, particularly for chronic or life-threatening disease, such as asthma. It should be ensured that the child's parents understand the prescription, its importance or how it should be taken. It is not enough to issue the dosage in the usual way; it must be translated and reinforced verbally whenever possible.

So, we have seen that children from the ethnic minorities have many of the same health needs as their white counterparts. However, they do need some extra provision or greater sensitivity to deal effectively with the specific factors that affect their health and service provision. Health workers must know their communities, must know how their cultures will affect the health and well-being of the members of the communities and must be sensitive to their needs. Racial discrimination, even in a covert form such as ignorance and insensitivity, must be eradicated, but Health Authorities should be prepared to be more proactive in addressing the needs of these communities. Members of the communities in any given area should form part of service planning groups. So many presumptions are made as to needs and fulfilling of needs; that is, if they are known. To discover/understand the needs of provide for them, the communities themselves must be consulted. They must be empowered to express the failings in service provision and to advise Health Authorities how best to correct these failings. Most Health Authorities have, until now, been white middle-class, British-led and ignorance of needs has been understandable. Nevertheless, in an increasingly multicultural society, this must no longer be the case. Planning and strategy groups and purchasing and commissioning teams should include black and/or Asian representation, not merely as tokenism but as real influences on provision.

Health workers who are in the business of delivery of services should be involved as they, too, can give of their own experiences, problems and successes.

Examples of good practice should be publicized in other areas wherever possible, so that they too can incorporate similar practices in local purchasing policy.

Theoretical issues are, of course, important in raising awareness and laying down guidelines. However, at a local level, nothing replaces direct experience, and this must influence policy formation and implementation. Having said this, so much research has been carried out in the ethnic minority communities that they have despaired of any significant change occurring. Intentions and theory must be reinforced by the real change and development based on the real experiences of the communities.

As always, education is a two-way process and there remains a lack of knowledge and low expectation of services and information among the communities. This, too, must be addressed and awareness and expectations raised and met by the appropriate service provision. It is often said that if we get it right for minority groups, we get it right for everyone.

People are people and children are children, regardless of their geographical or genetic origins and all of us, as individuals, have the right to expect the best in health care and health promotion. If that requires extra effort to make special provision, so be it. We are led to believe that we are entitled to this through such documents as the Patients' Charter. Health is a precious commodity and children's health should be protected, regardless of ethnic origin not only for the present, but for their and the nation's future.

Acknowledgement

I am grateful to my many friends from the South Asian, African and Caribbean communities in Northamptonshire.

References

Balarajan, R. and Soni Raleight, V. (1993) *Ethnicity and Health*. London: Department of Health.

Department of Health, (1992) *The Health of the Nation*. London: HMSO.

Health Education Authority (1994) *Health and Lifestyles: Black and Minority Ethnic Groups in England*. London: HEA.

Mares, P., Henley, A. and Baxter, C. (1985) *Health Care in Multiracial Britain*. Cambridge: Health Education Council and the National Extension College.

Townsend, P. and Davidson, N. (eds) (1982) Inequalities in Health: The Black Report. Penguin.

CHAPTER 8

Psychiatric Needs of Ethnic Minority Children

Dr Surya Bhate and Dr Soni Bhate

Introduction

It is estimated that over ten million foreigners, both adults and children, are living and working in Western European countries. The pattern of immigration and rules governing the arrival of these people vary from country to country, and depend upon historical links, such as a colonial past, as well as the need for labour due to post-War industrial expansion. In West Germany in the 1960s and 1970s, for example, an overwhelming proportion of 'guest workers' from Turkey and Yugoslavia arrived to take jobs in the motor industry. Most of these workers were supposed to return home on a rotating principle but, in practice, this failed to happen and gradually families began to arrive to join them.

The estimated composition of the population of the United Kingdom reflects the arrival of Jewish immigrants from Russia in the late nineteenth century, as a result of Pogrom, when millions of Jews fled to escape persecution. It is estimated that over 120,000 Jews settled in the United Kingdom. Similarly, the Irish have settled in large numbers, as did post-War refugees from a number of other European countries such as Poland and Hungary. Approximately 5 per cent of the population of the United Kingdom are non-whites from the Third World. This migration from the Third World countries commenced on a large scale in the 1950s and 1960s, and generally declined in the 1970s as a result of increasingly restrictive immigration laws. The only new immigrants now allowed to enter the United Kingdom are those with existing family ties, and no new immigration has been permitted since the laws were amended in 1971.

Migration

Migration, in simple terms, means a change of residence from one house to another, moving from one city to the next, or transporting oneself from one country to another. In understanding the effects of migration, time and scale are of vital significance. Migration occurs because immigrants, rightly or wrongly, believe that moving to a new town or country may offer them job opportunities that will improve their standard of living. These beliefs may or may not have a basis in reality. Insufficient information may be further compounded by the desire and attempt to escape hardship or persecution in the country of birth. That the improvement of financial circumstances was the key factor stimulating migration was recognized and commented upon in the nineteenth century, and migratory flow due to industrialization from rural areas to towns is well documented.

Who Migrates?

Usually migrants are not a random selection of people from the place of origin. The exception is when the whole population is deported, as was the case in Uganda when Idi Amin expelled all Asians. These people ultimately arrived in the United Kingdom, although some decided to return to their country of origin, India. In general, migrants tend to be young adult males arriving in search of work, followed by their wives and children. Hannan (1969) demonstrated that educational status plays a significant part in the individual's decision to migrate. Those who have spent a longer time in education are in general more likely to migrate compared with those who have had minimal education. This may be because those who are better educated have a greater chance of being allowed entry to the recipient country. There is clear evidence to back this statement in policies followed by Western countries in allowing and continuing to favour professional and white collar elements entry, although different countries adopt different policies in this regard. The United Kingdom authorities, in response to the post-War industrial boom, actively advertised and sought immigrants to take up unskilled low-level jobs as well as cheap labour to man factories.

Effect on Family and Communities

Asians

Although many Asians may have similar cultural background, there are important and distinct differences in culture between people from different parts of the Indian subcontinent. There are many religious groups, the main ones being Hinduism, Sikhism and Islam. These will have their own philosophical and social systems.

The importance of the traditional extended family system in the culture of the rural Indian subcontinent has been described in detail by various authors. It may consist of three generations, the husband, as head of the family, and his wife, their sons and their wives, and their children. The majority of immigrants who have arrived in the United Kingdom are from the rural population. These people tend to be religious and follow a traditional value system. The family structure is that of a joint family and as a result households are large and property ownership is often joint. The ethos of a family as a group is much more important than that of the constituent individual and relationships are developed and understood and valued in that context rather than on an individual basis which may be the case in Western countries. The individualism and independence valued by Western culture may appear selfish and even irresponsible in the context of the joint family, thus marriages are regarded as an agreement between two families and the prospective partners are often guided by the wishes and advice of the family. In turn, the family agrees to provide all the necessary material, as well as emotional support that the young couple will need. The choice of partner is based upon the suitability of their families, which may reflect social status, wealth, and the caste to which they belong.

Afro-Caribbeans

The majority of Caribbeans are of African origin. Thus, though there are distinct cultural differences within the Caribbean as it is made up of many separate islands, Afro-Caribbeans, like Asians, have some common aspects. West Indian immigrants to the United Kingdom are descendants of the enslaved Africans, brought forcibly to the Americas by Western Europeans. The relationship patterns of these slaves were forcibly interrupted and changed, they were encouraged to mate early and, if necessary, frequently to produce children, bringing additional wealth to the enslaver. This system allowed no real basis for family development, as slaves were not allowed to marry. Also, white men often forced black women to be their mistresses, resulting in the birth of mixed race children, which further compounded the problem. The West Indian matrifocal family, therefore, has evolved in response to forced circumstances. In this family, a strong bond is obvious through the female line, and children are seen to be the responsibility of the wider family in which maternal kin, usually the grandmother, plays an important, even vital part.

Stressors

All immigrants have to cope with numerous changes on arrival in the United Kingdom. The stresses faced by the immigrant family include lack of available housing, educational institutions that are ill-equipped to cope with the needs of their children, and racial discrimination in all walks of life, especially in the field of employment. Racial discrimination against the minority by the majority, is about power, oppression, and is essentially a de-humanizing experience. Ethnic minority immigrants may be considered inferior, or at least different. This racial prejudice and discrimination can often be re-inforced by the media, and reports by the Policy Studies Institute (1983) and Lord Scarman (1981) conclude that there is existence of racial prejudice and stereotyping amongst police at the lower echelon, but perhaps not amongst the higher ranks. Despite

the passing of the 1968 Race Relations Act by the British Parliament, discrimination in employment still continued. This Law was subsequently consolidated
in 1976, yet progress away from racial discrimination in recruitment has been
minimal. There is well-documented evidence of discrimination against minorities in employment at all levels in fields including Medicine, Law and the Civil
Service.

Effect on Education

Ken Fogelmann's national child development study *Growing up in Great Britain*
(1983) data examined four groups of immigrants from the Indian subcontinent,
the West Indies and the Caribbean, Northern Ireland and Europe. A large
difference was noticed between Asian children who were first and second
generation immigrants. The first generation immigrants, not surprisingly, lived
in large families many of them in crowded conditions, without appropriate
amenities, with a high proportion of male family members, and a much smaller
proportion of working female members. The second generation of Asians on
the other hand, appeared to be much closer to the indigenous populations;
although a similar proportion continued to live in large families with working
male members, a smaller proportion live in overcrowded conditions, the
proportion of mothers in paid employment is increased, and there is now even
the appearance of one parent families. With first and second generation West
Indian immigrants there was found to be less of a difference.

The educational system, particularly where there was a high concentration
of immigrants in the big cities in the South East of England, was ill prepared
to cope with the needs of these children from ethnic minorities. The educational
system reflecting the indigenous cultural and religious value system. Compara-
tively, the first generation immigrant children showed relatively poor attainment
in languages, particularly if they arrived in the country after the age of ten.
Although, with the exception of West Indian children, there is comparable
attainment, by immigrant children, when compared with those of similar
financial and other material circumstances. The poor school performance that
is found amongst the first generation Asian immigrant, but not the second, is
probably short term and language specific.

Single parent families have been topical recently. The majority of single
parents amongst immigrants are found in the second generation and these are
usually women. Apart from the usual religious, social and political stigma
attached to this status, these single parent families are subjected to considerable
financial and psychological stress because of the lack of support from the
extended family.

Cultural Values and Child Rearing

Newly arrived immigrants bring with them their own set of values, belief system and set of rules to live by, these cultural values are not static and are open to change. 'Culture' is defined by anthropologists as the plans and rules people use to interpret their own world and act purposefully within it. Cultural child rearing practices vary, with differences in the role of the mother, and other members of the extended family and their perception of their responsibility to the new born baby. Within the Indian subcontinent, especially in rural parts, where over 80 per cent of families live, children are born to joint families. Although in cities such as Bombay and Calcutta, as a result of the pressure of accommodation, many families are nuclear. In the traditional family system, all members of the extended family play an important part in the rearing of the child. But if the family becomes nuclear the pattern of child rearing, particularly where mother is working, will clearly vary from this traditional system.

The development of mother/child and other relationships can be best understood using the concept of attachment (Bowlby 1971). It is this biological process which protects and nurtures the child, with its subsequent capacity to develop social relationships being based on the success or otherwise with which this attachment behaviour is established. With an extended family, parents, uncles and aunts, siblings and grandparents all will assist with the task of bringing up the child. This does not mean that the mother fails to develop close emotional physical contact with the child, but the rest of the family, particularly female members, often develop fairly close bonds with the child. Child care tasks, particularly at night, are often more likely to be shared by the mother and grandmother of the child. The child therefore develops and grows to develop differential attachment to various members of the family, and from an early age begins to recognize and acknowledge his place within the hierarchy of the joint family. The child recognizes family members as special people from an early age, and develops warm and intense feelings towards them, as well as the expectation that the family members will meet his or her needs.

This warm, cosy protection and support offered by the joint family system (although not without its own problems) is not accessible to the migrant couple. The mother, in particular, may not have the skills needed to bring up her child, which a young mother in the host community may possess. This problem can often be compounded by an inability or unwillingness on the part of the young immigrant mother to seek appropriate support and help from professional agencies. In Asian culture child rearing practices and parenting style emphasizes obedience and indebtedness to one's parents. There is an expectation that children delay gratification, teaching them to control their impulses, and accept external controls put upon them, although there may be gender difference in parental expectation, with boys allowed greater latitude. In the West, non-controlling parenting is considered beneficial, and is found to be predictive of good school achievement. In view of this prediction, there is thus a paradox when one looks at educational achievements of Asian children in the educational setting of the United Kingdom. Their success may have to do with training ethos and high regard for education.

Epidemiology of Psychiatric Disorder

There have been several studies of the rates of emotional and behavioural psychiatric disorder of children living in the Asian and African continents. Broadly speaking these rates of disturbance are similar, although, not surprisingly, rates are higher in urban areas compared to rural, as has also been demonstrated in the West.

In the Indian subcontinent, a study by Verghese (1974) in the southern city of Vellore, surveyed over 700 children between the ages of 4 and 12 years of age, and reported that rates of disorder were approximately 7 to 8 per cent. This also included mental retardation, thought to be higher due to poor ante-natal and obstetric care, although the exact percentage was not recorded. Similarly, Lal and Sethi (1977) report rates of 11 per cent in 'neurotic and allied' disorder in an Indian urban community. A similar picture emerges in studies undertaken of Ugandan and Sudanese children. The former, using the Rutter questionnaire, shows an 18 per cent prevalence rate with 10 per cent in the Sudanese.

Immigrant children and young people appear to present with similar psychiatric symptomatology as that of indigenous (white) children. The presentation, however, may vary. Much has been written about the marked and rapid decline in the prevalence of hysteria amongst adults and to a lesser extent in children. Another point is the lack of equivalent words for depression and anxiety in certain languages. Somatization of emotional distress applies to depression and anxiety and is now well recognized in Asian patients. We have therefore arbitrarily chosen two disorders in children and young people to make salient points.

Conduct Disorder/Delinquency

Most children at some stage are likely to behave in a manner that contravenes the social norm. They are likely to lie, take things which do not belong to them, or display aggression. It is the extent and severity of this behaviour which warrants a psychiatric diagnosis to be made, and DSM IV (American Psychiatric Association 1994) and ICD 10 classify these. Essentially, this behaviour needs to be repetitive, persistent, violate others' basic rights, and to last at least six months. This behaviour includes severe temper tantrums, defiance of rules, anger, spitefulness and vindictiveness. There is also often the initiation of physical fights, cruelty to animals, truancy, running away from the home and offences against property. Many of these anti-social behaviours are not illegal, but the use of weapons, cruelty to other people, pyromania, sexual abuse and the confronting of victims, amongst others, are anti-social behaviours of higher legal concept. Thus they can be divided into non-delinquent and delinquent conduct disorders.

Compared to the indigenous population, there are lower rates of delinquency amongst Asian children and higher amongst those of West Indian origin. Higher rates of delinquency may be linked to higher unemployment (Rutter and Giller 1983). There is concern and belief that discrimination in courts is so rife that black offenders are twice as likely to receive a prison sentence than whites convicted of the same offence. The study undertaken by Roger Hood (1992) analyzed ethnic and white male offenders convicted and sentenced in 1989 in the Crown Court. He found Afro Caribbeans over-represented and received higher rates of custodial sentences, while Asians on the other hand were sentenced to custody less often than either whites or Afro Caribbeans. It reflected the less serious nature of the offences.

Case Study

A 15-year-old Afro Caribbean youth was recently moved from the South East of England by the social services department and placed with a special foster carer in the North East of England. The first three months were uneventful and there was a considerable degree of optimism. The foster carers were taken aback when the police telephoned them to tell them about the arrest of John (assumed name) for the offence of robbery. He was subsequently committed to the Court, whereupon the Magistrates requested a full psychiatric assessment.

The family background obtained from the voluminous social work records confirmed that John was born to an Afro Caribbean mother and a Ghanian father after a fleeting relationship. He was one of five children. His biological father left the scene and is said to have had a criminal record. The mother suffered from manic depressive illness which was complicated further by alcohol abuse. John and his siblings were on the At Risk Register and often had to be placed with members of the extended family, with the maternal grandmother often helping out. Eventually he was received into the care of the Local Authority at the age of five.

The developmental history suggested that John was born after a breech delivery; his temperament was said to be non-malleable and rigid. Milestones were within normal limits and there were no other major medical problems such as epilepsy or a head injury. But he was separated from his mother on several occasions for a protracted period ·of time before the age of three.

John was received into care and placed in a children's home. By the age of 11, as many of them had closed, he had been in five children's homes and experienced three broken foster placements. His behaviour in primary school was described as disruptive and difficult, with him being cheeky and unwilling and unable to accept adult authority. The move to secondary school, coinciding with the onset of adolescence, brought further management difficulties. He was suspended on several occasions, and ultimately excluded. He began to truant frequently in the company of other children, and there was a suspicion that he may have abused drugs.

The psychiatric assessments revealed a rather angry, sullen, hostile youth who appeared to have 'a chip on his shoulder'. Only in the third interview did he begin to trust and reflect on the present difficulties he found himself in. There was no evidence of a major psychiatric illness such as depression or anxiety, but he was nevertheless presenting with a severe conduct disorder. His delinquent patterns of behaviour dated back a number of years, and when invited to comment about his forays into delinquent patterns of behaviour John expressed angry and hostile views towards the police and the judiciary. He believed that he was often 'unjustly' treated by the police when he was in the South East and even the Magistrates gave him a custodial sentence of six months, when he was first taken before the Courts.

Commentary

This case demonstrates that delinquency is a universal phenomenon. John came from a large poor family, he experienced damaging life experiences at critical times in his upbringing, and appeared to be of a low/average intelligence. He had been presenting with unmanageable difficult behaviour within and outside the home for many years. The social worker report confirmed his failure to bond with his care takers, and that he came from a family where there was poor communication, lack of warmth and overt rejection. All these factors are known to contribute to a poor outcome in a child of whatever race or culture.

John's perception that his colour caused the police to treat him as they did, rang true, as did the fact that he received a custodial rather than non-custodial sentence from the judiciary. And luckily, it was possible in this instance, to argue for a Community Sentence Order, with supervision jointly by the social services and by attendance at the psychiatric clinic. Here attempts were made to help John with his repetitive offending and deal with his confused identity.

Views on trans-racial placement and/or adoption are polarized. The opinions of Thoburn being challenged by those of Tizard and Phoenix, Thoburn (1988) argues in favour of a delayed placement, if the same race family cannot be found. Essentially, his concerns are that black children placed with white families fail to develop positive identity and may grow up unable to relate to their country of origin, and white families may not be able to teach black children survival skills in a racist society. Tizard and Phoenix (1989) challenge this concept of positive black identity as too simplistic.

Given the age of John and, the absolute commitment and particular strengths of the white foster family, we were able to support him and the family and maintain his placement. For the following one year, when the unit was in contact with him, John had managed to remain out of trouble and had began to address some of the issues relating to him.

Anorexia Nervosa and Bulimia Nervosa

Anorexia Nervosa is a disorder characterized by self imposed excessive dieting, due to a relentless pursuit of thinness and fear of being fat. The result of this is a varying degree of emaciation with psychiatric sequelae and potential for significant medical consequences. Bulimia Nervosa on the other hand is a condition characterized by binge eating, a sense of loss of control, self deprecation and purging of ingested food. There is also a preoccupation with body weight, but patients suffering from this condition may not present with, or suffer from loss of weight which is a characteristic of patients with Anorexia Nervosa.

The aetiologies of these conditions are not known, although risk factors are acknowledged. Certain cultural factors are perceived to be of significance, such as the Western values of thinness which are particularly prevalent amongst females.

Ballet dancers, actors and fashion models are known to be at a higher risk of developing eating disorders. There is also a familial tendency with a high risk of siblings developing these conditions and this implicates possibly a genetic or environmental influence. Society and the media clearly influence significantly our concept of a desirable female shape which over the last two decades has become more androgenous.

Currently prevalence rates are around 1 per cent for Anorexia Nervosa and between 2 and 4.7 per cent for Bulimia Nervosa affecting predominantly females. Until recently there was a view that these conditions did not occur in Asians or Afro Caribbean people. Explanations for this include cultural differences in the concept of beauty and a desirable female body shape. But in the last decade or so reports have appeared in scientific journals describing a small number of cases of Anorexia Nervosa and Bulimia Nervosa among Asian schoolgirls (Bhadrinath 1990; Mumford, Whitehouse and Platts 1991).

The latter study used the Eating Attitude Test (EAT) and the Body Shape Questionnaire (BSQ). This well designed study has been criticized for using EAT and BSQ questionnaires, which are not standardized for the Asian culture and therefore the absence of the usual accompanying psychological distress usually reported by Caucasian patients. The low rates of these conditions in the

Asian continent may reflect the lack of acceptance by sufferers that these are psychiatric conditions and indeed they may seek help from physicians or obstetricians for physical problems resulting from chronic starvation and amenorrhoea. There has also been a strong association reported between eating disorders and a history of sexual abuse (Oppenheimer, Howells, Palmer and Chaloner 1985).

Case Study

A 16-year-old Asian female, Shamma (name changed), was referred by her physician subsequent to an overdose. She had taken 20 tablets of Paracetamol in circumstances which led to her immediate referral to hospital. This was her second admission following self-harm and fourth admission to a medical ward. The two medical admissions were related to investigations of epigastric pain following eating and the patient's mother observed that her previously 'healthy', but slightly overweight, Shamma had lost a significant amount of weight and that she had become less open in her manner.

Her history of food intake confirmed gradual but deliberate avoidance of carbohydrate and fatty food, with refusal to join the family at meal times and retching post prandially. She had also become miserable, irritable and began to display challenging behaviour, although she showed willingness to help her mother in the family catering business.

Detailed psychiatric examination as an in patient revealed two major areas of difficulty. Shamma attributed her overdoses to her family's unwillingness to allow her the freedom that her 'English' friends enjoyed, and that her family suspected, but not as yet openly acknowledged the existence of an English boyfriend. Shamma feared that if her family were to find out about her boyfriend, she would be shipped to Pakistan and forcibly married to a young man of her parent's choice. Her second major area of difficulty was her eating disorder, with her displaying a moderate to severe body image disturbance, believing that she was fat, even though she was 20 per cent below her ideal body weight. She revealed a history of excessive dieting, use of laxatives and exercising to keep her weight down. On direct inquiry she wanted the clinical team to find her a place away from her family to enable her to pursue her education, continue her relationship with her boyfriend and maintain her present body weight. She was unwilling to acknowledge that her body weight was substantially below her ideal body weight. Further inquiries unearthed the possibility of sexual abuse in the past but several attempts by her therapist failed to elicit further details.

Commentary

Shamma is a second generation 'immigrant' born to Muslim parents of low social class. She was exposed to the Western cultural view of desirable body weight as were her Caucasian schoolmates, and the development of Anorexia Nervosa is understandable. Her self-harm attempts happened in the context of the 'forbidden boy friend', her fear of being taken to Pakistan to be married off against her will and her general inner turmoil.

The multi-disciplinary team of the unit comprised only one member from an ethnic minority (the author) – the rest were Caucasions. Lively debate followed with strong proponents for receiving Shamma into care, helping her to individualize, and exercise her right to have a boy friend as she chose, include the option of sexual freedom, and ultimately live on her own or with a boy friend in the community. Conversely, arguments were put forward that Shamma may have underestimated the potential difficulties in pursuing a white boy friend about whose background and suitability she knew little, risking racial prejudice and social isolation from her 'community'.

It was agreed to share these views with Shamma and gradually, with her permission, take up specific issues with her family. Reassurance from her family was obtained that she would not be sent to Pakistan to marry for at least the following two years, as was agreement to attend family therapy at the unit regularly to 'understand' their daughter's problems, and help to improve communication. The author saw Shamma and key members of her family which included grandparents and an uncle, individually.

Two years later, Shamma had obtained high grades in her A levels, although decided not to pursue a University education and had broken off her relationship with her boy friend and become engaged to a devout Muslim boy brought up in the United Kingdom. It was, in this instance, possible to avoid inappropriate cultural solutions, and use the knowledge of cultural and religious beliefs to obtain the co-operation of the patient and her family. The temptation to offer her refuge and an opportunity to pursue her 'puppy love' was avoided, and individual therapy offered her the opportunity to consider and choose options whilst regarding dangers and rewards. The culturally appropriate approach of seeking the involvement of grandparents and an esteemed uncle improved the trust and co-operation of the family. Unfortunately, to date we remain unclear about the question of sexual abuse, as she chose not to reveal any further details.

Implications for Practice

Difficulties in communication can be one of the principal barriers to meeting the needs of the immigrant children and their families. These difficulties may be primary or secondary. Primary communication difficulties arise from a person's limited ability to speak or comprehend English. The secondary problems may arise due to cultural differences between client groups and professionals.

(1) Professionals have a legal duty under the Race Relations Act of 1976 to promote equal opportunities by communicating adequately. The Adoption Act of 1976 also requires the court to be satisfied that each parent or guardian fully understands what is involved in adopting a child. Similar safeguards exist under the Mental Health Act of 1983.

(2) Positive action – the effects of deprivation on black and white families is similar; however, as Lord Scarman pointed out there is group inequality and this cannot be redressed without positive action.

(3) The provision of day nursery care has become an emotive subject. This and the loss of working mothers to industry, has spurred businesses to start planning provision of creche and day care facilities. To cater for the needs of children from ethnic minorities, appropriate efforts need to be made to recruit staff from these ethnic minorities. Also, the kinds of food on offer should reflect the ethnic variation of population, and staff may need special training in a non-racist approach to children.

(4) Many people find it distasteful to make racial or ethnic distinction on the basis that children's needs are similar. The explanation for this attitude, apart from genuine concern for children, may be due to an unwillingness to acknowledge racial differences and the extent of racial prejudice. To quote Lord Tebbit 'to integrate existing communities into British Society,...to bring them to accept our culture, our language, our rules of Social Conduct' (The Times). The consequences of these attitudes are that a mother in Cleveland (as reported in the local press) described children of Asian immigrants born in the United Kingdom as 'Pakistanis' and not British. She became distressed that her daughter was 'learning Pakistani' (in fact it was Urdu or Hindustani) and was not pleased that her daughter was acquiring a second language. The difficulty here is that the indigenous community, and sometimes political leaders, insist that the task must be to Anglicize immigrants, and assimilate them as they are a 'threat' to British culture and not an enriching part of it.

(5) Fostering and adoption have been practised for centuries as a way of caring for children who have no parents, or whose parents cannot, or will not care for them. In all societies adoption and fostering is rooted in basic kinship rules. In the United Kingdom the practice is firmly rooted in law. These used to be working class activities but

have now spread to the middle classes. Adoption of 'black' children by white families has developed in response to the needs of children, and a readiness of white couples to adopt them in view of the shortage of white babies. It also coincided with the permanency movement and liberal tradition of rescuing 'children who wait'.

(6) The concept of mixed race children has become a separate entity, implying that these children are racially distinct. However, mixed race children are largely regarded as black by society. It is probably a mistake to believe that mixed race children will easily assimilate and adopt a 'white mask'.

(7) There have been many media headlines regarding the controversy generated by placement of black children with white parents. Mrs Virginia Bottomley (personal communication), in reply to a child psychiatrist, wrote that she 'takes the view that race and culture are important factors'. She also supports efforts to encourage people from ethnic minorities to come forward to foster or adopt. She cautions against rigid and dogmatic policies which place racial and cultural factors above the wider needs of the individual child, and emphasizes the current law, that is, the need to take account of the child's wishes and feelings. 'A placement with a family of different race can sometimes be in the child's interests, where that family is able to understand and meet all the child's needs, including those arising from his racial and cultural background.'

(8) Under-utilization of child and adolescent psychiatric facilities by ethnic minorities, particularly the Asian population, is recognised, and commented upon by Stern, Cottrell and Holmes (1990). The possible explanations are: (i) parents may not recognize certain types of behaviour as problems, (ii) Asian children having lower rates of disturbance generally, (iii) cultural norms are different and hence prevent help seeking, (iv) lack of fluency and inability to communicate with professionals working in the clinics. There is the need for epidemiological studies and room for innovative practices to emerge, for example; joint clinics with GP's and school health doctors, closer liaison with religious and community leaders, the advertising of services in immigrant languages.

Summary

People from the black and ethnic minorities now account for approximately 5 per cent of the population of the United Kingdom. As yet there is very little effort made to collect data in a systematic way to account for the possible different pattern of illnesses and different health service needs. In order to provide effective and appropriate care we need much better information than is currently available. Immigrant children and their psychiatric morbidity is a neglected area of research.

There is a strong association between the uptake of psychiatric services by adults (particularly in-patient beds) and variety of socio-demographic factors such as lower social class, social deprivation, isolation, overcrowding, low income and higher rates of unemployment. There is overwhelming evidence that immigrant families and their children share many of these difficulties. Yet this is not reflected in the uptake of psychiatric and psychological services available to children and young people. Concerted efforts are required if we are to succeed in providing prompt, efficient and culturally appropriate service to this vulnerable group of children and young people.

References

American Psychiatric Association (1994) *Diagnostic and Statistical Manual, 4th edition.* Washington, DC.: American Psychiatric Press.

Bhadrinath (1990) 'Anorexia nervosa in adolescents of Asian extraction.' *British Journal of Psychiatry* 565–568.

Bottomley, V. *Personal Communication.*

Bowlby, J. (1971) *Attachment and Loss. Volume 1 Attachment.* Harmondsworth: Penguin.

Fogelmann, K. (1983) *Growing up in Great Britain* (ed) Papers from the National Child Development Study. London: Macmillan. For the National Children's Bureau.

Hannan, D.F. (1969) 'Migration motives and migration differentials among Irish rural youth'. *Sociologia Ruralis 9*, 195–220

Hood, R. (1992) *Race and Sentencing.* Oxford: Clarendon Press.

Lal and Sethi (1977) 'Estimate of mental ill health in children of an urban community.' *Indian Journal of Paediatrics 44*, 55–64.

Mumford, D.B., Whitehouse, A.M. and Platts, M. (1991) 'Sociocultural correlates of eating disorders among Asian schoolgirls in Bradford.' *British Journal of Psychiatry 158*, 222–228.

Oppenheimer, R., Howells, K., Palmer, R.L. and Chaloner, D.A. (1985) 'Adverse sexual experience in childhood and clinical eating disorder – a preliminary description.' *Journal of Psychiatric Research 9*, 357–361.

Rutter and Giller, H. (1983) *Juvenile Delinquency: Trends and Perspectives.* Harmondsworth: Penguin.

Scarman, L. (1981) *The Brixton Disorders.* Cmnd 8427, London: HMSO.

Stern, G., Cottrell, D. and Holmes, J. (1990) 'Patterns of attendance of child psychiatry out patients with special reference to Asian families.' *British Journal of Psychiatry 156*, 384–387.

Thoburn, J. (1988) *Child Placement: Principles and Practice. Community Care Practice Handbook.* Aldershot: Wildwood House.

Tizard, B. and Phoenix, A. (1989) 'Black identity and transracial adoption.' *New Community 15*, 3, 427–437.

Verghese, A. and Beig A. (1974) 'Psychiatric disturbance in children – An epidemiological study.' *Indian Journal of Medical Research 62*, 1538–42.

CHAPTER 9

Children, Families and Therapists
Clinical Considerations and Ethnic Minority Cultures

Begum Maitra and Ann Miller

'It is a supposition of cultural psychology that when people live in the world differently, it may be that they live in different worlds.' (Shweder 1991, p.23)

Introduction

When therapist and patient meet, assumptions about the nature of problems and solutions are only one set of potentially dissonant belief systems that are conjured up. How each views the other may be dominated (and more so perhaps at the initial contact) by the professional world view. However, as questions probe the personal spheres, each character is given by the other a personality, a story, a past. The therapist may choose to see this as 'taking a history', as though it were a collage of discoverable, objective facts about the patient. How the child or parent views it is less often considered.

By making the choice to attend, no matter how reluctant the compliance, the parent gives substance to the assumption that it is s/he, or the family, that has the problem; depending on the parent's understanding of where the problem, if any, is located, s/he may believe that the child alone requires therapy. Another view, and one especially relevant to ethnic minority families, might be that the problem lies somewhere between the child/family and other systems, such as Western education or health care, that interact with it. Children themselves frequently have little power in directly influencing the course or nature of therapeutic interventions. Referred by adults (parents, teachers or other professionals), and taken to therapy by adults, the child's feelings and wishes are often overlaid by adult fears and hopes. For the ethnic minority family the relationship with Western/white systems is yet more complex, and the child's 'voice' may be drowned out completely. The ethnic minority child must face a particularly difficult problem in addition to all those that face her peers, namely that of negotiating a bicultural identity and existence.

Professional curiosity most often concentrates on problems and solutions, or sometimes on pathways to care. It rarely looks for the story the child or parent has discovered about the therapist, and how this has influenced the clinical session. That 'the person of the therapist' has a major impact on therapy has never really been doubted, even when much store was placed on the supposed 'neutrality', clinical dispassion and 'objectivity' of the therapist. Observe the markers of professional identity and status – the use of jargon, patterns of speech and other communication methods (letters, appointment systems, the ritual of professional meetings), and the white coats of the past. We work hard to control how we appear as therapists to our patients. Markers of professional status may be used, among other things, to introduce the patient to a particular world within whose metaphorical language change will, hopefully, be effected. However, the growing drive towards demystifying therapy not only makes therapists more visible, but opens them, as much as their professional discipline, to critical evaluation.

The idea that difference in ethnicity between patient and therapist is significant is indeed true, but if recorded at all, ethnicity is usually seen as a discrete, 'objective' variable (such as age or marital status), and relating to the patient alone. This is, of course, a vast oversimplification. Ethnicity has come to include both the ideas of 'race' or so-called intrinsic difference, and of 'culture' or derived difference. It contains the histories of both the therapist and the patient, and is selectively defined at each encounter between two persons, varying with the context and the need to assert sameness or difference. Thus, when in a foreign land we meet someone who looks like us, we may attempt to discover how much we share. Should the environment be seen as hostile it may be enough that we are 'Asians' together, or we may choose to unite with other people of colour as 'black'. On the other hand if one has painfully acquired a measure of accommodation to the host culture, such as through training as a therapist, one may wish to distance oneself from black groups or to 'pass' as white. With so much personal investment in the identification of one's ethnic group it becomes necessary to examine carefully the various ways in which it is constructed, deconstructed and interpreted in clinical encounters.

Taking a History

Individual and collective histories

The ethnic minority population in Britain at any time reflects current and remote historical events, both local and global. Today this compels us to consider the impact of wars and genocide in parts of Europe and Africa on families and unaccompanied children seeking refuge in Britain. The immediate psychological and physical tasks focus on survival. However, our knowledge of past wars and immigrant groups informs us that the psychological fragmentation caused by these events may linger for generations, emerging in later seemingly acculturated generations as a desperate search for 'roots' that were torn away.

While the impact of slavery and colonialism has been written about extensively these events in the distant past continue to influence how the 'other' is viewed (Said 1978; Nandy 1983) – whether as white master or oppressor, as exotic black or inscrutable Oriental. When discussing minority groups it is necessary to be alert to the distinction between those who have migrated voluntarily and others. Ogbu (1990) names 'involuntary minority groups' who, like the black and Native American Indian populations of the United States of America, exist within white cultures as a result of slavery, conquest or colonization.

We do not wish to suggest that the therapist working with minority groups must equip her/himself with all these stories; we do wish to draw attention to the need to explore these, and to how they influence the experience of the ethnic minority child and her/his family in Britain. It is important to add that a focus on cultural history as a ground for understanding the personal present needs to include not just the tragic stories but also the heroic ones, and also to remember that 'history' itself is constructed and interpreted in each telling.

These stories about the past express themselves in how people see and think about themselves and others, in body language, range of permitted facial expressions and verbal styles, forms of address, manners, taste and personal dress; they also influence ways in which new experiences are received and interpreted. These behaviours, rich as they are in meaning, are often ignored in clinical encounters as 'soft' data, even interfering noise, that masks the 'true' and objective exchange of verbal information. The anthropological study of modes of communication, and emotional expression in the West (e.g. Dreitzel 1981) restores a much needed sense of relativism to the Western clinical sciences. Speaking of the Indian sub-continent and the influence of oral-based traditions, Kakar (1989) emphasizes the predominance of the narrative style, the tendency to think and reason about complex situations through the medium of stories. It must be borne in mind that a Western professional preoccupation with abstract reasoning methods can, particularly in interaction with non-Western groups (or indeed with non-professional groups in the West), veil one of the practices of professional power that places the patient at a disadvantage.

While gender appears to be a much simpler proposition, it is rarely so. How does a female therapist approach issues of authority, autonomy and sexuality, to name a few areas, with a boy or with his father, when they hold strongly patriarchal values? How do therapists' assumptions about gender influence the interaction with ethnic minority families who have different sets of beliefs about gender roles and hierarchies? Are we completely convinced about the separateness of the sexes (Phillips 1994), or agreed about the correct allocations of powers and roles between the sexes (Perelberg and Miller 1990); or are these thoughts about how we would like things to be rather than how they are? Williamson's review (1976) reveals that the preference for male children is not restricted to particular cultural or religious groups alone. Medical technology now permits the determination of the sex of the early foetus, and high rates of abortion of female foetuses are recorded in many parts of the world; in other countries such technology is unavailable but female infanticide, whether by exposure or more direct means, remains a concern. Where a preference for boys is not quite so strong family practices may still treat girls unfavourably as compared with their brothers. These realities pose dilemmas in therapy that are not easily resolved by taking refuge in cultural relativism.

Public and Private Domains
Thinking about the setting
Many healing encounters in traditional Indian examples (Kakar 1982) are carried out in a public space and involve observers. However the 'gaze' of the observers is not usually deemed to be hostile or unsympathetic, but rather a part of the social fabric of such encounters, and serving often as witness to the righting of a social order that has been disturbed by, and manifest in, the illness being healed. In Western settings the gaze of the Western professional may be more ambiguous, and perhaps feared as intrusive, hostile and potentially damaging.

Alternatively, and no less problematically, white professionals may be courted as the only contact which will be acceptable, and this can occur when children or adolescents seek support from adults who they believe will disempower their parents. It can also happen with families who feel that the gaze of the local community (of which the professional of the same cultural group is seen to be a part) will create an experience of shaming with the attendant problems that this would bring for the reputation of the family and the prospects of the children.

Nasima

Mr Khan came to the Clinic with his 13-year-old daughter. They sat in the waiting room in a strained silence while Nasima glowered at her father, occasionally making spitting gestures in his direction. He was a slender Bangladeshi man in an ill-fitting suit, who sat hunched and helpless, face turned away from her. When the therapist walked into the waiting room she was horrified to discover that the girl's wrists were tightly tied together with her father's scarf. Her feet were bare. Professional concerns included fears of physical brutality and emotional abuse, and these persisted in reports on the family for several months. There were no other incidents on record of parental violence or abuse towards Nasima or the other children. Nasima was thought to be suffering from a either a psychotic illness or a severe conduct disorder; the therapist's opinion was that Mr and Mrs Khan were both excessively controlling and ineffectual as suggested by their inability to keep Nasima 'under parental control'. The parents attended sessions erratically, mother did so only rarely, and further anxieties were aroused about their lack of co-operation with treatment that was essential for their daughter.

A referral was made to BM and she rang the family to arrange an appointment. The conversation began in English; Nasima's father spoke in rather stilted phrases that did not make clear whether he could attend on the day suggested. BM switched to Bengali, but uncomfortably aware of curious looks from colleagues in the office she struggled to keep her voice and intonation under some sort of 'colour control'. His voice rising in helpless frustration Mr Khan insisted that he could not attend the Clinic any more. His daughter shamed him in public, kicking and scratching passers-by as he had walked her to the Clinic on the last visit. Failing to restrain her he had removed her shoes so as to protect anyone she kicked, also tying her hands for similar reasons. He and his wife were covered in bruises, but it was unthinkable that Nasima should be permitted to abuse others.

Mr Khan was very concerned about Nasima's rude and aggressive behaviour at home, but any display of this in public affected, in his mind, the family's standing in the community as well as casting a slur on Nasima herself. This, he feared would have long-term implications in that Nasima would fail to learn behaviour considered appropriate for a Bangladeshi woman, and may even be seen by the community as 'mad', with its inevitable consequences for her prospects of marriage and happiness. The ability to move clinical sessions into the home is a powerful strategic tool under such circumstances, as is access to the family's mother tongue. Both facilitate spontaneity of emotional expression and family interaction that is usually lost in the formality and 'public' nature of the clinic. Home visits also allow direct observation of the physical environment of the child, and clues about the emotional world the ethnic minority family live in (Maitra in press) – photographs and objects from 'home', religious icons, attention to beauty and order, or the equally informative absence of these. Admittedly, the validity of such impressions is greatly dependent on the therapist's experience of homes within that culture. Such observations may guide the exploration of exactly those areas of feeling and experience that the family may otherwise find difficult to verbalize.

The family's mother tongue is another powerful means of entry into their 'inner' emotional lives, and not always because it eases the speed or volume of what is communicated. While Mr Khan was able to conduct day-to-day business in English his emotional expressions were stilted, and sometimes bizarrely exaggerated or distorted by his limited fluency, or his attempts to find literal translations for Bengali expressions. Nasima clearly enjoyed speaking to BM in English, and excluding her parents in this way. But she was also relieved that in sharing with BM this power (to speak English) she shared also her sense of unease and guilt at overthrowing parental power and authority, underscoring their powerlessness in White society.

Private space – the home

> On a visit to a Bangladeshi home with an Asian colleague AM was surprised by the vehemence with which he commented on how 'dirty' the home was. AM, who had travelled and worked in the Indian sub-continent, had not been struck particularly by the levels of dust/grime.

> BM and an English colleague visited an Indian home. The parents were middle class Jains, members of a religious sect who live by a complex set of rules around purity and order. The meticulous attention to order and cleanliness in this home was obvious; lunch had just been served, but the kitchen was spotless and all evidence of cooking had been tidied away. The living room was bare of ornaments apart from two stone carvings of Hindu deities. In their young daughter's room dolls and soft toys were arranged in neat rows, bedroom slippers neatly parallel against the wall. The question arose of whether this was evidence of significantly obsessional traits, and a contributory factor in the child's feeding problems.

Observations of seemingly objective facts such as dirt, poverty, and levels of hygiene are influenced by the position of the observer. Offended by stereotypes of Third World poverty, and associations suggested between poverty, laziness, dishonesty and 'primitive cultures', more successful immigrants from these countries may seek to dissociate themselves from, or even pathologize, others who give apparent support to these stereotypes. The Western observer may rate degrees of cleanliness or organization based on comparisons with Western individual/group standards, on generalizations about practices in other groups that may be culturally remote, or on contemporary Western cultural beliefs about physical environments and 'health'. On the other hand to avoid making any observation at all would mean the loss of valuable opportunities for enquiry into the meaning of what is observed.

The idea of individual therapy for children has long been held by Western-trained professionals as a special kind of private space, crossing the boundary of which is surrounded by careful negotiation. For some ethnic minority families this may seem strange insofar as it conflicts with their own idea of privacy, not as an exclusive space but as a space shared with the notional family. Even when children are accorded a right to be seen on their own, the fact that their privacy is not exclusive, but shared with the family, means that many parents expect to have complete access, without the necessity to seek permission, to any information imparted by the child to the professional. With the exception of teachers, who are viewed in many cultures as surrogate parental figures in their role in the socialization of the child, parents may view with distrust the idea that other professionals may have access to their child that they do not themselves have.

Family therapy on the other hand has been a much more public event, not only with wider relatives being invited to therapy sessions but, with the advent of teams, screens, cameras and video, families are exposed to the gaze of a network of professionals (and 'viewing' machinery) who may not be in direct contact with the child and family, and may appear as disembodied voices commenting on the lives of those who have come to therapy. For some families a 'healthy cultural paranoia' (Grier and Cobbs 1986) will mean that they avoid such settings where they have the power to do so, or that they will want to check very carefully the safety of such a setting. There are still many black families, and others for that matter, who avoid statutory agencies on the basis that the risk of having their children 'taken away' is too high to chance.

Other private spaces – family relationships
Relationships within families are shaped by beliefs about the status of members, their duties, obligations and rights in relation to each other. The spaces between people, indicating closeness, formality and intimacy, are defined by rules that are shared by the cultural group, though modified by personal experience and choice. The relationship between parent and child is based on a mesh of beliefs – about the nature of parents and parenting, the nature of children and childhood, and are transmuted by experiences such as immigration, economic mobility, exposure to White (British) culture, the nuclearization of family units that had been 'joint', the movement of women into the public sphere, or by marrying into another cultural group.

A recurrent theme (and an article of faith in some circles) that dominates Western child psychology is the idea of the 'inner world of the child'. As sociologists and historians of Western childhood have amply documented this is a fairly recent development that has followed industrialization and subsequent economic forces (Lijlestrom 1983). Freed from the labour market children were re-created in sentimentalized images of innocence; the need to occupy them within educational institutions became the child's 'right' to an education, and a progression of needs and rights were identified. In other words, modern 'childhood' was created. It is wise to remember that while this definition of the role of children may be eminently suitable as preparation for urban Western society the ethnic minority family may continue to live, psychologically as well as in material terms (due to restricted employment choices), in a world that is somewhere between the country of origin and their new home. With little real understanding of Western ideals, of self-realization and individual freedom, the ethnic minority parent may continue to mould her child along traditional religious/cultural lines that value family and community connectedness and mutual responsibility. This is particularly relevant as the therapeutic goal of helping children (or helping families help their children) to develop in a manner appropriate to white British society may be in sharp conflict with the ethnic minority parent's wishes, and therapy may appear to be yet another attempt to 'colonize' the minds of their children.

That parents in other cultures hold very different views about what goes on inside children is revealed in their beliefs about the nature of childhood. Gil'adi (1992) discusses Islamic beliefs in the innocence of all children (as opposed to the Christian concept of original sin), and the need to teach them using sensory means of rewards and punishment (sweets and physical chastisement). With the development of 'tamyiz' – the ability to discern between good and evil, around the age of seven, the child is now ready to be taught using reasoning. While the child's understanding is still limited her main responsibility is her obligation of obedience towards her parents.

Yusuf

> Yusuf, age 12, was referred by the family doctor because he was completely out of the control of his Pakistani Muslim parents. They described themselves as very Westernized and for example, had stopped celebrating Eid and were now celebrating Christmas instead ('for the boy's sake'). Yusuf seemed obsessed with money and expensive gifts and his father thought he might be suffering from the same 'mental disorder' as his mother (she had a Western psychiatric diagnosis). Yusuf's explanation was 'it's like half of me is a devil'. When asked if he knew anything about 'jinns' he said he had heard of them. He added that he was dissatisfied with the results of his behaviour because money and toys did not really make him happy.

AM (the therapist) hypothesized that the problems in this family could reflect the seeming opposition of Western and Eastern/Muslim beliefs, and also contained within them differing notions of individual responsibility. Thus Yusuf's rejection of his behaviour was based on an idea of its non-human/non-self source (i.e. the devil, or 'jinns') and a cure would need recourse to religious/spiritual interventions; to his mother it was unpleasantly materialist and Westernized and in opposition to the family's Muslim spiritual heritage; to his father it was illness/disorder for which Western medicine had a name, and therefore possible control over. Western professional beliefs may propose an explanation from the individual psychological domain, and describe Yusuf's behaviour as stimulated by psychological pain.

The Concept of Age-Appropriate Behaviour

Normative views of children's behaviour are not confined to psychologists or indeed to professionals. Parents and relatives themselves compare their children with various local 'norms' and notice differences among their children. How they assign meaning to the differences governs parental expectation and anxiety about a particular child. For the professional, certain differences in child behaviour are assigned meanings which are quite different from those assigned by the parents. For example, rocking behaviour in a six-year-old may be seen by a professional as a sign of underlying emotional deprivation, and by a parent simply as an habitual but otherwise unremarkable behaviour, or in some cultural groups it may be seen as the rehearsal of a learnt religious practice. Similarly, the history of child-rearing practices reveals an enormous range of what are seen as age and gender appropriate behaviours on the part of children.

Ali

Ali was nine years old when his family fled from very traumatic experiences in the war in Iraq, finally arriving in Britain as refugees. On entering school, teachers noticed that Ali was extremely nervous, and appeared terrified each time an aeroplane flew overhead.

On referral Ali (now 10) was seen by AM and a bilingual worker with his parents and younger siblings. His father brought many documents with him as witness to the family's circumstances. They explained that Ali sometimes went to his room and screamed loudly. They had stopped remonstrating with him about it and his father explained apologetically, speaking for his wife and himself, 'we love our children but we are both so depressed, we can find no way to help them'. Ali sat silent and serious-faced throughout the conversation and when he did speak, it was in the measured and serious tones of an adult.

In line with the family's request Ali was seen on his own, but before this interview the therapist sought the parents' clarification on what they, as Iraqis, expected of a ten-year-old boy. They explained, as did the bilingual worker, that the boy at this stage would be treated as a young adult and expected to behave responsibly, looking after his younger siblings.

In the interview, Ali disclosed his belief that the dictator of his country had sent someone to London to capture and probably kill his family. He had not discussed this idea with his parents but he believed they would confirm it. He watched the news every night with his father, so he and father 'both understood the situation'.

When she fed this interview back to the father, in the boy's presence, the therapist complimented the father on Ali's sensitivity and loyalty to his parents in attempting to take on responsibility for himself and his feelings. He had not wanted to worry his father any further, but the therapist felt that despite this courage on his part he might have underestimated his parents' capacity to help him. She thought there were two ways in which his father in particular could help. First, to allow Ali for a short period to relinquish some of the responsibilities of a ten-year-old and to encourage him to act younger than his age, specifically in relation to his intellectual understanding of the complexities of the political situation in his country, and also in relation to the expression of his fears. With this in mind he should continue to watch the news with his father, but at the end of it his father should sit with him and carefully explain the meaning of everything on the news about his country and encourage Ali to ask questions about it. Ali's fears about Saddam Hussein were also explained to the father and he was asked if he thought this was likely. The father took Ali's fears seriously, but thought it highly unlikely that someone had been sent to kill him. He was again encouraged to explain this in detail to Ali and to answer his questions about it. Second, and after discussion between the therapist and the bilingual worker, it was suggested that he could call Ali to him at least twice a day and cuddle him for a few minutes, as he would a younger child.

Ali also had a problem about bed wetting and this was worked on with his mother helping him keep a chart of wet and dry days and rewarding him with special time when he was dry. In working with both parents to effect change in their son's fearful and traumatized behaviour, Ali regained his confidence in his parents' capacity to help him and protect him, and his parents, with a growing sense of success in relation to him, experienced a lifting of their paralyzing depression.

The idea that a child is treated as relatively adult at the age of ten is not a universal. By accommodating to it and respecting it, while at the same time suggesting a temporary 'regression' from part of it, a pathway was opened up for both the child and the parents to experience some degree of recovery from their highly traumatic experiences.

The Positioning of the Therapist

In the encounter between professional, and child and parent from an ethnic minority, the professional can be seen either as a member of the dominant culture, or linked to it by virtue of their position in a largely white organization. They will in addition be seen, potentially at least, as a repository of expert knowledge. For children still being inducted into cultural practices, the concept of a professional helper who is not a doctor or dentist is often either vague or non-existent. Permission from the family to talk to the stranger (when there are no examples of how to behave) is an important element in their readiness to do so. The child may be encouraged to adopt a 'fictive kin' position vis à vis the helper (Aziz 1979), and indeed families from some cultures may only feel comfortable in talking about intimate matters if they too can approach the therapist as kin or, at the very least as a friend (Bang 1987). How this becomes enacted will vary from culture to culture, but important elements of it will include modes of address used by therapists and clients, tone of voice and body language – particularly proximity and touching.

Christopher

Christopher was an African Caribbean boy aged ten, the late child of his single mother who had two other grown up children. He had been expelled twice from Primary schools due, apparently, to his unruly and 'disruptive' behaviour. His mother made a self-referral, explaining that she was dissatisfied with what had happened in the previous clinic to which she had taken him. She said she had been asked questions of a personal nature by the male therapist in front of Christopher which she felt were insensitive. These were about her white boyfriend. Christopher appeared detached and fed up, but put his complaint into words: 'I have had to come here because nobody understands me'.

AM sympathized with Ms Johnson in the way in which she had been disrespectfully treated in the last clinic. She also raised a discussion with her about her experience of seeing white professionals and how this fed into her expectations about seeing another one. While Ms. Johnson said she had no particular concern about the therapist being white, she did feel more comfortable with her being a woman. This discussion opened up the possibility of talking about how she perceived Christopher's treatment in his two previous schools, particularly in the light of the fact that he is a black child. The presence of black teachers in his school and what they felt about it was explored. What eventually, though not immediately, became clear was that she actually felt very strongly that Christopher had been discriminated against in his last school. This emerged in the third session and would probably not have done so without the therapist's clearly signalled readiness to entertain this possibility.

It also led to a discussion between Christopher, his mother and the therapist about those ways in which his family had prepared him for coping with racism. What became obvious in the discussion was that this was an area he had not shared much with his mother, and that he felt quite strongly at times that he was attacked because he was black. He had not felt that his mother would discuss this with him. There was an important generational issue here, in so far as Ms Johnson had managed her life in white society by adapting her self to it and by attempting to submerge and ignore difference and discrimination. Christopher on the other hand, like his older siblings, lived in a sub-culture which talked about racism and confronted it daily. At this point there was still the possibility of negotiation between himself and his mother about developing a different 'survival kit', more suited now to his needs. At the same time Ms Johnson decided to appeal his exclusion and to take the previous school to the Commission for Racial Equality (CRE).

For the white therapist, the experience of white racism can only be understood insofar as black people share it with her. In working with black children one possible position the white therapist can take is that of an explorer and facilitator of the child and family sharing with each other their different realities. So questions may be addressed to the parent – What do you teach the children about dealing with racism? Is it different from what you were taught? – to the child – Do you tell your mother when you've been upset by someone calling you racist names? What would your father think about the way you handle yourself in this situation? If your mother went to the CRE and complained that you had been treated unjustly in your last school what do you think the result would be? Would the adults do anything about it as a result? How would you feel about her doing that for you? How would your grandmother think about it, would she agree it was a good idea?

The white therapist can thus position herself as a person aware of the possible ramifications for a family living in a racist society. However, it seems likely that this can only be done successfully providing the therapist has gained the personal trust of the family members and providing also that she never loses sight of the paradox that she belongs to the dominant culture which is the source of the practices oppressing the family. In this way it sometimes becomes possible to open up a space in the therapy for the white therapist to be perceived either as 'neutral' in colour or alternatively as acknowledging (perhaps even challenging) racism in a way that the family and child can trust her to be sensitive to their ways of dealing with it without problematizing them.

Similarly, in working with white children, the white therapist can position herself as a questioner about racist or stereotypical attitudes in the child and family. When you say that all black people are the same, do you think your mother likes you to talk like that, do you think she approves of it? Do you have any black children in your class, what are their names? So if Delroy and Kwame are the same because they're black, in what way are they the same? I don't understand, are there any ways in which they are different? If your granddad heard the conversation we are having here, what would he say? What do you think your mum and dad will say about this conversation after they have left here? Do you think they will secretly agree with you talking in a racist way?

Sometimes the positioning of the therapist as a member of the dominant culture means that the family sees them, often rightly, as having more access to power in the organizations and institutions with which they deal. They can also be seen as a potential benefactor in helping the family gain access to services, goods or money. This view would fit well with the idea of the expectation of patronage. For example, within Bangladeshi society entitlement 'operates both above and below the self. A man is entitled to subsistence from the big people he is dependent upon, but similarly there are people entitled to dependence upon him, including family members' (Maloney 1986, p.42)

In working with the 'Miah/Begum' family (see below) AM wrote a letter to the Home Office supporting the application for a Bangladeshi mother's admission to Britain and also negotiated with the immigration lawyer on the family's behalf and at their request, as they had been unhappy with what they saw as his rather desultory attempts at processing their case. Although he treated the therapist with great courtesy when she called, he was obviously stung by what he saw as her implied criticism of his dealings with the family, and in fact he redoubled his obstructiveness in dealing with their case.

A well documented stance of the therapist (Hoffman 1993) may be one in which the professional sheds expertise by positioning herself as ignorant of or seeking knowledge from the family, particularly about their cultural norms. While this position of itself can be of immense value in transcultural work (Krause and Miller in press) it depends on the way in which the position is elaborated or enacted. If the therapist in adopting this position ignores hierarchies in the family, and treats children and adults in an egalitarian way then children from hierarchically organized families may themselves be placed in a curious position. They may feel that the 'expert' to whom their parents have brought them (or have been 'forced' to bring them) uses their authoritative position (as an adult and an 'expert') completely differently from the way in which their parents enact their own authoritative position.

For the older child or adolescent from an ethnic minority who may be in a struggle for control with her parents and already challenging the parents' traditional values, the encounter with such a professional may fuel the child's scorn for the parents' authority. For others, who are already socialized into their cultural hierarchies of authority, the Western therapist's 'democratic' stance may well appear insincere or dangerous. If the professional is from the dominant culture, there is considerable risk that the parents, in feeling disempowered by the therapist, may seek more rigid or extreme measures in their efforts to gain control in the battle with the child.

Soraya

> Soraya, a 16-year-old Pakistani Muslim girl, was taken into care after her uncle and father had beaten her for attempting to go out with an Indian Hindu boy of whom they disapproved. The white professionals involved strongly disapproved of the father's views and had made little effort to mediate between the various relatives who might have allowed for some rapprochement to be found between Soraya and her father without either having to harden their positions. By the time health professionals were asked to consult to the case, Soraya had made secret

arrangements to marry the boy, despite indications that neither of them was adequately ready for the marriage.

Rehana

Rehana was excluded from school for fighting with other children and for being abusive towards staff. BM wondered about the elderly Bangladeshi man seated with a young boy in the waiting room; the 'young boy' was Rehana. At 11 years she was a stocky, bright-eyed child, hair cut very short and dressed in the contemporary 'uniform' of her British peers – the baggy trousers and shapeless jacket. She looked curiously at BM's sari, her expression a mixture of defiant bravado and shy smiles. She sneered openly at her father's discomfort as he struggled to find a way of responding to conflicting sets of stimuli – the setting of the clinic, and the encouragement to discuss (in Bengali) his thoughts and feelings about his daughter.

At the second meeting, at their home, BM heard from both parents how furious they were at Rehana's bad, unfeminine behaviour. Mother, full term pregnant with their seventh child, was exhausted and tearful. The oldest daughter, a plump, pretty and light-skinned 19-year-old sat with her own infant, echoing her parents' complaints about how Rehana chose to dress in an immodest and revealing fashion 'like the English', refused to obey her parents, and chose to play football with boys. Rehana sat in a corner and hurled defiant responses at all of them. As the session wore on the parents allowed that indeed girls in Bangladesh might play football though perhaps not quite as well as Rehana did, and they would be giving it up by Rehana's age, especially as she had just reached menarche. Her mother was sad about how quickly girls reached puberty nowadays, and that life in Britain was making Rehana grow up so much faster. She didn't really want Rehana to marry early but was very concerned that she might grow further and further away from Bangladeshi values and expectations. Perhaps marriage would help her to return to the order and stability of the Bangladeshi world; their eldest daughter, who had never taken to school since they arrived in Britain, seemed very contented with a traditional marriage and motherhood.

BM asked about the family's experiences since they had decided to join Rehana's father in Britain four years ago. They were non-committal until BM spoke about what she had heard other immigrant parents say, about racism, about fears of admitting unhappiness in their new lives because it sharpened the pain of all that had been left behind. They talked then of a daughter left behind in Bangladesh by a bizarre confusion around proof of paternity, about an ageing mother that they feared might die before they had saved up for the fare to visit Bangladesh. Rehana listened intently; she had heard this many times before, wept with her mother, and hated her father as her older sister did, for his ineffectual helplessness; but never when the story and its sadness had been shared with an 'outsider'. BM shifted the conversation back to experiences in Britain and soon they were all discussing the difficulties experienced, with shared animation and rueful humour. BM got Rehana's mother to talk about her childhood in Bangladesh. Rehana, now much less angry, turned her face away in embarrassment when asked to tell her mother how it was to be a child in Britain. We discussed how Bengali a child could really be in this environment, whether in fact Rehana would have to be a new sort of Bengali, and what a difficult task that was if one had no idea of the shape such an identity would assume.

These vignettes reveal ways in which the therapist's self can be used in clinical encounters. For example, the therapist may emphasize her/his position in the political and social contexts within which treatment is being proposed; they may use their own racial/ethnic identity vis-à-vis the family to foster an exploration of the issues – of difference, of acquiring new/multicultural values or behaviours, of the temptation (or pressure) to acculturate or 'integrate'. Second, the therapist's use of tone of voice, body language, touching and direct emotional expression may permit and destigmatize alternative cultural ways of communicating or expressing feeling; culture being expanded here to include and explore professional and lay cultures as much as ethnic cultures.

The Patel family

After strenuous attempts in half a dozen sessions to encourage Mr and Mrs Patel (both Hindu, Indian but belonging to different regional and religious communities) to take 'parental responsibility' for their one-year-old child BM was exhausted and frustrated. They wished to spend every session angrily cataloguing each other's failings, citing events that had occurred between them and their families from the day they had married. In vain BM spoke of not wishing or being able to judge who was in the right, the couple just produced more evidence of how each had been let down or betrayed by the other. Eventually, with the uncomfortable task ahead of having to decide whether the child should be removed from their care because marital conflicts were interfering with child care, BM abandoned all effort to maintain the .stance of 'neutral' professional and with some impatience in her voice told the parents that they were behaving like children and not fulfilling their obligations to a child that had been given to them (by God). After a few moments of angry silence Mr Patel said that he 'didn't care', she

(BM) could do as she wished. For the first time Mrs Patel allied herself with him, pleading with BM not to take him seriously or be offended, because her husband was only speaking from hurt. This appeared to electrify him and he spoke with much intensity, but now about his own family of origin, their past power and status, though currently much reduced. The session ended in this state of intense emotion; for the first time it was not one of unremitting hostility between the couple.

Subtle but significant change followed this session and as suggested by Kakar (1982) and Roland (1988), we understand this as a response to the therapist's willingness to 'enter' the fray – as a family member or community elder who is visibly emotionally engaged. The neutral or dispassionate stance of the professional expert may be experienced as disengagement, or disinterest, and may wound or mystify the family that is desperately seeking help. To see the earlier endless locked argument as the couple's unwillingness to address their relationship (and their parental roles) would, indeed, be quite mistaken.

Cultural Relativism in Practice

Clinical work with other cultures frequently places the therapist in the uncomfortable position of not knowing how much 'cultural' information to gather, or how much is relevant. More difficult still is the emotional response aroused in the therapist by such information – whether of incomprehension, anxiety, disgust or admiration. One strategy is to take the stance that all cultural practices are equally valid and valuable – but this does not eliminate the need to act within British laws, nor does it eliminate the personal discomfort with beliefs that are dissonant with Western cultural expectations of moral and psychological health.

The 'Miah/Begum' family

This was a Bangladeshi family with three children aged eleven, seven and six who had recently arrived in London after being given permission to join their father and his first wife here. When their father had gone to Bangladesh to collect them he had dropped dead with a heart attack, but, knowing that the window allowing her children to emigrate would shortly close, their mother put them on the plane anyway. Their father's first (senior) wife, Hasina, was looking after them very well but they were understandably very distressed, and the behaviour of the middle child, a girl, was so difficult that her second mother did not know what to do with her. The health visitor referred them to AM. The woman had five children of her own and was, of course, also in mourning for her husband. Nevertheless she was remarkable in her tenderness with these children and in her general care of them.

Having established that she saw no real possibility of returning the children to their mother, since their mother was now without support and would be unable to care for the children properly, it also became clear that she was overwhelmed with the demands of their behaviour. She felt that both she and her husband's junior wife wanted to carry out her husband's last wishes and keep the children in London and she wondered if the therapist could find a way to get the Home Office to agree to allowing their mother entrance.

In talking to the children about their opinions, an activity which Hasina found unusual particularly for the five-year-old, the therapist discovered that the middle girl, the index child, was the closest of the three children to their mother. Her older sister was showing few signs of missing her mother, and indeed felt that she was treated more kindly by her second mother than she was by her own. The change in her ordinal position in the family (from oldest to one of the middle children) had clearly released her from responsibilities that she had found onerous. In enjoying her new found freedom, the eleven-year-old, instead of being protective to her eight-year-old sister, was annoyed with her because she felt that she may be jeopardizing their position in their new family. The youngest child was also clearly very upset, but he seemed to be able to attach himself to the new mother in a baby role and so was contained for the moment.

When these observations were fed back to Hasina and also the observations about how much the children appreciated her care, she redoubled her energies into attempting to activate various professionals to support the junior wife's application for entry to the country. In the meantime the children, bilingual worker and therapist, together with Hasina, composed a letter to be sent to the children's mother in Bangladesh giving her news of them and reassuring her that her co-wife was caring well for them. It also contained a request for the mother to send them some little object of hers (not a new purchase) for each child that they could have while they waited for the adults to sort things out.

AM's expression of a lively interest in discovering the relative positions of co-wives, the nature of their mutual responsibilities to the children of the other and the potential gains from family structures unfamiliar to Western society, indicated an acceptance of this family's frame of reference with regard to family relationships. This attitude can be genuinely curious (rather than a passive and theoretical acceptance of all difference as 'cultural', or a predisposition to dramatize and exoticize non-Western cultures) only after much exposure to non-Western families, and to a wide range of family structures and beliefs. The danger of seeing the other as exotic is that it is invariably accompanied by a view of them as regrettably primitive and therefore needing, however gently, to be Europeanized. Such negative assumptions may be visible in the tendency to translate 'co-wife' as 'stepmother'. The term stepmother, as evident in the fairy tales of many cultures, contains within it a value judgement of the negative sort, that is, that they are less kindly disposed to the children of the earlier wife, and does not acknowledge the bonds that exist between women and co-wives in non-monogamous cultures. This is not to suggest that certain structures should be idealized, rather that the areas of both strength and conflict, such as in the hierarchical positions, roles and reciprocal obligations between the senior and junior wives, be explored with the family, community elders or bicultural professionals.

Conclusion

Psychological, psychiatric and psychotherapy trainings need to look very carefully at models of, and values in, child development theory that are salient to ethnic minority children and families. In working with these families professionals need to appreciate the ways in which culture is an evolving process, rather than a static one, and to be alert to ways in which the professionalization of discourse can be coercive.

References

Aziz, K.M.A. (1979) *Kinship in Bangladesh.* Dacca: International Centre for Diarrhoeal Disease Research.

Bang, S. (1987) *We Come as a Friend.* Derby: Refugee Action.

Dreitzel, H.P. (1981) 'The socialization of Nature: Western attitudes towards body and emotions.' In P. Heelas and A. Lock (eds) *Indigenous Psychologies: The Anthropology of Self.* Berkeley: University of California Press.

Gil'adi, A. (1992) *Children of Islam: Concepts of Childhood in Medieval Muslim Society.* London: Macmillan.

Grier, W. and Cobbs, P. (1986) *Black Rage.* New York: Basic Books.

Hoffman, L. (1993) *Exchanging Voices: A Collaborative Approach to Family Therapy.* London: Karnac Books.

Kakar, S. (1982) *Shamans, Mystics, and Doctors.* London: Unwin Paperbacks.

Kakar, S. (1989) *Intimate Relations: Exploring Indian Sexuality.* Delhi: Viking.

Krause, I. B. and Miller, A.C. (in press) 'Culture and family therapy.' In S. Fernando (ed) *Mental Health in a Multi-Ethnic Society.* London: Routledge.

Lijlestrom, R. (1983) 'The public child, the commercial child, and our child.' In F.S. Kessel and A.W. Siegel (eds) *The Child and Other Cultural Inventions.* New York: Praeger.

Maitra, B. (in press) 'Giving due consideration to families' racial and cultural backgrounds.' In P. Reder and C. Lucey (eds) *Assessment of Parenting: Psychiatric and Psychological Contributions.* London: Routledge.

Maloney, C. (1986) *Behaviour and Poverty in Bangladesh.* Dhaka: The University Press.

Nandy, A. (1983) *The Intimate Enemy.* Delhi: Oxford University Press.

Ogbu, J.U. (1990) 'Cultural mode, identity and literacy.' In J.W. Stigler, R.A.Shweder and G. Herdt (eds) *Cultural Psychology: Essays on Comparative Human Development.* Cambridge: Cambridge University Press.

Perelberg, R.j. and Miller A.C. (eds) (1990) *Gender and Power in Families.* London: Routledge.

Phillips, A. (1994) 'Cross-Dressing.' In *On Flirtation.* London: Faber and Faber.

Roland, A. (1988) *In Search of Self in India and Japan: Toward a Cross-Cultural Psychology.* Guildford: Princeton University Press.

Said, E. (1978) *Orientalism.* New York: Vintage.

Shweder, R.A. (1991) *Thinking Through Cultures: Expeditions in Cultural Psychology.* Cambridge, MA: Harvard University Press.

Williamson, N.E. (1976) *Sons or Daughters: A Cross-Cultural Survey of Parental Preferences.* London: Sage.

CHAPTER 10

Emerging Ethnicity
A Tale of Three Cultures

John Burnham and Queenie Harris

Introduction

One of the main effects on us of writing this chapter together has been to enhance our belief that it is useful to think of our practice as always developing, always 'emergent'. Each time we have reached a position with which we felt 'satisfied' another experience would lead us to question, modify, elaborate or radically change our position. Our realization was that we are always adopting a position of changing position, not only because of our therapeutic curiosity (Cecchin 1987) but also due to the fact that ethnicity and culture are constantly emerging. We cannot hope that it will conveniently stay still so that we can count, categorize and describe in an absolute sense the characteristics of 'The Black Family' or 'The Irish Family' or 'The White Family'. Hence we will always be positioning rather than being loyal to any particular position (Langhove and Harre 1994)

One position that seems of enduring value is the view that meeting the needs of children from ethnic minorities can be construed as *creating a context in which those needs can be expressed to the services that aim to meet those needs*. Otherwise the needs that are being met are likely to be those that professionals hypothesize need to be met. Common ways of meeting the needs of children from ethnic minority family backgrounds include: engaging interpreters; matching therapist to child/ family; matching ethnicity in fostering/adoption; creating equal opportunities policies; race relations training; creating a welcoming environment; and the training of therapists from ethnic minorities. All of these measures create possibilities and constraints to achieving respectful and resourceful services. It is important to bear in mind the limitations of each practice so that services can continue to evolve in response to feedback from clients. For example, to maintain a general policy of matching clients and therapists in relation to ethnicity may not meet particular desires of individual clients. A Indian teenager expressed her fury at being 'matched' (without her consent) to an Indian social worker. She eventually chose to work (successfully) with a white, male, medical doctor arguing that nobody else would have allocated her to such a person!

General policies and practices are to be promoted and admired for the tremendous political profile that they introduce into the community at large. Professionals also require particular resources and practices that allow them to co-create ethnically sensitive practices with the families and individuals with whom they are working. In developing this it is useful to have working definitions of ethnicity in relation to culture and race. Phillips (1990) personal communication has suggested a useful distinction between race, ethnicity and culture. He describes race as a person's biological inheritance, ethnicity as the way a person thinks about that biological inheritance and culture as the social network within which conversations about race and ethnicity evolve. We would propose that ethnicity refers to a client/s 'definition of self' in relation to their race and culture at a particular point in time. As such it cannot be defined by 'another' and can only be created in a conversation between therapist and client/s. It may well include and reflect 'cosmopolitan ethnicity'. It may not be sufficient to define ethnicity as the colour of skin or the nationality of the person/s. It might be important to include particular national/regional affiliations expressed by the client/s, for example 'White/Northern English', 'Black/South Birmingham', 'Welsh Valleys\White'. The terms used and the ordering of those terms may be used to reflect how, *at this particular point*, the person/s constructs their ethnicity. A conversation about ethnicity may take place at one or more times in a therapy. It may assume different levels of importance within a particular therapy when compared with other clients. Therefore it cannot be prescribed when or how to have a conversation about ethnicity. It is desirable for such a conversation to be aesthetically useful in therapy rather than a 'research' or 'monitoring' question.

Interpersonal Team Process

The issue of how to become more culturally and racially sensitive in our practice and training courses, formed the basis of many discussions between us. An interesting aspect of these discussions and emerging practice was the realization that, as in the development of our practice as systemic therapists, we didn't have to be experts in order to make a start. We learnt that it was better to be 'clumsy' than not do anything, to be prepared to learn from our clients and from our mistakes. This was very liberating for both of us, and enabled the application of many of the concepts and ideas from our existing practice, instead of waiting to be properly trained or searching for an ideal way of intervening and 'doing therapy' in order to provide a better service to children from different ethnic or minority family backgrounds. All that we have been able to achieve has required working in teams and/or meeting with groups of people who have been prepared to create facilitative interpersonal processes, allowing mistakes to become contexts for curiosity rather than criticism. In this way team and group members have been able to be transparent about their prejudices, ideas and practices so that these ideas and biases may become more open and available for refreshment and reconstruction and learning from other people.

Theory for Practice

Over the past 17 years of our work together (see Harris 1994) there have been a number of theories that have been useful to us in developing our practice. Here we will highlight some of the ideas that have been most useful to us and refer readers to the source material for their further exploration.

Observed and observing systems

The shift from studying problems in an individual to understanding them in the context of the family, seemed to promote a view that the family is in some way 'dysfunctional' or the cause of the problems. This view guided therapists to work in ways to change the 'observed family' through direct and indirect ways.

The idea of the 'significant system' (Boscolo, Cecchin, Hoffman and Penn 1987) or the 'meaningful system' – that configuration of relationships and beliefs in which the family's problems and issues make sense was an influential and important development in the Milan based practice of systemic therapy. This thinking invited systemic therapists to avoid construing persons, families or cultures as dysfunctional and could be regarded as 'news of a difference that made a difference' (Bateson 1973) to how therapy and the relationship between families and therapists came to be viewed.

Other influential ideas throughout the 1980s came from second order cyberneticians such as Heinz von Foerster, Humberto Maturana, Francisco Varela and Ernst von Glasersfeld. These constructivists proposed that one could never know what is really 'out there' independently of one's own constructions. The idea that we can acquire objective knowledge about others and the world is being seriously and convincingly challenged by scientists. Mendez, Coddou and Maturana (1988) proposed the term '*multiverse*' to emphasize that there are many equally valid ways of perceiving the world though, one might add, not all equally desirable. Von Foerster (1981), offered the idea of the *observing system*, emphasizing that the observer is always 'in' what is observed. This concept invites us to step aside from the notion that an observer can describe something or somebody as separate from themselves. Each time we act as an observer, or group of observers, to describe we *inscribe* something of ourselves in the so called description.

Lyn Hoffman, a well known chronicler of developments in the field of systemic therapy draws our attention to the social nature of reality creation:

> Varela emphasizes that the observing system for him always means an observer community, never a single person, since we build up our perceptions of the world not only through our individual nervous systems but through the linguistic and cultural filters by which we learn. (Hoffman 1993, p.41)

This conceptual distinction between observed and observing systems becomes important when it helps a professional or team to recognize their descriptions as inscriptions and to see how their approach, methods and techniques (Burnham 1992) helps to co-create what kind of families they meet, see and work with.

Nevertheless, respect for the observed system position can have tremendous advantages when an observer(s) rigorously devotes time and effort to the apparently 'selfless' study of subjects. Knowledge is constructed which acts as general guidelines for practitioners who are contemplating working with families who are from a different ethnic group than themselves. For example, knowledge of resources needed for work with these families would include learning about different cultures, the employment of interpreters rather than using family members as interpreters, drawing on the experience of other families sharing the same cultural background. Knowledge and familiarity with the work of voluntary agencies working with families from ethnic minorities with particular problems, for example domestic violence, the care of the elderly, can help the therapist to enable particular families to connect with them.

This 'observed system' position has generated much useful information – for example, see Boyd-Franklin (1989), McGoldrick (1982), McGoldrick and Rohrbbaugh (1987), McGoldrick *et al.* (1991), Lau (1984, 1986, 1988). It has also enhanced awareness of differences between people from different ethnic groupings so that professionals have become more prepared to step aside from the comfortable assumption that 'we are all human beings' and therefore we treat everybody the same. This position tends to inhibit a therapist's ability to adopt a posture of contextual curiosity which we regard as an essential ability if therapeutic conversations are to created. It is important to bear in mind that gaining more knowledge of the culture can tempt the creation of a 'grand narrative' about cultures suggesting and promoting a static view of culture. One needs to guard against the development of a myth that more knowledge necessarily means less racism, or that more knowledge necessarily means more understanding.

Adopting an observing systems position invites single or groups of observers to reflexively examine how their own prejudices, values, passions and theories are situated within their own ethnicity and culture. Deconstructing their practice in these ways can help a practitioner to gain a more useful appreciation of their position and positioning in a particular network of clients, colleagues, agency and society. On the other hand the ideas of observing systems can lead one to think that the therapeutic system is created only between you and the client and so it is important to remember that these conversations are situated within broader political conversations that include immigration policies, racism and other oppressive practices of the ethnic majority (dominant) culture. A therapist who becomes preoccupied with the effect that they have on the family can become superficial in the sense that they fail to explore rigorously the client's situation for fear of being offensive and doing something that would be culturally insensitive. Wishing not to be the 'all-knowing expert', can lead one to adopt the 'not-knowing position' (Anderson and Goolishian 1992). This can lead to a swing from the 'knowing everything' position to a 'not-knowing anything' position. Either of these positions can become disingenuous and unhelpful.

> For instance, in an early attempt to ensure that he (JB) was being respectful to the cultural rules of one particular family he repeatedly asked them if it was all right to interview in the way that he did. Each time he noticed signs of discomfort on the part of family members he re-doubled his efforts to be sensitive and this pattern escalated until the father in the family said: 'We came here because the GP said that you might know something about how to deal with childhood problems. Would you please continue and we will tell you if you ask us to do something that is difficult for us!'

Ascribing all that one sees to cultural or ethnic factors, may lead one to overlook important personal difficulties experienced by one or more members of the family.

Inhabiting a second order world in which social realities are perceived to be socially constructed in many different ways, offers much scope for professionals working with people from different cultures. The worker is freed from the idea of fitting everyone into the same set of beliefs and practices and therefore is less likely to commit 'cultural violence' by imposing the values and practices of the dominant (majority) culture upon persons from a minority culture. This freedom can also be experienced as a practical constraint since it can be difficult to know how to proceed in the absence of clear frameworks. In this situation it is useful to have a theoretical framework which is sufficiently clear to follow at a general level yet is sufficiently flexible to respond at a 'local' level with each family that is being seen. Such a model for us continues to be the Coordinated Management of Meaning (CMM) developed by Pearce and Cronen (1980) with many further developments. Most recently see Pearce (1994) and Cronen and Lang (1994). Most specifically in relation to culture see Hannah (1994).

A Communication Perspective

Social constructionism proposes that social realities are constructed locally, between people in communication over time (for up to date reviews see Pearce

1992, 1994 and Gergen 1992). In this perspective communication is regarded as the primary process rather than a tool that can be picked up, used and put down.

Multiple levels of meaning

Bateson's dictum (1973) that there is 'no meaning without context' has been elegantly elaborated and clarified by Pearce and Cronen (1980) and Cronen, Johnson and Lannaman (1982) in their coordinated management of meaning (CMM). This model has been further developed into a working tool for therapists in published works by such practitioners as Cronen and Pearce (1985), Burnham (1986), Cronen, Pearce and Tomm (1985), Burnham and Harris (1988), McAdam and Hannah (1991), Hannah and McAdam (1991), Oliver (1992), Roper-Hall (1993) and Hannah (1994). Cronen and Pearce propose a hypothetical hierarchy of levels of context in which the meaning of any level can be understood by reference to a higher level.

The contexts that give meaning can be arranged as follows in ascending order; **content** (of a statement); **the speech act** (the utterance as a whole); **episode** (the particular social encounter); **interpersonal relationship** (the definition of the relationship between the people creating the episode); **life story** (stories people have about themselves); **family narratives** (family mottos and ways of behaving in the world); **social mores** (laws, regulations and social prescription for the citizens of a particular society); and **cultural patterns** (the beliefs, values and practices that distinguish a culture as unique, different from other cultures). Although the higher levels exert a stronger (contextual) force downwards, the lower levels also exert a weaker (implicative) force upwards. **It is proposed that the relationship between levels is circular and reflexive over time** (Boscolo and Bertrando 1993) **rather than vertical and linear.** Cronen, in Cronen and Lang (1994), repeated the message that this arrangement should be viewed as fluid, where any level of context can be privileged in discerning the meaning of a given episode. Scaife (1993) proposed using the term *heterarchy* to replace the word hierarchy with the same intention of accentuating the 'living' qualities of the relationship between the levels. It is unlikely that any two cultures will have corresponding details in the levels but that each culture will 'have something to say' in relation to each of these levels.

The impression of a 'regular' hierarchy is easy to understand since the levels are usually presented in the form of a ladder as in Figure 10.1 in which the loops indicate the reflexive connections between the levels. Alternatively, Figure 10.2 maps these aspects of experience in a way which may seem to many readers as closer to how they experience their day to day experience of living. The map in Figure 10.2 intends to convey that the aspects of experience are not separate and distinct but are more likely be lived as 'tapestry' (Lang, personal communication), 'kaleidoscope' (Pearce 1992) or 'seascape' Shotter (1994). Figure 10.2 is much more difficult text to read and this difficulty is intended to convey the difference between 'lived experience' and 'told experience'. It is this kind of 'lived experience' which can only be 'read' in conversation with the persons concerned. Both maps can be useful when talking with a particular family/child. A therapist would explore each of the aspects of experience as shown in Figure 10.2 but would intend to interview so as to bring forth the particular map (of the persons seeking help) organized like Figure 10.1. In this way the therapist is clear about what they are doing *and* the clients' experience of their own experience is privileged. The therapist will endeavour to use the terms, descriptions and orderings that the client thinks are important, which may change during the course of a session, therapy or lifetime. For example

> An Indian teenager said that mapping out her family tree with her *and then* inviting her to connect her personal and family experience to the broader level of culture was the best way round as it ensured that discussion about culture was always related to a person's particular family situation rather than culture as an abstract generalisation.

A child moving between home, school and different peer groups is likely to organize their map of experience differently depending on the particular context they are in at any particular in time in the day. For instance, they will participate in several different cultures during the day, each with different 'language games' (Wittgenstein 1953), requiring different grammatical abilities (Cronen and Lang 1994) and ways of behaving. Thus their life story is not likely to be a 'singular' internal entity and 'self' may emerge in the coordination between these different contextual demands/resources.

CMM can be useful in many ways. Here we are emphasizing its potential for helping practitioners:

- to be constantly aware of the complexity of experience;
- have a way of visually mapping experience;
- have ways of organizing and re-organizing the coherence of different aspects of experience;
- exploring the 'seascape' of consciousness and action (after Bruner 1986)

To use this structure effectively a therapist will need to develop several abilities including: to explore within each level; to orient herself to the local arrangement of the levels; to elicit the patterned connections between the levels; to bring forth which levels are most influential and how in relation to the reason the family are seeking help. These abilities are coherent with and are facilitated by the postures and practices known as circular interviewing (Selvini, Palazolli, Boscolo, Cecchin and Prata 1980; Burnham 1986; Penn 1983, 1985; Tomm 1987a,b, 1988; Cecchin 1987; Burnham in press) some of which are demonstrated in the following case example. This case example is intended to illustrate some of these ideas in action. The examples are best regarded as a series of

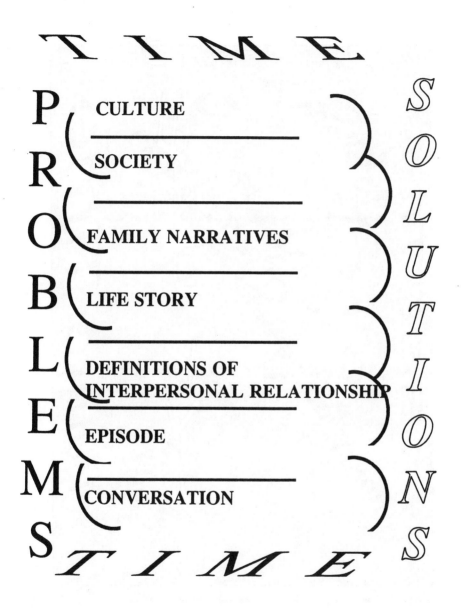

Figure 10.1

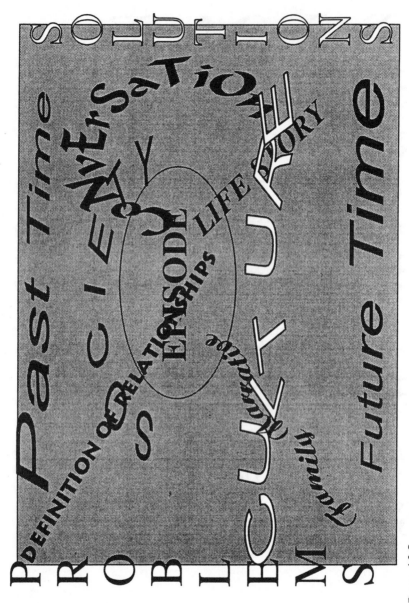

Figure 10.2

'snap shots' from a therapy that covered other important aspects of the family's life that are not re-presented here. Vignettes from the therapy have been chosen in relation to the themes of ethnicity, culture, CMM and circular questioning. Details have been changed to protect the identity of the family members.

Case Example

This therapeutic interview was conducted by the therapy team of the authors with Dr Queenie Harris as therapist. The family consisted of a family of four: mother, father, son 1, son 2. The social services department were contacted by the Headmistress of the school son 2 attended, following Mr X's request for help because of son 2's difficult and outrageous behaviour at home. The family doctor who was consulted later described son 2 as having a very controlling role in the family. The problems presented by son 2 were set in the context of a family where Mrs X suffered a mental health problem requiring hospitaliza- tion and follow up. Mr X came alone at first to discuss his problems with son 2. He described how he would replace expensive items that son 2 had destroyed when in a temper. As he talked he began to realize he was not helping his son by giving in to him.

From this therapy we have extracted several episodes in which we directly work with the dilemmas faced by children, parent and therapists in co-creating new forms of coherence within emerging cultures. These dilemmas present different challenges to each participant in the therapeutic endeavour.

Section 1: assumptions and curiosity

The therapist enters the conversation with the intention of being aware of her own assumptions and trying to maintain her curiosity in the context of those assumptions. Part of the pre-session preparation is often to declare and look at the team members' own maps of their cultural, personal and professional values in relation to the dilemmas presented by the family members. These assump- tions, once publicly declared as hypotheses, hunches or musings, then become more available for deconstruction and exploration as to their usefulness in this particular situation. These assumptions are often reconstructed into questions intended to explore the relational theme connected to the assumption without being restrained by the cultural content which is particular to the therapist or team.

The text has been arranged with a transcript of the interview on the left hand side and a *deconstruction* of the therapists/team thinking about the interview on the right hand side. The transcript begins with an exploration of the sleeping arrangements of the family as they are related to the difficulties experienced within the family.

Therapist: In your setting, in Chinese families, what age would you, let me put this in a different way. In different cultures it varies as to whether children sleep with their parents. For you, in Chinese families, what is the sort of rule, the norm?

Father: We are quite liberal in the sense that the children normally sleep with the parent until they themselves decide to go. They decide to; when Son 1 decided he wanted his own room it was just out of the blue. Son 1 was a mature age, his voice started to change and he said, 'I want my own room'. You know the rules are all there but for us we have never made a conscious effort to tell them.

Here, the therapist reflexively 'catches herself' and opens a more neutral space through recontextualising her question and re-presents herself as a therapist who accepts that different cultures may think differently and that there is no 'universal' way of handling this situation.

Therapist: Yes, that's what I wanted to know because it's important, you see.

Validates answer and the inherent difference

Father: But with son 2 it wasn't so much I did not want to sleep with him but because his impositions were too rigid. I mean, I couldn't read my paper, he would take my papers out, my things out, my books out and he even wanted to empty my top drawer where I put all my little private things. I found that too much I mean *(laughing)* if I can't read in my own bed.

Therapist: So in your family you (father) are deciding when to leave (the bed).

Father: Yes, I have been, you know, eased out. I have been made to do more or less all the donkey work.

Therapist: So generally the norm is that children leave the bed, your bed, when *they* are ready.

Father: Yes, yes, when they are ready themselves.

Therapist reconstructs the problem as dilemma about the relationship between following traditional cultural rules and personal experience.

Therapist: And that is a practice that would be adhered to in your brother's family, your sister's family?

Father: Well not so much with my sister's family because they have been here longer than us and they have adopted the Western style, you know, to put the children in their own beds when they are young so that they get used to that.

Therapist: So do they give you advice? do they kind of say…?

Father: Well they tend to look at us and tell us.

Therapist: So they kind of put the pressure on you, do you think?

Father: They used to mention it but I never used to take much notice. Because I thought that if they'd be happy *(pointing to his two sons)*…because we all liked to sleep in one big room *(pointing to the whole family group)* it's like one big room, it used to be two rooms, now it's joined together. I think it was quite good in a way.

Therapist *(to Mother)*: So you don't feel under pressure from his relatives to do something different?

Mother: *(quietly)* No.

Therapist: It's quite OK by you?

Mother: *(hesitantly)* OK.

Therapist question places discussion in the context of others who are likely to be significant in the process of making 'cultural stories told' into 'family stories lived.'

How do cultural rules become mediated within particular extended family narratives?

What are the contextual influences?

This sequence of conversation juxtaposes several contexts which are influential in creating the dilemma about which the father speaks. The therapist's attitude of cultural curiosity from a multi-versal posture brings forth a richer story than might have been created by adherence to the dominant cultural values relating to the issue of sleeping arrangements for parents and children.

The therapist notes the 'quiet' voice of the mother both literally and metaphorically.

Section 2: Inter-Intra Generational Conflicts: Between Cultures, Between People
The therapist picks up the father's cue: '…my sister's family because they have been here longer than us and they have adopted the western style, you know, to put the children in their own beds…' and spends some time asking the two sons which of their parents has adapted more to the Western culture. Both children have some difficulty answering the question even though they say they understand what the therapist is talking about. This may indicate a rule 'not in front of the parents'. Finally the youngest (and boldest?) says it is his mother.

Therapist: (son 2) We were hearing something just now, your mum and dad come from a way of life that's different from here, it isn't like what they had in Malaysia?	*Tone of voice creates a speech act of 'interested curiosity' (tell me more) rather than 'interrogative curiosity' (what is the problem here?)*
Son 2: Oh yes, actually she speaks this funny accent. (He looks at son 1 and mother, laughing.)	
Mother looks at therapist.	*The content and manner of what is said indicates a speech act of 'mockery' and gives another understanding of mother's 'quiet voice'.*
Therapist: Yes, OK. You have to follow certain rules like your dad said just now to show respect to older brothers and mums and dads and all the rest of it, OK? Which of them is having difficulty in having to settle down here with things the way they are here?	*The therapist notes the mother's 'appeal' to her but decides not to openly 'challenge this challenge' by the children to the mother but quietly resolves to make sure that she persists in including the mother in the conversation and openly demonstrates respect for her.*
Son 2: Mmm, my mum, my mum,	
Therapist: Do you think your mother? (*to the children and then switches to the parents*): In your opinion, which of you two have had most difficulty in keeping to Chinese traditions and the way of life in a Chinese family since coming here?	*The therapist decides not to amplify the children's criticism and instead accepts/places parents' life script stories in the context of the parental relationship and the movement between cultures.*

Mother: He (*pointing to her husband*), he tries to keep to the Chinese ways of life, to the customs and all that but me, I am inbetween, sometimes I follow, sometimes I don't, but he (*continuing to point to the husband*) at Chinese New Year he will get all those Chinese crackers but I wanted to follow the English custom by having a Christmas tree do you see, but he follows Chinese custom like with the respect for his older brother, do you see?

The mother seems to feel encouraged and 'finds' her voice in the session.

Therapist: So you are more half and half but he, your husband, is more Chinese if I can put it that way.

Mother: He is very Chinese but also he is quite Western.

Differences between parents are brought forth within a broader context that gives meaning to 'parental inconsistency'.

Therapist: Yes, but suppose we say Chinese and Western, he is 60 per cent Chinese, 40 per cent Western and you (mother)?

Distinction creating questions brings forth different personal realities

Mother: I am 60 per cent Western, no 70 per cent Western and 30 per cent Chinese.

Therapist: 70 per cent Western and 30 per cent Chinese, I see. So has this come about recently, what do you think?

Mother: No, it has always been like that.

Therapist introduces time into these changing relationships between parents and between loyalty to 'old' culture and engagement with 'new' culture

Therapist: Even from the first time you came would you say that you are more Western than Chinese and he was more Chinese that Western.

Mother: Yes, yes, that's right.

Therapist: Do you think he would agree?

Mother: I don't know, why don't you ask him (*laughing*)?

Therapist asks husband

Therapist accepts mother's question as a 'teasing challenge'

Father: I don't know about the percentage but from my own personal experience there are some types of behaviour that I have always been brought up to.

'**Therapist:** But would you say you are more Chinese than Western?

Father: Depending on the type of situation, I mean I would try to maintain some form of, you know, our own culture and tradition but I don't expect them (*gestures towards the children*), you know, to be against Western culture, the British culture but I do expect them to understand our own.

Therapist: So how does your lifetime's experience influence your relationships?

Father: Well, my wife doesn't know very much about our Chinese culture because her parents lived in Malaysia for the past 30 to 40 years, but I was born in China, I emigrated to Malaysia although I was only seven but my family always lived in Chinese culture. That's why she, in fact she doesn't understand the culture, that's why she doesn't appreciate it but now sometimes when I explain to her why I am doing something she is now beginning to understand. (*Mother is nodding*)

Therapist (*to mother*): Do you agree, would you go along with that?

Mother (*nodding*): Yes I would.

The questioning brings forth through the eyes of the parents the issues of movement between cultures and the contextual influence of this movement on the emerging autobiographies and daily episodes between family members. There are no simple differences between two cultures but an emerging seascape of culture within a 'single family unit'. Each individual is relating to multiple cultural contexts simultaneously. The influence of these different cultures are mediated through the autobiographies of each of the individuals as they together create the family story. The next section shows how these multiple influences create a definition of relationship between the couple in relation to the problem they brought to the clinic...

Section 3: Multiple levels of relationship

The seascape of cultural contextual influences has real and practical effects within creating the 'local' relationships between the members of a family. The effects on parenting of the parental preferences for different blends between Western and Eastern cultures is vividly illustrated in the next section which is from the next session three weeks later.

Father: Well, it (the problems at home) is much less. My concern is now that when he comes back (from school) he behaves towards him in a way that belittles him, I don't like that.	
Therapist: So he doesn't act like a Chinese brother?	*Therapist places child's actions in a context of father's cultural expectations of how to do 'brotherhood'*
Father: Well, he is so much younger, he is no competitor. He (the eldest son) doesn't have to prove to me...he should be protective toward him (the youngest son) like last week, he (the youngest son)...	
Therapist: So if he was to listen to you he would be more like how you would like Chinese brothers to be?	
Father: Yes, there are only two of them and if they are not going to have a good relationship, well...	
Mother (*to father*): They will have it (a good relationship) when they are older; now they are still young and this fighting it is sibling rivalry, (*to therapist*) that is quite normal in most families.	*Mother appears more able even with her 'funny voice' to express her views.*
Therapist (*to mother*): Do you see that as normal in most families? Do you see that as normal in Chinese families too?	
Mother: Yes, it's umm, in all families it's bound to, all children have sibling rivalry.	
Therapist: So your idea is whether it's Western or whether it's Chinese this kind of thing takes place?	
Mother: Yes, most, yes.	

Therapist: Yes, whatever culture it might be... So what kind of solution do you think needs to be applied, a Malaysian solution to this problem, a Chinese solution to this problem or a Western solution? **Mother:** Solution? I think...(pauses in a thoughtful looking way) **Therapist** (*to father*)**:** OK, let me ask you this question because your wife doesn't see this as a problem, she sees it as a kind of temporary sibling rivalry common in all cultures, right, but you see it differently. So what solution do you think needs to be applied, Malaysian, Chinese, Western?	*The therapist avoids the temptation of constructing the influence of three cultures as a problem or offering a solution from a position of expert as to which culture should be chosen (ie the 'When in Rome' posture). Instead she moves the conversation from problem formation to solution creation while still remaining within the intercultural framework and thus brings equal privilege to the three strands of culture that are may be resources to this family now.*

The father tells a long and interesting story about how he wants his children to feel free to express their views and that he respects their views. If they experience respect they will behave well.

Therapist: When you respect the (children), will that be a kind of Chinese way? **Father:** No, traditional Chinese will never let very young children express their views, they wouldn't let them talk. **Therapist:** So when you are doing that you are being more Western than Chinese? **Father:** Yes, I keep my children as friends, I hear what they want to tell me. **Therapist:** So that would not be acting within your strict...(Chinese culture) **Father:** No, not in that strict...(*looking very thoughtful*) **Therapist:** Not like it was for you? **Father:** Not like in Chinese tradition.	*The therapist highlights through her question the emergent nature of culture when the context for relationships is cosmopolitan rather than ethnocentric. In struggling to achieve a both–and position there will (inevitably?) be difficult moments when it will appear that to do something (for example brotherhood, respect, father–son relationships) within the rules of one culture will compromise a person's ability to do it in another.*

Therapist: Would you see that being more Western?

Father: Yes, more Western.

Therapist: You would see that as being more on 'this side' (Western), so you try to listen to them to be on 'this side'.

Father: Yes, to find out what upsets them and what they want. But you see this disrespectfulness to each other, no matter what culture, if you don't respect each other you are going to have this. The problem comes from this continual fighting.

Therapist (*to father*): Can I ask you your view on this because I know your view (*to the mother*) that it's sibling rivalry and that it will all come all right in the end and at the moment it's sibling rivalry because you see it in that way. I want to come to you, the father, because you see it differently. If you were to somehow think like your wife that this is sibling rivalry and this kind of fighting is something that lots of brothers in Western cultures do, what difference would that make to you? Would you come to consider it as healthy development or not healthy development if you were to kind of push yourself to think 'this is Western, this is a way of adapting to this culture and this was no more than what for most families takes place between brothers'. Would that make you regard that as a kind of healthy development or not?

Father: I don't mind so long as they don't eventually become a physical battle.

The therapist constructs a reflexive (Tomm 1987b) question inviting the father to imagine that he agrees with the mother's view and to speculate what effect that would have on how he construes his sons' behaviour. This may be important for the mother and sons to hear the therapist begin this way instead of inviting the mother to take the father's position. Simultaneously, it also fits with the father's expressed wish to have a more 'Western' father–son relationship.

The therapist, through using distinction-clarifying questions, facilitates the family members to struggle towards a more 'cosmopolitan' form of communication.

Like all other forms of communication, 'cosmopolitan' is a means of achieving coordination, coherence, and mystery within the constraints imposed by the 'facts of life' and in response to particular social and material conditions. Its distinctive features derive from giving primacy to coordination rather than coherence, and from its unusual means of achieving mystery. (Pearce 1989)

Thus while the therapist endeavours to respect the family's wish to be coherent with being Chinese she is also facilitating the parents to achieve coordination between their different adaptations to what they see as Western culture. This may make it easier for the children to know which cultural rules they are supposed to be following in different social contexts and what kinds of behaviours those rules require of them.

Section 4: explanations for change

At the next session the mother and father attended without the two children. The parents agree that things have been much improved with the boys at home.

Father: Well I think that during the last two months, to me anyway he has made quite a lot of improvement from the last time when we saw you. He still once in a while reverts back to his old ways, his old character, but that could be just because by his own personality he has got a very strong, very determined kind of personality and that comes through and his unwillingness to submit to his older brother. If you have got a situation where the youngest child accepts the authority of the oldest child they will play well and the older child will fit in but because before I was playing the wrong role with him (son 2), this overprotection and he sees me as the person that fights on his behalf, he yells and I go, but now I don't. **Therapist:** How did you stop doing that?	*The father tells a story in which he both remains loyal to the Chinese idea of how to 'do brotherhood' and introduces the idea of 'strong personality' which he had previously seen as more of a Western idea. He also recognises his former position in the interaction between brothers as not helping the rules of brotherhood to operate successfully.*

Father: Since when you asked us to 'imagine what would happen if I said no'. and we tried to introduce 'no', eg, he has been keen on collecting all those stickers for those Beanos and Dandy, last year he was collecting football cards, he wanted the cards every day, he would go to the shop and not just buy one packet he would buy as many as he thinks he can get, but now I don't.	*Cites the influence of hypothetical questions in generating change and speaks of a shift from 'I' to 'we', indicating a greater coordination between parents. He refers to particular episodes that have been generated, in this emergent context.*

Section 5: Which Culture? Both–And (the therapist's personal position)

Two months later there was a final session arranged as a follow-up attended by father and mother and youngest son. The episodes of success were repeated and confirmed with a much happier story emerging among all family members. The therapist invites the family members to look forward to the future. The therapist's own experience of immigration and evolving family and personal values are evident in the interview and provide much food for reflection.

Therapist (*to father*): What about eight years' time, how do you imagine your family will be? **Father:** Well I imagine that they, as time goes on, we will eventually emerge as, for me anyway, as a reasonably average family.	*Future oriented questions (Penn 1985) invites family members to escape current difficulties and create a preferred story for the future which can recursively regenerate the present.*
Therapist: Do you think your children will be more like your wife in her views and attitudes or more like you in your views and attitudes? **Father:** I think they will have adopted both. (*Mother and father look at each other nodding in agreement*) **Therapist:** So they will have half and half whereas you, the mother, are 80 per cent Western and 20 per cent Chinese and you, the father, have 20 per cent Western 80 per cent Chinese. They (the children) will have half and half.	*A question which explores the coordination between the parents' influence to their children's emerging ethnic identity.* *A new story emerges both verbally and non-verbally which indicates the parents are privileging coordination between rather than coherence within their different ethnic heritages.* *Therapist confirms a multi-versal position through further questioning within the metaphor of percentage which was used earlier in the therapy.*

Father: Probably they will have less of mine because it is easier to be Western here. I take them to ancestral worship and they go through the rituals but they don't understand the whole concept. Not that I'm Buddhist, I am more Christian in my outlook but I carry on in traditions because I was able to understand these things...

An apparent support and confirmation of the contextual influence of the mother's cultural (more western) position in the current context **as well as** *the father's ability to continue to enjoin the children with connection with his heritage in the present.*

Therapist (*to mother*): In eight years' time, do you think the children are more likely to be Western?

Tone of voice and non-verbal posture is of curiosity rather than predictive or advisory.

Both mother and father nod indicating that the children will be more Western.

Father: (*continuing*) Yes, it's a trend with immigrants to any country the minority will be absorbed, you know, if their parents come from traditional values then some of the tradition will be kept on or you segregate them like the Jew does.

Therapist (*to the mother*): What do you think, are you in agreement?

Therapist persists in hearing mother's voice in the session.

Mother: Yes, they are in this country, my children, and they came very young. They are more likely to adopt the English way, they mix with English boys, they are less likely to be Chinese than us.

The mother seems more confident to express her opinions than previously and the father and son are both listening to her compared to previous episodes when their attitude was to discount her contribution.

Therapist: Do you think it is a good idea that they have some Chinese?

Mother: Umm, I don't know if I can really say that (*she sounds very uncertain*)

Therapist takes a complementary position to explore the continuity of culture as well as the changes.

Therapist (*to youngest boy*): What do you think in eight years' time, your parents say that they think you will be more Westernised, do you think it will be very sad if you don't have a little bit of Chinese.

Future hypothetical questions explore some of the potential disadvantages for individuals and family groups of disconnecting from cultural heritage for children raised in a different culture from their parents

Younger son (*nodding*): Yes, very sad.	
Therapist: Who do you think will be more sad?	*Exploring emotion as socially constructed in the context of significant family relationships.*
Younger son: Both of them.	
Therapist: Both of them? What do you think about yourself, how will it be for you, will you want to give up everything, every bit of Chinese in you or what?	*Drawing out the distinction of individual experience the therapist explores further the idea of the child's future ethnicity.*
Younger son: (*answers immediately in a definite tone of voice*) Probably.	
Therapist: Probably? Why is that? There must be some attractive bits you want to keep.	*The therapist expresses surprised curiosity at the definite tone of the boy's answer and he becomes a little less certain in his response.*
Younger son: I don't know.	*The therapist recognizes her position and attempts to keeps the topic open by acknowledging the uncertainty of what the future might hold so as to avoid pushing the boy into a definite 'anti-Chinese' position.*
Therapist: It's a hard question, I know. It's kind of guessing about the future.	

Reflections

This session and the therapy drew to a close shortly after this episode and in the post session discussion the therapeutic team reflected on how complex and exciting the issue of ethnicity is when one comes to regard it in a postmodern sense as *always emerging*. Therapists who wish to knowingly participate in this emergence can adopt an observing systems position through developing reflexive abilities. In this last vignette it may be seen how therapists from different cultural positions may have responded differently. A therapist from the 'host' country might have inscribed the expediency of adapting to the 'Western' culture, whereas a therapist with personal experience of immigration might be inclined to inscribe the advantages of maintaining connections with the parents cultural heritage. And yet the positions could also have been reversed. A reflexive therapist is likely to monitor their participation in the creation of conversations so that many possibilities are considered for the present without closing down future possibilities.

Readers of these vignettes might say 'But this is just like any two parents disagreeing' (this is a comment often made when a 'local' similarity is inscribed in such a way that a larger difference is disguised). The difference between the parents is set within a multi-layered discourse which is more likely to degenerate into cultural confusion than generate choice. In this situation silencing the voice of the mother might be seen as an attempt to create an acceptable universe. This kind of situation might invite therapists to say which is best, instruct the parents to choose one way (to be consistent) We prefer to ask reflexive questions or create rituals (Selvini Palazzoli, Boscolo, Cecchin and Prata 1978; Imber-Black, Roberts and Whiting 1988) which invite people in such dilemmas to 'step out' of their current position and 'step into' the position of another person, time, relationship and so forth. and consider the dilemma from that position. When they take up their 'own position' again they may well have more options than they had previously imagined. An important part of the work *for the children* was to bring forth the discounted voice of the mother who was categorized as: female 'mental' patient with a 'funny' voice (the kind of voice which is so often caricatured by comedians in the British culture in which the boys were engaging). To silence the voice of the mother could in a way be construed as silencing the voice of the culture which the mother re-presents when she is talking to/for the children.

Meeting the needs of children from ethnic minorities requires the therapist or professional to first examine their own needs. By needs we mean the professional might usefully ask themselves the question 'In order to work effectively for this child what do I need to know, what do I need to be able to do?' In our working together in this area we have found that our differences and similarities have both been immensely useful in developing practice. To put it a different way, it is how we use the relationship between our differences and similarities that is most likely to help us in developing practice in this and other areas. Our differences relate to our race, gender, spiritual beliefs and original training. During our 17-year working partnership we have developed similarities in how to coordinate the relationship between our differences so that 'news of these differences become a difference that makes a difference in our practice'.

Conclusion

Professionals wishing to explore, confirm and amplify their abilities in meeting the needs of children from ethnic minorities are assisted in this mission by theoretical postures and practices which are both reliable and flexible. We do not see ethnicity as a static entity but as a narrative which is constantly emerging through the relationships between people, groups of people and nations. Professionals may find practical theories such as CMM valuable in this emerging field of work. Perhaps we can end with ten guidelines on culture and ethnicity that we use to guide our practice:

(1) CULTURE AND ETHNICITY ARE ALWAYS IMPORTANT BUT NOT ALWAYS OBVIOUS: Explore issues such as culture and ethnicity even when professional and client 'look' the same.

(2) PEOPLE WHO ARE DIFFERENT (FROM YOU) ARE NOT NECESSARILY THE SAME (AS EACH OTHER): Avoid assuming that all people from the 'same' country, family, or local culture follow the same rules of behaviour, preferences, etc.

(3) ETHNICITY AND CULTURE ARE SOCIALLY CONSTRUCTED: As well as asking 'what is' ask 'how do you do...sadness, joy, saying hello, saying goodbye, being the eldest daughter, leaving home...?

(4) HYPOTHESIZING: Through the process of hypothesizing make your ideas, assumptions, values and prejudices open to colleagues and clients so they can be examined as to their usefulness and relevance.

(5) SUSPEND YOUR BELIEF: Step outside your own cultural rules that are often 'taken for granted'.

(6) SUSPEND YOUR DISBELIEF: Step into other people's ideas, customs and patterns.

(7) BE 'CLUMSY' RATHER THAN 'CLEVER': The value of 'not knowing' and the potential of curiosity.

(8) NOT AN EDUCATION LESSON FOR THE PROFESSIONAL: Curiosity of the professional is most useful to the family when it is related to the reason that the family are consulting you.

(9) BE SENSITIVE NOT SUPERFICIAL: You have a job to do. How to take risks safely?

(10) THIS LIST IS ALWAYS EMERGING AND SO WHAT WOULD YOU ADD TO THIS LIST?

References

Anderson, H. and Goolishian, H. (1992) 'The client is the expert: A not-knowing approach to therapy.' In S. Mcnamee and K.J. Gergen (eds) *Therapy as Social Construction*. London: Sage.

Bateson, G. (1973) *Steps to an Ecology of Mind*. London: Paladin, Granada Publishing.

Bateson, G. (1980) *Mind and Nature: A Necessary Unity*. London: Fontana.

Boscolo, L. and Bertrando, P. (1993) *The Times of Time: A New Perspective in Systemic Therapy and Consultation*. New York: Norton Press.

Boscolo, L. (1989) 'Falling in love with ideas: An interview with Luigi Boscolo by Max Cornwall.' *Australian and new Zealand Journal of Family Therapy 10*, 2, 97–103.

Boscolo, L., Cecchin, G., Hoffman, L. and Penn, P. (1987) *Milan Systemic Family Therapy: Conversations in Theory and Practice.* New York: Basic Books.

Boyd-Franklin, N. (1989) *Black Families in Therapy: A Multisystems Approach.* New York: Guilford Press.

Bruner, J. (1986) *Actual Minds, Possible Worlds.* Cambridge, MA: Harvard University Press.

Burnham, J. (1986) *Family Therapy: First Steps Towards a Systemic Approach.* London: Tavistock Publications.

Burnham, J. (1992) 'Approach – method – technique: Making distinctions and creating connections.' *Human Systems 3*, 1, 3–26

Burnham (in press) 'Co-constructing effective interviews with clients.' *Humans Systems: The Journal of Systemic Management and Consultation.*

Burnham and Harris (1988) 'Systemic family therapy: The Milan approach.' In E. Street and W. Dryden (eds) *Family Therapy in Britain.* Buckingham: Open University Press.

Cecchin, G (1987) 'Hypothesizing – circularity – neutrality revisited: An invitation to curiosity.' *Family Process 26*, 405–413.

Cronen, V. and Lang, W.P. (1994) 'Language and action: Wittgenstein and Dewey in the practice of therapy and consultation.' *Human Systems 5*, no.1–2.

Cronen, V., Pearce, B.P. and Tomm, K. (1985) 'A dialectical view of personal change.' In K.J. Gergen and K.E. Davis (eds) *The Social Construction of the Person.* London: Sage.

Cronen, V.E. and Pearce, W.B. (1980) 'Toward an explanation of how the Milan method works: An invitation to a systemic epistemology and the evolution of family systems.' In D. Campbell and R. Draper (eds) *Applications of Systemic Therapy: The Milan Approach.* London: Grune and Stratton.

Cronen, V. (1992) 'Ethical implications of the theory of "Coordinated Management of Meaning"' Pre publication copy.

Cronen, V. (1992) 'Coordinated management of meaning: Practical theory for the complexities and contradictions of everyday life.' In J. Siegfried (ed) *The Status of Common Sense in Psychology.* Ablex Press.

Cronen, V., Johnson, K. and Lannaman, J. (1982) 'Paradoxes, double binds and reflexive loops: An alternative theoretical perspective.' *Family Process 21*, 1.

Gergen, K. (1992) 'Social constructionism in question.' In B. Pearce (ed) *Social Constructionism. A special edition of Human Systems: The Journal of Systemic Consultation and Management 3*, 3–4.

Hannah, C. and McAdam, E. (1991) 'Violence – Part 1.' *Human Systems 2, 3 and 4.*

Hannah, C. (1994) 'The context of culture in systemic therapy: An application of CMM.' *Human Systems 5*, 1 and 2.

Hare-Mustin, R. T. (1994) 'Discourses in the mirrored room: A postmodern analysis of therapy.' *Family Process 33*, 19–35.

Harris (1994) 'A systemic approach to working with families from ethnic minority backgrounds.' *Context 20*, Autumn.

Hoffman, L. (1993) *Exchanging Voices: A Collaborative Approach to Family Therapy in Systemic Thinking and Practice Series*. Edited by David Campbell and Ros Draper. London: Karnac Books.

Imber-Black, E., Roberts, J. and Whiting, R. (1988) (eds) *Rituals in Families and Family Therapy*. London: Norton Press. Chapters 1 and 2.

Langhove, L. and Harre, R. (1994) 'Positioning and autobiography: Telling your life.' In N. Coupland and A. Nussbaum (eds) *Discourse and Lifespan Identity*. London: Sage.

Lau, A. (1984) Transcultural issues in Family Therapy *JFT 6*, 2. Rhodes, M. Family Therapy and The Problem of Cultural Relativism: A Reply to Dr Lau, *JFT 7*, 3.

Lau, A. Cultural relativism – relative agreement *JFT 7*, 3, 273–276.

Lau, A. (1986) 'Family therapy across cultures.' In *Trancultural Psychiatry*. London: Croom Helm.

Lau, A. (1988) 'Family therapy and ethnic minorities.' In E. Street and W. Dryden (eds) *Family Therapy in Britain*. Buckingham: Open University Press.

Maturana, H.R. and Varela, F.J. (1987) *The Tree of Knowledge: The Biological Roots of Human Understanding*. London: New Science Library.

Maturana, H. (1990) 'Reality: the search for objectivity or the quest for a compelling argument.' *Irish Journal of Psychology 1*, 9, 25–58.

Maturana, H.R. and Varela, F.J. (1980) *Autopoiesis and Cognition*. D Reidell: Dordrecht, Holland.

McAdam, E. and Hannah, C. (1991) Violence – Part 2: Creating the best context to work with clients who have found themselves in violent situations.' *Human Systems 2*, 3 and 4, 217–226.

McGoldrick, M. (1982) 'Normal families: An ethnic perspective.' In F. Walsh (ed) *Normal Processes*. New York: Guildford Press.

McGoldrick, M. and Rohrbbaugh, M. (1987) 'Researching ethnic family stereotypes.' *Family Process 26*, 89–99.

McGoldrick, M., Pearce, J.K. and Giordano, J. (1982) *Ethnicity and Family Therapy*. New York. The Guildford Press.

McGoldrick, M., Almeida, R., Moore-Hines, Rosen, E., Garcia-Preto, and Lee, E. (1991) 'Mourning in different cultures.' In F. Walsh and M. McGoldrick (eds) *Living Beyond Loss*. New York: Norton Publications.

Mendez, C., Coddou, F. and Maturana, H. (1988) 'The bringing forth of pathology.' *Irish Journal of Psychology*, Special Edition. 9, 1.

Oliver, C. (1992) 'A focus on moral story making in therapy using coordinated management of meaning (CMM).' *Human Systems 3*, 3 and 4.

Pearce, W.B. (1989) *Communication and the Human Condition*. Southern Illinois University Press

Pearce, W.B. (1992) *Social Constructionism.* A Special Edition of Human Systems: The Journal of Systemic Consultation and Management, by Leeds Family Therapy and Research Centre and Kensington Consultation Centre.

Pearce, W.B. (1994) *Interpersonal Communication.* London: Harper Collins.

Pearce, B. and Cronen, V. (1980) *Communication, Action and Meaning: The Creation of Social Realities.* New York: Praeger.

Penn, P. (1983) 'Circular questioning.' *Family Process 21,* 3.

Penn, P. (1985) 'Feedforward: Future questions, future maps.' *Family process 24,* 3, 299–310.

Roper-Hall, A. (1993) 'Developing family therapy services with older adults.' In J. Carpenter and A. Treacher (eds) *Using Family Therapy in the 90s.* Oxford: Blackwell Publications.

Scaife, J. (1993) From Hierarchy to Heterarchy. Unpublished Dissertation University of Birmingham/Charles Burns Clinic Diploma in Systemic Therapy.

Selvini Palazzoli, M., Boscolo, L., Cecchin, G. and Prata, G. (1978) 'A ritualised prescription: Odd days and even days.' *Journal of Marriage and Family Counselling 3,* 3–9.

Selvini Palazolli, M, Boscolo, L, Cecchin, G, and Prata, G. (1980) 'Hypothesizing – circularity – neutrality: Three guidelines for the conductor of the session.' *Family process 19,* 3–12.

Shotter (1994) 'Becoming someone: Identity and belonging.' In N. Coupland and Nussbaum *Discourse and Lifespan Identity.* London: Sage Publications.

Shotter, J. (1993) *Conversational Realities.* London: Sage Publications.

Tomm, K. (1987a) 'Interventive interviewing: Part 1: Strategizing as a fourth guideline for the therapist.' *Family Process 26,* 3–13.

Tomm, K. (1987b) 'Interventive interviewing: Part II: Reflexive questioning as a means to enable self healing.' *Family Process 26,* 167–183.

Tomm, K. (1988) 'Interventive interviewing: Part III: Intending to ask lineal, circular, strategic or reflexive questions.' *Family Process 27,* 1–15.

Varela, F.J. (1989) 'Reflections on the circulation of concepts between a biology of cognition and systemic family therapy.' *Family Process 28,* 1.

von Foester, H. (1981) 'On constructing a reality.' Republished in *Observing Systems.* Seaside, CA: Intersystems Publications.

von Glaserfeld: (1989) 'On the difficulty of changing a way of thinking.' *The Irish Journal of Psychology.* Special Edition.

Wittgenstein, L. (1953) *Philosophical Investigations.* Oxford: Basil Blackwell.

CHAPTER 11

Family Therapy and Ethnic Minorities

Annie Lau

Introduction

Family therapists from a Western European ethno-cultural background working with ethnic minority families need to pay attention to the tensions in the interface between them and their client families. An understanding and respect for the cultural and religious differences between them and their client families will help therapists to gain credibility, and use culturally determined materials in a way that will enhance the family's problem-solving skills, and mobilize strengths derived from traditional values and practices.

Family Therapy Assumptions

Family therapists are trained to regard the family unit as the primary focus for assessment and interventions. Behavioural or emotional disturbance in a family member is regarded as symptomatic of family disturbance. All family therapy schools have a basic grounding in family systems theory, which informs both theory and practice. Thus one would look for stress-related changes in the family system in order to understand the causes that led to the precipitation of distress, or disease, in a particular family member. Similarly, for example, it would be through exploration of family system characteristics, for example belief systems, role attributions, subsystem alliances, boundaries, authority, that one understands why the family appears to be stuck in a series of maladaptive problem-solving sequences and end up perpetuating and maintaining the identified patient in a sick or disabled role.

Different family therapy schools would emphasize different aspects of family system in both assessment and intervention. Structural family therapists work in the here and now, use observations of family interactions as a primary means of gathering information about the family, and intervene through empowering in the present by guiding the family through the change process. An example would be Minuchin's work on unbalancing the system by taking the family past their usual points of lack of problem resolution; he directly challenges parental perceptions of the patient that have paralyzed parental authority and goes for more effective problem-solving in the present.

Both Strategic and Systemic schools work on underlying rules and belief systems that have led to family paralysis and ineffective functioning. Circular questioning, developed by the Milan School, elucidates differences in perception and understanding by various family members, and the therapist tries to maintain a position of therapeutic neutrality. Strategic family therapists work on the power of the belief system, sometimes by the use of paradoxical interventions. Brief solution-focused approaches regard the problem as an attempted solution gone wrong; the therapist tries to reframe the problem with the family in order to mobilize potential for change.

All the schools are interested in life-cycle issues and developmental tasks, also in stresses that arise from crises in the family life-cycle. An understanding of family history, myths, and intergenerational patterns is of particular importance to therapists influenced by psychodynamic considerations. In recent years there has been considerable critique of family systems theory for not taking into account disparities of power in the family system, for example child abuse, domestic violence. Gender differences and access to power mean men and women cannot be regarded as having equal weight in their contributions to, say, wife-battering. Feminist writers have stressed that the experiences of men and women are different and that this needs to be taken on board in the process of devising strategies for working with the family.

In a similar vein I suggest that family therapy theory and practice need to be modified in working with ethnic minority families. Existing practice tends to be Eurocentric, based on Western European norms and values, which in turn inform practice and research.

Bridging the Gulf; Acknowledging and Working with Difference Culture

A working definition of culture has been offered by Leighton (1981) as follows:

> Culture consists in the knowledge, values, perceptions and practices that are
>
> (1) shared among the members of a given society
>
> (2) passed on from one generation to the next. (pp.522–529)

The components of a culture are interrelated in such a way as to constitute a whole that governs the functioning of the pertinent society. Culture directs the behaviour of individuals within the group, enabling the group to survive.

In cross-cultural family work we need to address the areas of tension in the interface between the therapist and the family from a different ethno-cultural and racial background. These will be;

- differences in race
- differences in symbolic and belief systems

- differences in family structure and organisation
- differences in language and communication.

Race

Here one needs to consider both conscious and unconscious racial attitudes, also the fact that different racial tensions exist between different racial groups. For example, the historical experience of slavery has led to attitudes based on the master/slave dynamic in the tensions between American whites and blacks. Over generations this has led to a lowering of self-esteem in vulnerable clinical populations, with the influence of negative racial stereotypes perpetuating feelings of learned helplessness and despair. It is important that this paradigm, based on the Afro-Carribean experience, not be applied indiscriminately to all non-white groups, for example Chinese and Vietnamese. So, for example, just because black or mixed race children in care will often feel ashamed of being black as this is associated with negative stereotypes, it does not follow that a Chinese, Indian or West African child will have the same psychological difficulties with regard to racial awareness, or even define himself or herself as 'black'. Power disparities between the therapist and the client family may, however, need to be addressed early on in the session.

Differences in Symbolic and Belief Systems

The cultural and religious traditions of a group organize the perception of experience, give shape and form to myths and beliefs, and determine the limits of appropriate behaviour and family roles. The symbolic belief system of the group also provides explanations of health and illness, definitions of normality and deviance, also guidelines for how to be acceptably deviant within a recognized pattern (Lau 1990).

Value orientations that are culturally determined organize the individual's view of the proper relationship between self and context. Differences in basic assumptions between the Western and Eastern views of self (Lin 1986; Rao 1986) are as follows: the Western view emphasizes independence, self-sufficiency, assertiveness and competition, clear and direct verbal communication, while the Eastern view emphasizes interdependence, harmony and cooperation in relationships, with more emphasis on non-verbal and indirect communication through the use of shared symbols.

Embedded in the system of cultural meanings for traditional societies is the central role of religious beliefs. Family therapy and the understanding of family systems have developed largely in an a religious, secular context, with the erosion of the authority of the Church in contemporary Western society. In religious communities, the authority of religious teaching cannot be discounted by the family therapist. For example, adherence to the principles of the Halacha is a central tenet of individual and family life for the Orthodox Jewish communities, and the Rabbi wields considerable personal and community authority. Similar powers are invested in the Imam by Muslim communities.

Family Structure and Organisation

Value orientations determine structural relationships; hence family organization following the ideal of the pre-eminence of the group would be along extended family lines, with a primary emphasis on connectedness. For example, in the traditional Chinese family an important organizing principle is filial piety, where loyalties to parents take precedence over loyalties to spouse and children.

Families will need to be located along a continuum between the traditional, hierarchical family with adherence to extended family values and the Western, contemporary, egalitarian family. In the non-Western European family there are important differences in the construction of 'family' as a concept and the role of the individual within the family. The importance given to interdependence and the need to preserve harmonious family relationships has given rise to structures that do not conform to Western European norms, for example extended family groups within the same household. Life-cycle transitions are managed in the context of different rules with regard to authority, continuity and interdependence. In the traditional Asian or Oriental family, relationships are hierachical between the sexes as well as between the generations. Authority is invested in grandparents or the most senior male members; elder siblings have authority over younger siblings, and responsibility for their welfare. The presence of the aged provides continuity and a link between the generations. Where kinship systems are highly structured, kinship terms delineate the individual's place in the family, including duties and expected obligations, within a system of mutual dependence. Where religion is an important organizing factor, as in Islam, strict religious guidelines may exist for sex-role behaviour including the ideal of segregation of the sexes, particularly after puberty.

Differences in Ideas of Individual and Family Competence

Current definitions of family competence used in research into family functioning, for example the Timberlawn study of working class black families in America (Lewis and Looney 1983), are based on nuclear family norms. They do not include, for example, the concept of a network of reciprocal obligations characteristic of ethnic groups with highly structured kinship systems (Lau 1988). It is important to clarify ethnocultural differences in competence for individuals throughout the life-cycle, as this has implications for expected stage-specific individual and family tasks.

Preparation for Parenting

As part of learning about adult roles, the adolescent growing up in a traditional extended family in which three generations are present is exposed to childrearing practices and learns from examples around her, as well as from 'supervised practice' in helping with the upbringing of younger siblings and cousins. Parenting does not come as a nasty shock. Rather it is an expected and a welcome event, for which her mother will have prepared her. In contrast, in the industrialized West, parenting may be experienced as an interruption, or a threat to a comfortable life-style, rather than a raison d'etre.

Producing a child, especially a male child, still signifies security for many a young wife in an arranged marriage, and an entry into full social status of the parental couple. In the traditional family the pregnant young wife will also be surrounded by a host of her female kinfolk whose task is to ensure that things go well and that, where necessary, the expectant mother can be relieved of tiring domestic responsibilities.

Infancy and Early Childhood

Given the importance of inter-dependence and family connectedness as a goal for the socialization of the young, it should not be surprising that patterns of childrearing in traditional extended families would be different. The child from a traditional Asian or Vietnamese family could be sleeping with mother or grandmother for many years (Bassa 1978). Indeed co-sleeping arrangements may be preferred in these families even though there may be adequate space for individual bedrooms. Parenting may be shared, and this provides for the young child a wider variety of parental figures, and an increased range of models for age and sex role identifications. Childhood stories, often with religious underpinnings, stress the importance of family, and reinforce family interdependence (Lau 1995). The child learns the overriding importance of being dependable, of being loyal. Through regular participation in family rituals such as meals, outings, festivals, religious events, the child learns its place in the kinship system and the rules governing relationships and expected behaviour. For example, in a well functioning extended family in the Far East, the young child will have grown up noticing that respect for the grandparents will be shown not only by terms of address, but also by the fact that one often waits for the grandparents to be seated before the meal begins, and that as the elders they have an assumed right to the choicest bits of food.

Middle Childhood

The child starting school is taught to accord the teacher the same respect due to its parents, and that good behaviour in school will reflect well on the family name. An older sibling will be expected to take responsibility for a younger sibling, or to contribute to the family welfare by helping in the shop on the weekends. It will be a source of pride to 'so behave that your parents will be proud of you'. Within the family boundary, the child will also learn the importance of manoeuvres for diffusing tension in the family. Through example, the child learns that it is normal and healthy to regard the wider family as an important emotional resource; a temporary refuge from one's angry parents, for example, or a place where one can practice strategies for using on one's parents. Also worries can be shared with a favourite aunt or uncle if one's parents are for any reason emotionally unavailable at the time.

Adolescence

The competent adolescent from a traditional, non-Western European extended family background is one who will have been prepared to meet his/her obligations to the family, which often include the obligation to look after one's parents and younger siblings. Within the family he/she will have been socialized to know the importance of being dependable, and to be expected to have a behavioural repertoire which includes respectful behaviour to one's elders, and strategies for tension diffusion and conflict avoidance within the immediate and wider family. These skills prepare the young person for adult roles within a value orientation that stresses the importance of maintaining the integrity of the family group. Other issues to do with individuation and separation, as well as distance regulation, will be negotiated differently. Preparation for leaving home is an important difference for adolescents from different ethnocultural groups (Lau 1990).

Marriage

Marriage in traditional families also raises differences in stage-specific family tasks. Where arranged marriage is an expected event in the family life-cycle, the wider family has to provide a facilitating environment for stabilizing and nurturing the couple relationship, particularly in the first year of marriage. There are also gender differences in the levels of adjustment required of the individuals concerned. The new wife moving into a joint household must invest emotionally in the relationship with her mother-in-law and sisters-in-law, and work out power relations within the female network. Competence in these tasks is vital towards ensuring her survival in the new family.

Case 1

A young family presented with feeding difficulties in the young child of six months. This was an Asian family where the mother-in-law lived in the same household as the young couple. Exploration revealed that there was disagreement between the wife and her mother-in-law on feeding routines and weaning practices, arising from different family traditions. The power struggle between the two women had got to the point where the child was becoming distressed and confused, particularly as the young wife was working on a part-time basis, and mother-in-law was involved with childcare.

Case 2

A mixed-race adolescent girl presented with extreme behavioural disturbance, including wrist-slashing and suicidal behaviour. The background history was one of poor relationships with her English mother ever since the family moved to Hong Kong to stay with her Chinese father's extended family. According to the mother, her Chinese in-laws forced her to accept a situation in which she and her husband had to leave the children in Hong Kong with the grandparents, while the couple went back to England to carry on the family business. Each time she saw her daughter again, on a brief visit to Hong Kong, the mother felt an increasing gulf between her and her daughter. It was difficult to relate to her, as the child would speak Chinese and very little English. As a result of mother-in-law's sudden illness and death, the child had to return to England. At this point she had been in a Chinese-speaking environment from age two to eight. Mother started shouting at the girl in order to 'get her to understand'. The child turned to her Chinese father for comfort and protection, and the two of them would speak to each other in Chinese. This had the effect of making mother feel increasingly excluded. In addition, the parental relationship was undergoing severe strain; the English wife wanted more physical demonstrativeness, she said, which her husband would not provide. In fact she found it strange that her Chinese in-laws did not touch and hug the way her own family did. The child ended up being the casualty of the conflicts in the parental marriage, as well as the inability of the family system to integrate the foreign daughter-in-law.

Afro-Carribean Family Structure

The Afro-Carribean extended family functions by different rules compared to the extended families of Asia and Africa. Functional relationships are not necessarily defined by formal kinship (Lau 1990; Littlewood and Lipsedge 1982). Contemporary studies of the American black family find a heterogeneity of structure and function. Particular strengths have included role adaptability, strong kinship bonds, a strong religious orientation and church affiliation, and strong work and achievement orientation (Hill 1972). Extended family values are an important element in the family assessment. Traditionally the single parent mother would have depended on male relatives in her own family to provide appropriate male models and authority for her sons. Where the family attends church, religious authority wielded by church elders has been an important source of family support.

Language and Communication

Proper assessment of family needs, vulnerabilities and strengths is difficult where language presents a barrier to communication. If an interpreter is used, he/she needs to be familiar with the therapist's theoretical and conceptual base, otherwise important information may be screened out. In my experience, one can gain considerable information through the use of an interpreter, especially where the techniques used involve the therapist asking questions of various family members in order to elucidate differences. Once family transactions (interactions between family members) start to occur, however, it is impossible to slow the action down in order to intervene. In these situations the therapist is unable to gain direct access to information in a family assessment situation, as immediate feedback becomes impossible.

Communicational Modes

There may also be differences in expected communication modes. The Western trained therapist's expectation of clear, direct verbal communication is often at variance with cultural rules where direct communication and confrontation are avoided because this may lead to loss of face within the family group (McGoldrick 1982). In the East, a well-known ideal of maturity is the capacity on the part of the individual to tolerate psychic pain and discomfort without 'inflicting' his/her pain onto the environment. This means that qualities like patience and endurance are highly valued, as is silence, contemplation and introspection. Children are praised for 'showing understanding', anticipating the needs of significant others and taking initiative. Thus a child is more praiseworthy if he offers tea to a parent on the parent's return from work, without being told to do so. My own mother used to say, 'Empty vessels make the most noise'. Thus a child who asks too many questions may well be asked to be quiet and to try and work out some answers by himself, after which he may then check out the logic of this reasoning with the adult. Western therapists unused to these concepts may well regard these processes as dysfunctional; 'Family members show withdrawal and a lack of communication between them'.

Therapeutic Goals

Therapeutic goals may differ between the therapist and the family. The preferred direction of change for families from traditional backgrounds will be in the direction of integration of the family group, rather than towards differentiation and increasing separation of the individual from his/her family (Tamura and Lau 1992). This has potential for conflict for therapists and their supervisors from a different value orientation. Acceptance of these differences in norms implies the use of different therapeutic strategies, with different aims; for example, diffusing and containing conflict rather than amplifying it. Thus a therapist who was working within cultural rules might put more energy into exploring possible areas of agreement, and finding the middle ground. The reader is encouraged to refer to the paper by Tamura and Lau for case examples where differences in perception and cultural orientation emerged between the therapist, of Japanese ethnic origin, and a Western European supervisory team.

Working with Families with Adolescents

The ethnic family with an adolescent member whose views on autonomy conflict with family norms poses by far one of the most challenging dilemmas for the Western therapist. A common response is to 'rescue' the young person, often a girl, from a family that is 'stifling' her. I do not dispute that sometimes it may well be necessary to remove the girl from her family, at least temporarily, especially if there is a serious risk of physical abuse. What often comes into play which prematurely punctuates discussion around possible outcomes, however, are beliefs held by Western workers about issues like arranged marriages (e.g. they are evil and oppressive patriachal practices) or the role of the adolescent in the family. This often includes the idea that all young people should leave home and set up independent living as soon as possible, or, that a young woman needs to be able to make her own choices about sexual partners from around the age of 16. This ignores the psychic reality of the young person, who will have tried to maintain a dual identity in which she maintained a balance between the demands of the school environment and home. I believe one should attempt as far as possible to open up all possibilities for negotiation and airing of differences. This needs to be handled in an atmosphere in which levels of hostility and criticism are managed and kept within tolerable limits. One needs to recognize that, in the majority of cases, it will be in the client's long-term interests to be enabled to stay within the family and ethnic community.

Insider Therapists

A therapist from a similar ethno-cultural background may well find it easier to engage the family, also be more prepared to engage the cultural material in a way that facilitates therapeutic change. Weiselberg describes work with Ortho-dox Jewish families in which the therapist was able to engage the family in trading religious metaphors (Weiselberg 1992). Similarly, Lau has described work with a Chinese family using a cultural ritual that facilitated commitment to change (Lau 1988).

Working with Parents

All parents, whatever their ethnic background, have similar expectations of what constitute the results of successful parenting. Indeed, in an address to the National Children's Bureau conference on 'Confident Parents, Confident Children' in 1993, Virginia Bottomley, the Secretary of State for Health, said all parents expected their children to grow up to be happy, healthy, literate, confident and law-abiding. The difference, however, with working cross-culturally, is that these categories are subject to definitions within the boundaries allowed by the ethno-cultural group. Bassa (1978), in making observations on Indian child rearing practices and identity formation, says, 'Self-fulfilment (ie happiness) is thus to be sought for and found within the family, not in a frantic search for love outside it' (pp.333–343). For the traditional Muslim family, literacy will include being able to read the Koran as well as conforming to the requirements of the National Curriculum. Similarly, the traditional Chinese parent will expect his/her child to be able to read and write in Chinese. Health may also be defined differently, with different explanatory models, as in the Ayurvedic traditions of India and the classical medical traditions of China. For example a Chinese mother, brought up traditionally in Hong Kong, found it difficult to accept the advice of her health visitor not to give her infant barley water when it was colicky. Her family traditions would suggest that barley water would serve to restore the yin-yang imbalance that ailed the baby. This was however in conflict with the idea, deriving from Western medicine, that barley water might introduce another allergen into the baby's diet, on the assumption that the colic was of allergic origin.

Family Ritual Maintenance

I have found it extremely useful to inquire about the levels of ritualization in ethnic minority families. Family rituals provide support, continuity with family, cultural and religious tradition, and affirm membership for participants. Life-cycle rituals mark and celebrate movement of the individual from one stage of his/her life cycle to another. Where this is a publicly celebrated event, like a naming ceremony for an infant, or the coming of age of an adolescent, for example Barmitzvah, the family are also making a public statement to the community. For Jewish parents, it is a declaration that somehow they have succeeded in holding together fragments for the next generation. They have also discharged their duty of responsibility for their child's religious education.

Family rituals, whether religious or secular, provide opportunities for family members to meet on a regular basis and to communicate. The pattern and regularity is important. Do the family eat together, watch TV together, go out together? Is there a central family dinner time, are there holiday celebration rituals? Has the impact of immigration and the loss of supportive networks led to a loss of cultural rituals, for example celebration of Chinese New Year? All these factors may have bearing on the meaning and significance to the family of the problem that has precipitated the crisis leading to referral.

Conflicts in Mixed Marriages

Intergenerational conflict in families with a mixed racial/cultural background may be compounded by the child's sense of confusion regarding racial or ethnic identity. Where the parental sub-system has a poorly maintained boundary, with ineffective emotional containment, the child or young person's frustrations may give rise to a wide range of deviant behavioural disturbances. There may be parental conflict over which family cultural traditions, rituals, values and loyalties are more important; cultural differences in the expected roles of spouses, including kinship obligations, may not have been resolved. The child or young person may end up being triangulated in the parental conflict, or expected to make up for the losses incurred by the parent of ethnic origin in the process of immigration. The young person will end up being unable to resolve the racial diversity in his/her background; it becomes a source of adversity instead of strength.

Refugee Families

Families with a refugee background will need to be handled with particular understanding for the traumatic stresses that have been part of the family's recent experience, and allowances made for apparently uncooperative behaviour. Adults will to varying extents carry features of Post Traumatic Stress Disorder, particularly if they have been raped or tortured. My own experience suggests that one can expect a long engagement process, as often these families find it difficult to trust authority and establishment figures, given their previous highly traumatic experiences. Bereft of personal networks, crises in daily living, for example inability to heed the final written demand for payment, may lead to the supply of electricity being cut off. Health Visitors often report being frustrated as people never seem to be home when they call. It is unfortunately all too common that as soon as a refugee family is housed in this country, that supports are withdrawn and services that may make a difference to the family's adjustment, for example counselling, are not offered. The adults' unresolved losses, for example personal networks and family, social and financial status, and sense of helplessness and an inability to take control over their own affairs, often leads to a depressive withdrawal from the children and their psychological needs. Where language is a problem, and this is often the case, it means the parents are inadequately involved with their children's school life. They are then unable to support their children's needs for integration with an appropriate peer group, which would enhance a sense of belonging.

Case 3

An eight-year-old girl from a French speaking refugee family from Zaire was referred from the GP for 'bizarre behaviour' including apparent auditory hallucinations, lack of concentration and disruptive behaviour in the classroom. She was also described as having learning difficulties, and for the past year had received fairly intensive remedial help for which she had responded well; the school said she was beginning to acquire literacy skills. She was the eldest of four children. The family had enjoyed a comfortable middle-class life back home. The father spoke good English and was a political refugee, now attempting to retrain at a local community college. The mother was extremely isolated. She spoke little English, despite attending English classes. She missed the life back home and had not really wanted to come. They had left several children behind with the grandparents. The identified patient was readily able to tell us that she thought her mother was sad and unhappy at having to be in this country, and particularly missed the other children, as well her extended family. The process of leaving had been precipitous and extremely dramatic, with no time for proper leavetaking. We felt the child's behavioural disturbance was a predictable response to the family's sense of loss of practically everything they had taken for granted back home; a good life, adequate accommodation, status and a good job, supportive social networks.

The mother felt abandoned by her husband who was out most of the time at college and also cultivating social networks from which she was excluded. She was reluctant to encourage her children to bring friends home, out of a sense of insecurity and a fear that things may go out of control. She wanted her oldest daughter to demonstrate a capacity for helping her with housework and childcare, and felt ignored and rejected by her. In turn, a lot of her frustrations were vented on her daughter, who felt more was expected of her than her same age peers at school.

The team working with the family consisted of a psychiatrist and a psychiatric social worker. In working with this family we found we had to engage individual members of the family by ensuring that each one had space to articulate their separate concerns and views. This was particularly important for the parents. We also had to work through a French speaking interpreter, and it was fortunate that both the therapists spoke some French, as this meant we could follow the dialogue between the mother and the interpreter (a French teacher at the school the children attended) to some extent.

Guidelines for Family Assessment

While assessing families it would be useful to keep following questions in mind;

(1) What belief systems and values (including religion) influence role expectations, define and set limits of appropriate behaviour?

(2) What are the structures relevant to authority and decision-making in the family? Are there formal kinship patterns? What key relationships have important supportive and homeostatic functions? What is the relevant family network to be worked with?

(3) What are the stage-specific developmental tasks at different life-cycle stages for this family? How does this family negotiate life-cycle transitions, continuities and discontinuities with the past and present? What are traditional solutions and mechanisms used for conflict resolution and to what extent does the family use them?

(4) How is the living unit organized to enable essential tasks to be performed?

(5) What activities, including family rituals of ethnocultural and religious origin, maintain and support structural relationships? What traditional networks supported and enabled traditional family tasks to be performed? Which of these networks or rituals have been lost?

(6) What are significant stresses and losses arising from the family's own experience, from the environment of origin, or from adaptation to host country? What racial or cultural factors confer advantage or disadvantage in the host culture?

(7) The clinical hypothesis must take into account the meaning and function of the disturbance for the family, the cultural group, and the wider community.

(8) Therapeutic interventions must engage the authority structure in the family and be congruent with the family's world view. For example, it is important to enable the identified client and his/her family to work out the right balance of separation /attachment consistent with family and societal norms. It is often helpful to reframe the problem within a developmental context, in order to make it more manageable.

Existing therapeutic techniques and methods can be successfully used in work with ethnic minority families, providing the therapist is sensitive to the importance of respecting cultural rules and prepared to modify his/her clinical approach. This may mean more flexibility in working with sub-systems, for example the group of sisters-in-law, rather than with the whole family. Ethnic minority families respond more readily to therapists who are directive and assertive (Yung 1984; Rao 1986; Tseng 1975; Tamura and Lau 1992) as this conforms to traditional expectations of the learning process. Structural family therapy with its emphasis on problem solving in the present has been described as highly successful with Chinese families in the USA (Yung 1984), where the therapist works on modifying communication patterns while supportive of parents' traditional beliefs. Gestalt-type work and sculpting was described by Lau (1988) including the use of metaphors and family rituals (Levick, Jalali and Strauss 1981; Scheff 1979; Pesechkian 1986). Wolin and Bennett (1984) link the importance of maintenance of family ritual to the continuity of family heritage. All these strategies attempt to mobilize strengths and assert competencies within an ethnocultural context.

References

Bassa, D.M. (1978) 'From the traditional to the modern; Some observations on changes in Indian child-rearing and parental attitudes, with special reference to identity formation.' In E.J. Anthony and C. Chiland (eds) *The Child in his Family – Children and Parents in a Changing World.* New York: J. Wiley.

Cohen, N. (1982) 'Same or different? A problem of identity in cross cultural marriages.' *Journal of Family Therapy 4*, 177–99.

Henriques, F. (1949) 'West Indian family organisation.' *American Journal of Sociology 55*, 30–7.

Hill, R. (1972) *The Strengths of Black Families.* New York: Emerson-Hall.

Lau, A. (1988) 'Family therapy and ethnic minorities.' In E. Street and W. Dryden (eds) *Family Therapy in Britain.* Buckingham: Open University Press.

Lau, A. (1990) 'Psychological problems in adolescents from ethnic minorities.' *British Journal of Hospital Medicine 44*, 201–205.

Lau, A. (1995) 'Ethnocultural and religious issues.' In C. Burck and B. Speed (eds) *Gender Power and Relationships.* London: Routledge.

Leighton, A.H. (1981) 'Culture and psychiatry.' *Canadian Journal of Psychiatry 26*, 8, 522–529.

Levick, S.E., Jalali, B. and Strauss, J.S. (1981) 'Onions and tears; a mutidimensional analysis of a counter-ritual.' *Family Process 20*, 77–83.

Lewis, J.M. and Looney, J.G. (1983) *The Long Struggle: Well-Functioning Working-Class Black Families.* New York: Brunner-Mazel.

Lin, T.Y. (1986) 'Multiculturalism and Canadian psychiatry: opportunities and challenges.' *Canadian Journal of Psychiatry 31*, 681–90.

Littlewood, R. and Lipsedge, M. (1982) *Aliens and Alienists.* Harmondsworth: Penguin.

McGoldrick, M. (1982) 'Ethnicity and family therapy: An overview.' (pp 3–30). In M. McGoldrick, J.K. Pearce, and J. Giordano (eds) *Ethnicity and Family Therapy.* New York: Guilford Press.

Peseschkian, N. (1986) *Positive Family Therapy.* Berlin, Heidelberg: Springer-Verlag.

Rao, A.V. (1986) 'Indian and western psychiatry: a comparison.' In J.L. Cox (ed) *Transcultural Psychiatry.* London: Croom Helm.

Scheff, T.J. (1979) *Catharsis in Healing, Ritual and Drama.* Berkeley, CA: University of California Press.

Tamura, T. and Lau, A. (1992) 'Connectedness versus separateness: Applicability of family therapy to Japanese families.' *Family Process 31*, 319–340.

Tseng, W. (1975) 'The nature of somatic complaints among psychiatric patients; the Chinese case.' *Comprehensive Psychiatry 16*, 237–45.

Weiselberg, H. (1992) 'Family therapy and ultra-orthodox Jewish families: a structural approach.' *Journal of Family Therapy 14*, 305–330.

Wolin, S. and Bennett, L.A. (1984) 'Family rituals.' *Family Process 23*, 401–20.

Yung, M. (1984) 'Structural family therapy; its application to Chinese families.' *Family Process 23*, 365–74.

CHAPTER 12

Community and Youth Work with Asian Women and Girls

Radha Dwivedi

Background

Most of the women who migrated from the Indian subcontinent – India, Bangladesh and Pakistan – usually had to suffer long separations before they could join their husbands. They had to travel huge distances to the British High Commissions and then undergo rigorous and intensive interrogative interviews, much of which felt totally irrelevant and impertinent. On arrival in the UK their experiences of further interrogation by the immigration officials, humiliating medical examinations and some times even detentions and fear of deportation added to their distress. Asians who migrated here from East Africa came mainly from Uganda, because the Idie Amin government forced them to leave suddenly and they could not even bring their belongings or properties with them, and the whole experience was extremely emotionally traumatic.

On arrival here the adjustment to the new environment is not very easy. Not only is the weather astonishingly different, but so are the dress code, social and welfare structure, health service provisions, cultural values and so on. These and many other issues can easily become very stressful. Many are shocked by some of the things they see here. Even the sight of animal carcasses hanging in butcher's shops can be extremely shocking and unbelievable for many who have recently arrived.

For many women the language barrier can be a formidable obstacle. Some may be able to read or write English but not able to speak. They have always had a poor grasp of English, but not only do they find it difficult to talk to the British residents, but also to the other Asians settled from abroad. These may be equally difficult to talk to because of the large variety of languages spoken within the Indian subcontinent. They may not be able to approach or find anyone with whom they could share or express their feelings and difficulties. There are therefore immense problems in dealing with official bodies such as the social security, social services, police, school and so on. They may not even be aware of such agencies or the advice bureaus that could offer them support. Becoming aware of opportunities for training or jobs and applying for such things are therefore very difficult tasks.

Similarly, a number of other things in day to day life such as public transport, road crossings and traffic, buying clothes, food or even ordering milk can be very different and unfamiliar. Shopping can be equally difficult in the beginning as one may not know where to go to buy the desired items. One may not think of a post office in a grocery store. Many have language barriers too and cannot read the names of items or ask for them in English. They may get confused by the appearance of things. For example, shoes for men and for women may sometimes seem very similar and they may purchase the wrong type through being too shy to ask. Most shops look alike and finding what they are looking for may be a very daunting process. Returning goods is even harder as this involves some understanding of the system and rituals involved in such transactions.

Even little things like what saris to wear for different occasions can become problematic. In their previous environments these decisions were straightforward, but those social cues are no longer available or applicable here. The result is that some can be overdressed for the occasion, such as visiting their doctor wearing an expensive silk sari along with all the jewellery. The disorientation they feel from not knowing what is and what is not acceptable or the 'done thing' can be very unsettling. This can also lead to being ridiculed by others.

Thus, the day to day activities which were in fact the high point of the day in their previous societies, now become difficult and burdensome in the UK. The shopping trip was a great social occasion, getting on a rickshaw and visiting the hustle and bustle of the market. The shopkeepers were well known to them and they often went in groups and chatted. Such activities provided a nice relaxing change and a light relief from other demanding tasks. Here, the life and excitement in such an outing is usually missing and it becomes just another fearful and burdensome task. They are no longer able to have long chats with the milkmen, argue with the laundryladies, or haggle with the vegetable sellers. Such social interactions played a highly supportive role in women's emotional stability and its loss is a major contributory factor to their loneliness and isolation.

Another factor causing isolation here is their work environment. The job situation is such that Asians find it difficult to find jobs, let alone good jobs. The women with little or no skills sometimes find unskilled, repetitive types of jobs with poor working conditions and pay. Even women with University degrees from the Indian subcontinent are usually not recognized for their potential and fall into doing some menial jobs from lack of encouragement or opportunities for further training. The employers or bosses invariably put extra pressure on in these jobs demanding completion of even more work in the same time allowed. These women don't feel confident in standing up for their rights.

They often in fact have very little or no idea of their own rights and feel helpless and trapped. Sometimes these women work from home and this leads to further isolation and vulnerability.

In the Indian subcontinent where they lived before, the roles and responsibilities of men and women were very clearly differentiated. The housework was usually shared by all the women. They also knew what other work was or was not appropriate for them to undertake. For example, some women could fetch water from the well, feed and milk their goats, buffaloes or cows, sow seeds and so on. Some activities, for example, driving (especially tractors, vans, minibuses or rickshaws), digging or ploughing and policing were, however, seen as inappropriate, heavy and burdensome and were not undertaken by women. There was usually a good understanding between employer and employee to accommodate the needs of special circumstances that may arise such as pregnancy, illness, death of a relative and other life events. There was also a great deal of team approach to work. Women from the same household or neighbourhood in a village could approach a potential employer together for work such as planting rice in a group. Thus knowing each other so well gave them support and strength and this approach was further enthused by group singing. If disagreements arose, the quarrels were rarely suppressed, in fact, these were expressed immediately so that a resolution of conflicts could take place more openly and spontaneously.

In Britain, this isolation is further exacerbated by their husbands working unsociable shifts and over-time to maintain a living wage. Much of the housework and chores are then left for the wives, the burden being very substantial if they take on some employment themselves. These are rarely anything other than of the very lowly paid types already described. The pressures may be even worse if they are to look after aged parents in extended family situations.

Of immediate significance to their welfare is housing. If they are lucky enough to have a house of their own then more often than not it will be cold with faulty heating, draughty, in a poor state of repair and unkempt. Often families have to make do with rented accommodation with just one room. Here they cook, work, live and sleep in crowded conditions. They also have to answer to the landlord who may make excessive demands and take advantage of such helpless immigrants. Moving in with relatives or friends is very impractical as they are often themselves trying to cope with already crowded conditions. The waiting lists for council houses is high and availability is very low. Sometimes they are forced to stay in make-shift accommodation including Bed and Breakfast or cheap hotels. This is obviously stressful and has serious implications for their health and interpersonal relationships within the family. It also has serious effects on the quality of the children's education. Schooling may become haphazard and children find it difficult to do any work at home in such conditions.

It is true that not all Asians emigrating here undergo such hardships, but a significant proportion do. It seems that the immigrants from Bangladesh arriving here have experienced the maximum difficulties. They also have the greatest level of unemployment.

Another serious problem is the experience of racial harassment and abuse which leads to enormous suffering, isolation, hatred and discomfort felt by these families. They develop fear and anxiety through having to live in the environment that such attacks create. The families most affected include those just settled and widowed or single women. They live in constant fear of verbal and physical abuse and are afraid to let their children go out. There are numerous examples of such incidents including sealing doors from the outside and smashing windows with stones at night. Racist elements may try to beat up Asian children on the way home from school. In the area I work I have come across many examples of harassment. For example one incident involved the house of a Bengali family which was completely sealed with tape and all their rubbish scattered in the back garden. Another Punjabi family suffered for some time with stones being thrown through their windows. This turned out to be by a nine-year-old boy. They therefore find it very difficult to feel part of their new environment. They feel threatened and extremely isolated.

The dramatic difference in almost every aspect of their lives in comparison to what they were used to before and the loss of the supportive social network means that they find very little to hold on to and there is an intense feeling of insecurity. This is compounded by the lack of communication due to a very poor grasp of English and other Asian languages. Before, in their societies of origin, they took part in a variety of rituals, customs, traditions and celebrations, which were immensely helpful in dealing with their feelings and stress. For example, crying together was the most natural way between close friends and relatives to express sympathy or share each other's feelings. Usually a large number of people participated in celebrations of child birth, weddings, funerals and so on and shared various responsibilities for organizing these things. Such things are no longer possible in Britain because of the loss of the close links between the neighbours that existed in their societies of origin. Here it would appear very awkward and out of place if dozens of women got together and started to cry with someone recently bereaved.

When they lived in the Indian subcontinent the family included the whole of the extended family; uncles, aunts, parents, children and grandparents often living together in large and complex households. The women felt very secure and well supported and knew who to turn to if they had any problems. Before marriage the girl felt well protected. They received proper guidance as regards education, morality and behaviours appropriate for girls, expectations of roles and responsibilities in marriage, various domestic skills and so on. Old people were seen as experienced, wise, important and highly respected. They usually lived with their children and grandchildren in an atmosphere of care, warmth and affection for each other and of striving for harmony. The theme of familiarity extended to the village life as well because people living in a village knew each other extremely well. The relationships were very close, almost like an extended family. People learnt about the way various relationships should be formed. For example, the relationships between parents and their children, mother-in-law and daughter-in-law, younger ones and the old ones, students and teachers, and between the neighbours and village kinsmen and so on. These relationships were governed by well known rules which were learnt through observing others, and through parental guidance. Thus these codes of conduct became as if instinctive with a natural sense of what is right and what is wrong in a particular situation.

One of the additional worries for the Asian parents is about the fear that their children may reject their family values as regards education, marriage, interpersonal relationships, self-development and so on. As they themselves had a rather different upbringing which instilled rigorous moral standards, they begin to feel apprehensive about the possibility of their children not persevering with these traditional moral values. When the children's presentation, manners, attitudes, thoughts and ideas diverge markedly from traditional patterns and from what the parents perceive as culturally appropriate and correct, they may fear the loss of their close links with their children.

The children may feel that other children have more freedom such as about being out late and may think that their parents are being unfair or unkind. On the other hand, the parents may not have had any experience of childhood in this country and may not know what is safe and could be permissible. Their fears may also be fuelled by the stories of violence, kidnapping or road accidents as portrayed in the media. In their countries of origin they would have felt comfortable to allow children to go out to the market, see friends or attend festivals and so on because of the security of a close knit community and of knowing what they were likely to encounter. Here they are now very unsure.

Sometimes in desperation, some parents put pressure on their children to comply, but this may only make matters worse and the children may become more distant due to the lack of a close social network that could help them appreciate each others points of view and feelings, as might have happened in their previous societies. The so-called helping professionals may further strain the relationships in the name of teaching children independence or of 'rescuing' them. Family arguments can cause the home environment to deteriorate and this can become so stressful that the youngster may run away from home.

Community and Youthwork Principles

Social and community work with such a community requires the right attitude, if it is to be successful. A community or youth worker trying to help such a community needs to develop enough understanding, respect and commitment to the community. A thorough understanding of both the complex problems and their enormous cultural strength has to be the basis of the whole approach. Only through knowing how they feel and the traumas that they are going through and have suffered already, can the worker make a resolute effort to help. If a worker is simply going through the motions of running a community project, without a sincere commitment to the community and real people involved, the project is likely to fail, no matter how hard it is 'sold' or how many leaflets and other publicity materials are distributed. I have personally seen numerous examples of failed attempts at such community work. Although the workers may blame the community for their lack of cooperation, I feel that this is more likely to be due to the lack of sincerity and unskilful and uninformed approach of the worker involved.

In the beginning one has to get to know some individuals from the community, who are in need of support and help them as far as possible. This would help to establish the sincerity and the credentials of the worker. In community work actions speak louder than words. Because of auto-extension and the sense of curiosity in the community, the news of the worker's sincerity begins to spread around. Thus by interacting on a personal basis with individuals the workers have to expose themselves, their values and commitment to the community in order to build up a good working relationship with members of the community on a larger scale. Even in organizing group programmes it is essential to make personal contact with people, making them feel respected and valued for what they are. On the contrary I have known workers who have been arrogant in their approach. They have felt uncomfortable visiting peoples homes or mixing with the community. There is not only the need for a constantly supportive attitude but also great sensitivity to people's feelings and above all immense humility. If enough preparation and work with individuals in the community has not been accomplished the planned group programmes will be difficult to start or such groups are likely to break down.

In organizing group activities or programmes the worker initially needs to be personally available to see through all aspects of the group's activities, such as collecting members from their homes to the meeting point, personal contact out of hours and being present at every activity, function or outing. This is more difficult to keep up than it sounds as people can create many obstacles even in the face of the worker's very good intentions. In fact, these are testing times. One can fail by losing temper or patience under such pressures. Any inappropriate or noncooperative behaviour, instead of being reacted to with sanctions or telling off, has to be taken up in group discussions to explore various perceptions, points of view, underlying feelings and so on. This then becomes a social learning opportunity for individuals and worker alike.

When the members begin to develop trust in the worker they start to disclose their underlying feelings (such as of frustration, anger, hate and jealousy) as and when they arise in the group settings. Eventually their chronic and complex difficulties and also the reasons for their certain behaviours are shared in this supportive atmosphere. By being aware of the mood of the group in the context of their culture and language, the worker can begin to avoid potentially difficult situations by intervening at right time in a skilful way. If excessive or uncontrolled quarrelling or disputes break out without resolution, the members will see the worker as weak and incompetent. Loss of trust in the worker can easily lead to the collapse of the group.

As more and more problems, simple or complex, come to be shared, the strategies for solving these are evolved. Some would need active help from the worker, others for the mobilization of group resources. This can easily test the limits of the worker's capabilities and may include work outside the worker's understanding or competence. It is especially important to ensure that these particular problems are solved even if they require extra time and effort and gathering of external resources. This will further help the strengthening of trust. Some, however, may not express their desires or wishes but may still expect the worker to fulfil them regardless.

It is also essential to arrange opportunities for learning certain skills, and for outings, recreational events, festival celebrations, use of local leisure facilities and staging of group events. The idea may be to get them into activities such as swimming or learning sewing which they would enjoy but had been hesitant to get involved in before. In organizing such activities or lessons it is essential to make sure that the instructors or teachers are very skilled, competent and sensitive to the particular needs of the group. It is therefore crucial that these classes are very professionally led. This means, for example, a professional sewing teacher is employed and the proper equipment is used in the sewing classes, or that talks are given by professionals or experts who specialize in their fields.

Initially there may be a great deal of resistance but it is the enthusiasm of the worker that helps them to attend at least the first few sessions. Once they manage to get a taste of these few sessions and start to enjoy the activities and the opportunities gained by coming out of the house, they quickly become self-motivated. After the first few classes they become confident in the worker as they see the deeper benefits of the activities. This confidence helps the worker in establishing further trust. They also begin to see that it may be possible to start to break the vicious cycle of depression and isolation. As they begin to appreciate the benefits of such activities for social interaction they themselves start to put in their own efforts to make sure that they attend, such as making their own transport arrangements.

The effect of such activities, along with groupwork with its emphasis on interpersonal social education and counselling can be extremely profound on the entire community. The benefits of careful preparations for establishing the group, solving of individual problems with due care and other such interventions begin to spread throughout the community outside the group. The positive changes in individual's behaviours also have an impact on the relationships in the community and become examples for them. This leads to the recruitment of new members and the spread of self help activities. These developments can be enhanced by working outside the group environment in liaison with key community members to smooth the progress of change.

Groups for children follow similar principles. They are best started after the adult groups are established to allow the mothers to gain confidence and trust in the worker. When the adults have begun to trust the worker and feel safe with the worker's values and attitudes, they would then feel comfortable in allowing their children to join the groups organized by the worker. The content of the psycho-educational activities of such groups should again depend on the group's perceived needs. If such activities are not made interesting or adequately researched they will not be supported by the youngsters and will fail to continue. The worker should be careful to respect the parents' wishes and the cultural needs of the children and use the opportunities to explain the parents' traditional values, norms, and the parental behaviours. Similarly, it is essential to explore, understand and empathize with the youngsters' feelings, points of view, hurts, dilemma and so on.

Sometimes it is not obvious to the children that their parents, to whom the wisdom of their traditions has been passed on for many generations, are trying to do the same for the children's benefit. The children, because of the outside influences of the school, media and so on may not fully appreciate this, leading to conflicts between the children and their parents. Similarly, when a child does not adopt the traditional dress, food or hair style the parents may fear that their child has become alienated. Thus both children and their parents need help in understanding each other better and appreciating each other's difficulties. Parents need help in transmitting their culture to their children in a new environment like this, in a way that will be acceptable and understandable to the children.

The worker should also remember that the children do not have enough opportunities for going out and it is because of the fact that the parents have developed enough trust in the worker that the children are attending these group activities, with their recreational or educational opportunities. As it is a precious time, every effort should be made to use the time as constructively and enjoyably as possible.

Community and Youth Work: An Example

When I did not succeed in obtaining a paid job here for several years, although I had a post graduate qualification (MA) from one of the best Indian universities, I started to do some unpaid voluntary sessions to teach English as a second language to Asians in a small town. At the end of these sessions the women gradually began to approach me with some of their practical problems. For example, someone's child was being racially abused at school or someone had received a letter from the school regarding a child's irregular attendance, poor home work or school dress. They wanted me to accompany them to the school, which I did. Someone had difficulty with getting permission for their close relative (such as a son's wife) to come to the country and I helped them contact the appropriate helping agency.

Seema, a Punjabi woman, was extremely worried about her 11-year-old young child, Reeta. Reeta, who was a very withdrawn and quiet child, did not mix with other children. Reeta's older brother had already been taken into care and Seema was very angry with and suspicious of the so-called helping agencies. I gave her a listening ear. Similarly, women needed my help in dealing with their bank, social security office, arranging appointments with their doctors, approaching the Racial Equality Officer, clarifying problems with their gas, electricity and so on. Many had sleepless nights, others suffered from various aches and pains. Someone didn't get enough house-keeping money from her husband, someone's husband was very violent, someone's child was being refused school dinner and so on. Most of these were single women. Those who were married also had a number of difficulties. Their minds were too preoccupied with such difficulties to be able to concentrate with English lessons. I myself had plenty of time, so I began to spend a couple of hours listening to the difficulties, giving whatever advice I could offer and afterwards took them to the relevant agencies and helped them in their dealings with these agencies.

I then decided to organize a social group for these ladies and approached the social services for help. The local social services department, too, were aware of the problem and had already made several unsuccessful attempts to organize such a group. Their previous attempts had failed because they concentrated more on gathering the women together to form a big crowd than on genuinely helping them with their difficulties. The educational activities that they had organized were rather insensitive to the women's actual needs and abilities. For example, a sewing teacher used numerous handouts that the women could not read. Having personally known many of these women and their difficulties, I was more in touch with their needs, their strength, their abilities and their suffering.

With the help of the local social services department, I managed to organize a group for the women. These included both Hindus and Muslims, young and old, women who had originated from Bangladesh, Punjab, Pakistan, Gujarat or East Africa. The group activities began to take place in the local social services accommodation, so that the women would come in contact with the social workers to provide opportunities for mutual familiarity and learning from each other. I made sure that there was enough space and comfortable sitting arrangements, facilities for refreshments and transport provided by the department. I personally looked after them with a lot of affection, humour, regard and respect.

In the beginning I picked them up from their homes but they were seldom ready when I went to their houses to pick them up. In fact, they would wait for me to arrive at their house before they would start to get ready. Later I learnt that they did not actually believe that I would really turn up. They had had so many disappointments in their lives that they had become so sensitive. During the group discussions I began to discuss these issues. Then we also talked about the time that could be saved if people were ready. To my delight, it really began to happen. Then they began to wait in small groups and even to telephone our receptionist to apologise if they could not attend, so that we didn't make any wasted journeys. Similarly, they began not to mind being collected by someone else and at times made their own way.

The same pattern of response was reflected in a number of other areas while working with this group. Initially, I personally made tea and snacks and offered to each one of them treating each person as the most respected guest. Gradually we turned this into a learning and teaching exercise about different regional dishes. Someone would teach others how to cook a certain dish. They all began to be involved with great curiosity and enjoyment and most of the tasks related to cooking, serving, washing up, shopping and so on began to be shared. Similarly, people began to try out different regional songs and even dance, humour and jokes. Although they had different mother tongues such as Gujarati, Bengali, Punjabi, Hindi and Urdu, we began to manage somehow through Hindi/Urdu as a link language. This became the high time of their week, providing the enjoyment they had so sadly been missing from their lives before.

In the beginning, whenever I organized any skill-based educational activities (e.g. sewing, swimming and so on) I met with a great deal of resistance. But I made sure that the teacher was professionally skilled and qualified and that I fully prepared and supported the teacher in the lessons. Soon the women began to enjoy learning, also because the social atmosphere that had already been created was maintained in the new environment as well.

I organized day trips to places, lectures by visiting speakers on relevant topics such as health issues, benefits, police and so on. We began to visit some of these agencies together and, in fact, we even enjoyed a week's holiday together. They began to help each other more, for example, looking after someone's child, pushing a disabled person's wheel chair, taking care of an elderly person and so on. A number of small subgroups across age, language or religions began to form. They began to pick up a bit of English, a lot of confidence in approaching agencies and great deal of understanding about so many other things. Things like not asking the minibus driver to turn or to stop immediately without due notice had to be learnt on these trips. Even little achievements were fully acknowledged like managing to make or cancel an appointment with their doctor or policewoman entirely by themselves with the use of broken English.

Most important, they began to tolerate each other's idiosyncracies, moods, manners, customs and so on. They began to notice and support each other, share their pain with and comfort each other. Either individually or in the group setting, they began to discuss a number of their deep rooted difficulties.

Uma, a 28-year-old single depressed young mother with a young child had also been attending this group. I knew her from my English as a second language classes. She had had a violent husband with a drinking problem who deserted her when she became pregnant. She had grown up in India and had no other support here. She went to the Women's Refuge and finally found a council house to live but felt extremely hurt, bitter, isolated and depressed. She had frequently visited the surgery with various aches and pains and fears of all sorts of infections. She was frequently suicidal. However, through attending the sewing classes that I organized for the group, she turned out to be very skilled in sewing. She had never touched a sewing machine before but she put in a great deal of effort in learning it. She began to make dresses for her child and for herself, in fact, very professionally. Before she would have been seen as rather unkempt and neglected and was unnoticed by other community members, however now, people began to take a great deal of notice of her and of her tailoring talent. The sewing teacher was also very pleased with her. Her hair style changed and she began to look really smart. Similarly, when I organized swimming classes, she became equally interested.

Uma began to share with the group her intimate feelings, about her relationship with her child, her confidence or lack of it before, her anger and her life, her new found pride in her sewing skills and so on. Her relationship with and her handling of her child was now unbelievably better. She at times would still get bouts of depression but now realizes that she can recognize these earlier and can do things to manage her feelings better. She is now become interested in learning for her GCSEs and in training to become an instructor.

One could see a gradual and similar transformation in almost all the women. As mentioned earlier, Seema had been extremely angry and full of hate for the social work agencies. She was also a single mother with three children. Her son had a medical condition for which he received treatment but then began to exhibit behaviour problems which gradually escalated and led to the involvement of a social worker. Seema felt that her son became delinquent because of the fact that the social worker arranged for him to go on a holiday with other extremely delinquent boys. He was now in care with negligible contact with the family and she felt that she had now lost him. Her daughter Reeta was often withdrawn, quiet, and shy and Seema felt that she might lose her too. Through attending the groups Seema developed a great deal of confidence and a tremendous improvement in her self-esteem. Her relationship with Reeta began to improve as she began to enjoy the group and then enjoy the company of her daughter too.

Seema became very keen for her daughter to experience similar groups as well. Other women felt the same for their children, especially their girls. I therefore started a weekly girls' group after school for the youth of 12 years and above. The girls appeared really motivated to attend and very keen in various educational, recreational, social and other activities that we arranged. They valued the opportunity to discuss their feelings and understand their parents' point of view, working out ways of clarifying, sharing, exploring and negotiating with their family members and others. There were nearly twenty girls attending and more wanted to come but we could not find a bigger place. I then started another girls' group through the Youth Service. Many had had enormous difficulties, some had recently arrived from Bangladesh, some missed their fathers, some felt extremely restricted, some were scapegoated in their community, some were still feeling hurt by the family violence that they had witnessed a long time ago.

Reeta remembered the physical abuse she and her mother experienced in the hands of her drunk father. Although it happened several years ago and her parents were no longer living together, the memory of these traumatic experiences were still very distressing for her. As she began to share these feelings either in the group or outside with me she began to take interest in her day to day activities as well. She talked about her worries for her mother and how her mother felt lonely. She felt angry about the freedom her brother had. She was annoyed by the visitors in the house and how this interfered with her homework. As I began to take interest in her educational progress she began to use these opportunities with more and more delight. She shared her fantasies and fears. She had recently attended some weddings where some of her relatives had enquired about her wishes. She became very anxious thinking that her mother was going to arrange and force her to marry soon. The intensity of her feelings tended to stop her from discussing a lot of these things with her mother. She would wonder 'Does my mother not like me?' 'Does she want to get rid of me?' and so on. I tried to explain that most Asian parents tend to feel responsible for their children's marriage out of their true love for their children. They have their children's welfare at heart and would hate to force any thing like this. My suggestion was 'try to explain your feelings, your likes and dislikes to your mother, I am sure she would not like to do any thing against your wishes.' Gradually she began to try. Reeta's experience of her father was so negative that she worried that her own husband could turn out to be like him. Through the discussions in the group and her relationships outside she gradually began to learn that all men may not be like her father. She began to enjoy other things in her day to day life as well and to realize that there was more to life than constantly worrying about one's future marriage or husband. In the women's group I encouraged Seema to listen and to explain her feelings to Reeta. In the girl's group I encouraged Reeta to do the same with her mother, with occasional comments on how they appreciated their heart-to-heart talks. I still treasure the happiness that it brought into every aspect of their lives.

I have continued running both the groups but they in fact now have a life and independence of their own. I enjoy being a part of them and keep them running smoothly. Many new members have joined the groups. Others have emotionally matured and left. These groups do a great deal for the community as a whole, as the members also take interest in the welfare of the community.

When I went to do my course in Community and Youth Work for a year, both the women's group as well as the girls' group dwindled. This is because the social workers concerned, in their wisdom, began to restructure the proceedings, such as, splitting the group into some 'logical' categories of certain age bands, family circumstances or mental states. Afterwards I had to pick up the pieces again and restart the womans' group in a voluntary organization, on a voluntary basis! Many of the girls, however, managed to join my Youth Service group.

The Contributors

Carolyn Bailey, BA (hons), MSc (Health Education), Cert. in counselling theory, works as a Health Promotion specialist for Mental Health with Northamptonshire Health Authority. She previously worked as Health Promotion Facilitator for older people and ethnic minorities and as a Community Development Facilitator and an Adult Education Tutor and artist. She has taken ethnic minority issues as a specialist area of work and has researched particularly the needs of the South Asian Communities in the county. In so doing, she has also developed many close and valuable friendships within this community, giving her a broader perspective of life in personal as well as professional terms.

Dr Soni Bhate MBBS, is a part-time trainee Psychiatrist at the City Health Trust, Newcastle-upon-Tyne. Having arrived in the UK at the age of two, she soon became acclimatised to the North-East Geordie culture, and moved with her parents to Leicester and then to the North East. She graduated from the Royal Free Medical School and married and has a young baby. Soni grew up in two cultures: the Indian culture at home, and the British culture outside. Having married an Englishman, she is acutely aware of differences in cultural nuances.

Dr Surya Bhate MBBS, DPM, FRCPsych, is Consultant and Senior Lecturer in Child and Adolescent Forensic Psychiatry Service, Kolvin Unit, Newcastle-upon-Tyne. He graduated in medicine from Nagpur University, India and trained in Psychiatry in India as well as in the UK with Sir Martin Roth and later with Professor Kolvin. He worked as a Consultant in Adolescent Psychiatry in Leicester for seven years before moving to the North East where he has developed the forensic services for children, young people and their families in response to the Reed Committee recommendations. He has been a member of various committees including the chairmanship of the Royal College of Psychiatrists Committee for Overseas Doctors. He has published on the subjects of school phobia, depression and racism in medicine.

John Burnham is employed by the South Birmingham Mental Health (NHS) Trust as a Principal Family Therapist working in The Charles Burns Family Clinic at the West Midlands Centre for Children, Young People, and Families. Together with Queenie Harris he co-organizes the therapeutic and training services in the Family Clinic and Sexual Abuse Project. In the independent sector John works at the Kensington Consultation Centre in London as a supervisor and director of the Diploma in Systemic Teaching, Training and Supervision.

Waveney Bushell has an Honours degree in Psychology and a Masters' degree in Child Development. She has thirty year's experience of working with children and has worked with Surrey and Croydon local authorities as an Educational Psychologist. She is now retired.

Dr Kedar Nath Dwivedi, MBBS, MD, DPM, FRCPsych, is a Consultant in Child, Adolescent and Family Psychiatry at the Child and Family Consultation Service and the Ken Stewart Family Centre, Northampton, and is also a Clinical Teacher in the Faculty of Medicine, University of Leicester. He graduated in Medicine from the Institute of Medical Sciences, Varanasi, India and served as Assistant Professor in Preventive and Social Medicine in Simla before coming to the UK in 1974. Since then he has worked in psychiatry and is a member of more than a dozen professional associations, including the Transcultural Psychiatry Society and the Group Analytic Society, and has contributed extensively to the literature (nearly 40 publications) including editing *Groupwork with Children and Adolescents* (1993, Jessica Kingsley Publishers), *A Handbook of Childhood Anxiety Management* (Arena, in press) and *Depression in Children and Adolescents* (Whurr, in press). He teaches on the Midland Course on Groupwork and Family Therapy and is the Director of Courses on Groupwork with Children and Adolescents in Northampton. He is also interested in Eastern, particularly Buddhist, approaches to mental health.

Mrs Radha Dwivedi, MA (Pali), Cert. in Youth and Community Work, works as a Health Care Worker for Ethnic Minorities in the Northampton Family Health Services Authority. She graduated in Sociology, Pali and Hindi and obtained a Master's degree in Pali from the Banaras Hindu University in Varanasi. She came to the UK in 1975 and has worked in a voluntary capacity and as an Adult Education Tutor, and in Youth Service and Social Services.

Gerry German, BA, Dip.Educ, Dip. Philosophy of Educ., has long experience of teaching in Jamaica and London. He has also worked as a Comprehensive School Head in Clwyd, as Principal Education Officer in Nigeria and with the Commission for Racial Equality, London for twelve years as Principal Education Officer. He is now Honorary Secretary for the Working Group Against Racism in Children's Resources and also provides, on a voluntary basis, advice, support and representational services to people experiencing problems in education and employment.

Dr Queenie Harris came to this country in the early 1960s to join her husband soon after qualifying in medicine in south India. She works as a Consultant Child and Adolescent Psychiatrist in The Charles Burns Family Clinic at the West Midlands Centre for Children, Young People, and Families and at the City

Hospital, a large general hospital in the inner city area of Birmingham. She is also a Senior Clinical Lecturer in Child and Adolescent Psychiatry. Her special interests are systemic therapy, child sexual abuse and transcultural psychiatry/practice. Together with John Burnham she co-organizes the therapeutic and training services in the Family Clinic and Sexual Abuse Project.

Dr Annie Lau MD, FRCPC, was born in Australia and grew up in Singapore and Malaysia. She graduated in medicine in Canada and worked in the Royal Ottawa Hospital before coming to England in 1978. She is a Consultant in Child and Adolescent Psychiatry and Clinical Director in Child and Adolescent Mental Health Services, the Redbridge Health Care Trust, London. She continues to be actively involved in contributing to the literature and teaching in transcultural issues in individual and family life.

Dr Begum Maitra, MBBS, DPM, MRCPsych, MD, is a Consultant Child Psychiatrist at the Child and Family Consulation Centre in Hammersmith, London, and a Jungian Analyst. Her training and clinical experience in India and her subsequent experience in the UK has fostered an interest in the impact of cultural systems on psychiatric practice and on health service provision. A significant portion of her work involves the assessment of children at risk and their families, and she teaches and writes on the complex issues around cross-cultural assessment.

Harish Mehra came to this country in 1973 after completing his BSc. He worked in industry for a few years before gaining his Diploma in Social Work in 1984 and also did the Marriage Guidance Counselling Course at Rugby in 1987. He worked as a social worker in Coventry and then as a training officer with Sandwell Social Services before taking up his position as a Principal Officer (Ethnic Minorities) with Northampton Social Services Department in 1989. At present he is employed as a Principal at the Education Welfare Service Birmingham. He also has a Master's Degree in Race and Ethnic Studies from Warwick University and is currently doing a PhD study on Exclusion of Asian Children from Secondary Schools at Birmingham University. Harish is also a journalist and has written three books in Panjabi; a fourth is in press. His articles on various issues are frequently published in the Panjabi press in the UK and in India.

Ann Miller BA (Hons), AFBPS, is a Consultant Clinical Psychologist and Registered Family Therapist at the Marlborough Family Service and at the Institute of Family Therapy, London. She is also an Honorary Research Fellow at University College, London. She originally trained in Australia and has had a wide teaching experience in family therapy both in the UK and abroad. She is particularly interested in relating training to intercultural work. She was co-editor of *Gender and Power in Families* (Routledge 1990).

Dr Ved Prakash Varma PhD was an educational psychologist at the Institute of Education, University of London, the Tavistock Clinic London, London Boroughs of Richmond-upon-Thames and Brent. His 30 previous books include *How and Why Children Fail, How and Why Children Hate, Troubles of Children and Adolescents,* and, as Co-editor with Professor Barbara Tizard, *Vulnerability and Resilience in Human Development.*

Dr Harry Zeitlin BSc, MPhil, MD, FRCP, FRCPsych is Professor of Child and Adolescent Psychiatry at University College London and Honorary Consultant to the North Essex Child and Family Consultation Service. He graduated at London University and trained in psychiatry at The Maudsley Hospital. He has written on various subjects including the links between child and adult disorder, child abuse and drug and substance abuse. He has special interest in teaching on forensic and transcultural psychiatry.

Subject
Index

Author Index